Public Speaking in the City

Also by Janet Stewart

FASHIONING VIENNA: Adolf Loos's Cultural Criticism

BLUEPRINTS FOR NO-MAN'S LAND: Connections in Contemporary Austrian Culture (co-edited)

Public Speaking in the City

Debating and Shaping the Urban Experience

Janet Stewart
University of Aberdeen, UK

First published 2009 by
PALGRAVE MACMILLAN

Palgrave Macmillan in the UK is an imprint of Macmillan Publishers Limited,
registered in England, company number 785998, of Houndmills, Basingstoke,
Hampshire RG21 6XS.

Palgrave Macmillan in the US is a division of St Martin's Press LLC,
175 Fifth Avenue, New York, NY 10010.

Palgrave Macmillan is the global academic imprint of the above companies
and has companies and representatives throughout the world.

Palgrave® and Macmillan® are registered trademarks in the United States,
the United Kingdom, Europe and other countries.

ISBN-13: 978-0-230-21809-3   hardback
ISBN-10: 0-230-21809-1   hardback

This book is printed on paper suitable for recycling and made from fully
managed and sustained forest sources. Logging, pulping and manufacturing
processes are expected to conform to the environmental regulations of the
country of origin.

A catalogue record for this book is available from the British Library.

A catalog record for this book is available from the Library of Congress.

10   9   8   7   6   5   4   3   2   1
18   17   16   15   14   13   12   11   10   09

Printed and bound in Great Britain by
CPI Antony Rowe, Chippenham and Eastbourne

Dedication

*For Verity and Dominic, who arrived in the
middle of things*

Contents

List of Figures		viii
Acknowledgements		x
Introduction: Public Speaking in the Modern City		1
1	Look Who's Talking	13
2	Architects and the Urban Public	51
3	Appearing in Public	87
4	Locating the Voices	120
Epilogue: Public Speaking and the City of the Future		168
Notes		180
Works Cited		182
Index		199

Figures

I.1 American moving walkway at the Berlin Trade
Exhibition, 1896   5

I.2 Imperial Jubilee Exhibition, Vienna 1898: Bird's-eye
view of the exhibition site   6

1.1 Alfred Hagel: Karl Kraus lecturing   28

2.1 Final scenes from *Der Weltbaumeister*   75

2.2 Information about the 1910 General Municipal
Exhibition in Berlin, with handwritten notes
listing speakers by Muthesius   80

3.1 Georg Simmel at the lectern, 1906   108

3.2 Poster advertising Loos's 1913 lecture,
'Ornament and Crime'   118

4.1 Interior of the Romanisches Café. Architect:
Franz Schwechten: *Berliner Architekturwelt* IV (1901/02)   129

4.2 Sophiensäle: Grand hall in use as a swimming pool   134

4.3 Arbeiterheim. A concert in the big hall, 1902   136

4.4 Weinhaus Rheingold, Kaisersaal. Architect:
Bruno Schmitz   137

4.5 Weinhaus Rheingold, high relief sculpture.
Artist: Franz Metzner   140

4.6 Zoological Garden Berlin. Site plan of the entertainment
complex showing the promenade   142

4.7 *Raumbühne* in the Konzerthaus in Vienna, 1924:
Platform for public speaking. Architect: Friedrich Kiesler   147

4.8 'Everything is spinning, everything is moving':
Die Raumbühne. Caricature by L. Tuzynsky
(originally in *Der Goetz von Berlichingen*,
24 October 1924)   148

4.9 Berlin, Masurenallee 8–14. 'Haus des Rundfunks'
(Berliner Rundfunk)   153

4.10 Urania, Berlin: Scientific Theatre and laboratory for
optics and acoustics   157

4.11 Frontal view of the newly built Volksheim in
Ottakring, 1905   159

E.1 Rebecca Nesson lecturing at Langdell Hall, Harvard,
2008, with Second Life projected on a screen in
the background   176

Acknowledgements

This book would not have been possible without the support of the Arts and Humanities Research Council and the Leverhulme Trust, both of whom facilitated periods of dedicated research time, while grants from the British Academy and the Carnegie Trust for the Universities of Scotland enabled research to be carried out in Berlin and Vienna. The British Academy also provided assistance with the costs of illustrations, as did the College of Arts and Social Sciences at the University of Aberdeen.

This book is the product of extensive library and archival work and I owe gratitude to the staff of the following institutions: the Zentrum für Berlin Studien, the Staatsbibliothek and the Bildarchiv Preussischer Kulturbesitz in Berlin; the Deutsches Literaturarchiv in Marbach; the Austrian National Library in Vienna; the Albertina in Vienna; the Arbeiterkammerbibliothek in Vienna; the library of the Technische Universität in Vienna; the Wien Museum; and the Wiener Stadt- und Landesbibliothek.

The material presented in this book is original. However, in Chapter 3, I have drawn on two existing articles – 'Georg Simmel at the Lectern: The Lecture as Embodiment of Text', *Body and Society* 5/4: 1–16 and 'Talking of Modernity: The Viennese "Vortrag" as Form', *German Life and Letters* 51/4: 455–69 – while the analysis of the Weinhaus Rheingold in Chapter 4 appeared in an earlier form in *Imagining the City*, ed. Emden, Keen and Midgeley (Oxford: Lang 2006). In all cases, this material has been revised and adapted for the purpose of this book. For permission to reproduce illustrations, I owe gratitude to the Picture Archive of the Austrian National Library, the Wien Museum, the Werkbundarchiv Museum der Dinge in Berlin and the Federal Archives of Germany. As this book is intended for an English-speaking audience, I have used standard translations where available. Unless otherwise indicated, the translations are my own.

This book would not have been completed without the intellectual encouragement and advice, at various stages of the project, of David Frisby, Roger Stephenson, Andrew Benjamin, Elizabeth Boa, Leo Lensing, Gilbert Carr, Andrew Barker and the anonymous reader at

Palgrave Macmillan. I would also like to thank supportive colleagues, old and new, at Aberdeen; in particular, Chris Fynsk and Michael Syrotinski both encouraged and enabled me to rework the project; Kriss Ravetto and Liz Hallam provided fresh intellectual stimulus; Finn Brunton offered insights for the epilogue. Beyond Aberdeen, thanks are also due to Paul Bishop for both his illuminating references and his deep pessimism. Thanks also to Philippa Gould at Palgrave Macmillan for giving this book a home. Finally, my thanks go to Simon. Without his encouragement, translations skills and overwhelming support, there would have been no *Public Speaking in the City*.

Introduction: Public Speaking in the Modern City

> Words are in space, yet not in space. They speak of
> space, and enclose it.
>
> Lefebvre (1991: 251)

The spectacular modern metropolis

Little did Georg Simmel know when he rose to give a lecture on 'The Metropolis and Mental Life' in 1903 at the invitation of the Gehe Foundation in Dresden, that this work would become a canonical text in the field of urban sociology and indeed, in the wider context of academic writing on the city. The enduring influence of his deliberations is due to the manner in which they combine philosophical, psychological and sociological insights to reflect on the experience and aesthetics of modern urban life. His lecture focused on the rationalisation of social relations brought about through the increasingly objectified relationship between producer and consumer in the mature money economy of the modern city. This process of rationalisation shapes both temporal and spatial dimensions of urban life: it necessitates the 'stable and impersonal time schedule' that makes 'all economic life and communication of the city' possible, while also affecting the relationship between city dwellers (Simmel [1903] 1997: 177). Simmel characterised the attitude of city dwellers to one another as 'reserve', the 'inner aspect' of which is 'a slight aversion, a mutual strangeness and repulsion, which will break into hatred and fight at the moment of a closer contact, however caused' (179). He then described the metropolis as comprising an 'extensive communicative life', in which 'reserve with its overtone of hidden aversion' figures as a 'cloak [that ...] grants to the individual a kind and an amount of personal freedom which has no analogy whatsoever under other conditions', but in which, simultaneously, 'one nowhere feels as lonely and lost as in the metropolitan crowd' (180–1). His point was that, as a prime site of modernity, the metropolis is a location that exemplifies the compression of time and space made possible through processes of modernisation, such as the development of new forms of communication technology. These in turn are responsible for the changed nature of communication in the metropolis, whose 'most significant characteristic [...] is [the] functional extension beyond its physical boundaries' (182). This extension of influence is partly the result of flows of capital, goods and services, but is also connected to the flow of ideas, or circulation of discourse, facilitated by the development of new communication technology such as the railway, the telegraph system and the telephone.

Simmel's lecture was part of a series of talks organised in conjunction with the First German Municipal Exhibition held in Dresden in 1903 (Petermann 1903; Frisby 2001: 133–9). This exhibition, like its predecessors, the Berlin Trade Exhibition of 1896 and the Vienna Imperial Jubilee Exhibition of 1898, provided a vision of the modern city of the future, with a particular emphasis on its communicative potential. Addressing the Society of Economists in Berlin, Julius Lessing (1900) described the latter half of the nineteenth century as the time of the World Exhibition. This gives weight to Paul Greenhalgh's (1988: 1) description of events such as the London Great Exhibition of 1851, the Chicago World's Fair of 1893 and the Paris Expositions Universelle of 1900 as some of the most important historical phenomena of the late nineteenth and early twentieth centuries, through which cities sought to consolidate or establish their status as modern metropolises. Despite not achieving their initially hoped for status of World Exhibition, both the Berlin Trade Exhibition of 1896 and the Imperial Jubilee Exhibition of 1898 were celebrated as significant events that served to confirm that Berlin and Vienna had now joined the ranks of the 'world city' (*Weltstadt*), although in rather different ways. In the foreword to the *Official Guidebook through the Imperial Jubilee Exhibition*, an effort was made to steer a course between celebrating Vienna's newly found modernity and underlining the role of the Emperor in creating the political stability that allowed trade and industry to flourish (Ausstellungs-Commission 1898). In contrast, reviews of the Berlin Trade Exhibition focused almost exclusively on its role in heralding Berlin's sudden emergence onto the global stage as a thoroughly modern city (Stein and Metzsch 1896).

Writing in the Viennese weekly paper, *Die Zeit*, Simmel maintained that the Berlin Trade Exhibition signified Berlin's accession to the rank of 'world city', which he defined as 'a single city to which the whole world sends its products and where all the important styles of the present cultural world are put on display' ([1896] 1997: 256). The unique character of the exhibition, according to Simmel, is that there it became apparent how 'through its own production a city can represent itself as a copy and a sample of the manufacturing forces of world culture' (256). The exhibition, in other words, formed a microcosm of its host city, and served, above all, to highlight how a particular city was enmeshed in the increasingly global phenomenon of commodity capitalism. This was, however, not the only way that the relationship between exhibition and city was characterised by contemporary commentators. In 'The Exhibition Style', the first of a series of articles on the Imperial Jubilee Exhibition first published in the *Neue Freie Presse* (Vienna's leading daily newspaper), Adolf Loos described the exhibition as a prime location of modernity, as the herald of a 'new style', which, for the time being, would have to remain *ante portas*, on the threshold of the city itself (1983: 43). Here, the exhibition represents an ideal image of modernity, to which the existing city can aspire. The enduring fascination of exhibitions lies in the juxtaposition of these two views with their relationship to the city itself: exhibitions were simultaneously visual representations of the existing form of urban modernity and also sites in which reflection upon the future of the city could be provided and experienced.

Dovetailing with the view of exhibitions as sites that could herald the urban future, one of the main themes of the industrial exhibitions of the late nineteenth and early twentieth centuries was progress. Exhibitions were exemplary instances of what Walter Benjamin described as the remythification of Europe that was brought about by the rise of capitalism and, as such, were material manifestations of the dominant myth of history-as-progress (1999: 391). In the Berlin Trade Exhibition, the Imperial Jubilee Exhibition in Vienna and the

First German Municipal Exhibition in Dresden, technology was clearly on display as a prime means of achieving progress, as it was in similar exhibitions the world over:

> Technology would transform the world, bring plenty, peace, unity, all in the foreseeable future. [...] Universal advance of civilization via the achievement of science was both a canon and an assumption at exhibitions.
>
> Greenhalgh (1988: 23–4)

A striking feature of the display of technology at the Berlin, Vienna and Dresden exhibitions was the emphasis on modern mediated communication, meaning that these exhibitions were primarily communicative phenomena (communicating a particular view of the modern metropolis) in which new directions in communication technology were on display.

Central to the exhibitions' display of new directions in communication technology were advances in transportation and in telecommunications. All three events included the formal exhibition of new modes of transport and were catalysts for the extension and improvement of existing public transport networks in each city. In addition, they offered visitors a number of opportunities to experience new modes of transportation in action. One novel form of transport in use at the Berlin Trade Exhibition was the 'American moving walkway', which served to bridge the Park Allee that ran through the centre of the exhibition site, linking two popular amusement sites located within the exhibition ground: the Pleasure Park and 'Old-Berlin' (Berliner Gewerbe-Ausstellung 1896: 191).

This contraption, which had first been on display at the Chicago World's Fair in 1893, consisted of two platforms that were constantly in motion, one travelling at walking speed, the other, which was fitted with seats, moving twice as fast. The idea was that passengers walked from a stationary platform onto the first platform, then from the first onto the second. Just before arrival at its destination, passengers would move from the second, to the first, before disembarking onto a stationary platform. Meanwhile at the Imperial Jubilee Exhibition in Vienna, particularly adventurous visitors were given the chance to take a trip in a modified balloon, while others could ride the aerial tramway that ran across the main entrance to the site, connecting the Education

Figure I.1 American moving walkway at the Berlin Trade Exhibition, 1896; *Source*: Berliner Gewerbe-Ausstellung 1896: 191

Pavilion to the Air-Travel Exhibition, or take a trip in an anchored balloon that rose to a position 300 metres above the main square of the exhibition (Ausstellungs-Commission 1898: 88). At night, this balloon took on a symbolic character: lit by two giant electrical floodlights, the balloon became 'a colossal emblem of the exhibition, visible from miles around' (87) thereby underlining the central representative role of this kind of communication technology in these exhibitions.

Figure I.2   Imperial Jubilee Exhibition, Vienna 1898: Bird's-eye view of the exhibition site; *Source:* Austrian National Library/ Picture Archive, Vienna

The new communication technology on display at the exhibitions was, of course, not limited to transportation; a significant amount of space was also devoted to developments in the field of telecommunications. For many visitors, this form of communication was the more fascinating, but also potentially the more disorientating. Suggesting a possible reason for this reaction, Franz Kafka noted in a letter to Milena Jesenka that while new advances in transportation seemed to aid natural communication by bringing people together, telecommunications – a field devoted to the circulation of messages, sounds and images, rather than of people – was about the much stranger phenomenon of facilitating disembodied communication (1953: 229). As was the case with transportation, exhibitions supplemented the formal display of new developments and products in the field of telecommunications, by offering visitors and exhibitors opportunities to avail themselves of new communicative possibilities. They could, for example, see how telecommunications offered a way of helping to control and make sense of the increasingly insecure modern world. Telegraph operators working at the exhibition intercepted all telegrams sent in the city concerning important police matters, which they printed out and displayed under the title 'Events of the Day' (Ausstellungs-Commission 1898: 73).

Events such as the Berlin Trade Exhibition, the Vienna Imperial Jubilee Exhibition and the First German Municipal Exhibition that exhibited innovations in the fields of transportation and telecommunications, presented a particular view of modernity and, concomitantly, of the present and the future of the modern metropolis. As such, they help cement the idea that modernity should be understood primarily as the birthplace of modern mediated communication, in which the circulation of individuals and the circulation of disembodied messages, images and sounds were increasing in importance. To use Friedrich Kittler's (1999) terminology, this was the 'Mediengründerzeit', which we might gloss as an era that laid the basis for mass communication in the modern world. As communicative phenomena that themselves displayed new communication technology, exhibitions presented the spectacle of the modern metropolis as a place built on the promise of what Simmel described as 'space-conquering technology', as a place in which mankind's age-old dream of communicating over space and time could begin to be satisfied ([1903] 1997: 184).

Exhibitions as speech sites

Before we get too carried away with the seductive image of the late nineteenth and early twentieth century exhibition as the place where the dream of communicating over space and time could be realised, however, we would do well to recall that Simmel's deliberations on the metropolis that accompanied the 1903 First German Municipal Exhibition were first delivered in the form of face-to-face communication. Apart from Frisby's detailed account of 'The Metropolis and Mental Life' (2001: 100–58), most analyses of Simmel's work either ignore this fact or deem it unworthy of comment, yet the mode of delivery of his reflections provides a practical example of the continuing importance of public speaking in the modern city. Simmel had already taken up this point in his remarks on the Berlin Trade Exhibition, where he argued that like all world exhibitions, this was a clear example of a particular historical phenomenon, which saw people continue to gather together in certain places long after the original reason for the gathering had become obsolete (1997: 255). The more durable purpose of any gathering is to provide possibilities for 'sociability', which is a 'fundamental type of human sociation' (255). The kind of 'sociability' taking place at the Berlin Trade Exhibition was, according to Simmel, based on consumption – and mainly on the consumption of visual images and experiences. More pertinently, however, for this investigation of the possibilities for embodied communication in the modern city, the exhibition also facilitated the consumption of the spoken word. The importance of the Berlin Trade Exhibition essay, then, is that it puts sociability and public speaking right at the core of the modern technology-oriented exhibition and, by extension, at the core of the modern city.

In the early twentieth century, new possibilities for non-corporeal communication on display at trade exhibitions were not yet matched by opportunities for attaining that dream, and so public speaking remained a primary form of communicating ideas in and about the modern city. To take but one example, the success of Alexander Graham Bell's telephone was apparently attributable to his prowess as a public speaker as much as to the publicity that he gained from demonstrating his invention at the Philadelphia Exhibition in 1875 (Winston 1998: 54). In fact, public speaking was 'among the least noticeable but most influential of elements at exhibitions' (Greenhalgh 1988: 21);

the entire exhibition site at the Chicago World Exposition of 1893 was made available as a conference venue, and in 1900, the Paris World Exhibition played host to a number of conferences on subjects as varied as photography, ornithology and memismatics. The First German Municipal Exhibition in Dresden was heralded by a related series of public lectures, while during the course of the Berlin Trade Exhibition, public lectures on a wide variety of disciplines were delivered daily. A number of lecturers in this series took the city as their subject, including the dermatologist, Oskar Lassar, whose lecture on 13 May was devoted to the topic of 'Public Baths'; Julius Lessing, who elected to speak about 'Art and Hygiene in the Home' on 2 June and the professor of architecture, [Carl] Schäfer, whose lecture on 31 August was entitled 'Architecture Now and in the Future' (*Deutsche Bauzeitung* 1896). These exhibitions, then, provided a space in which ideas about the modern city could be disseminated through the medium of the spoken word, as well as through spectacle. Not only that, but as a space that provided opportunities for 'sociability', the exhibition was also the location of an urban public to which these ideas were addressed and which played its role in what we could call the discursive construction of the modern city. In other words, exhibitions were not only sites in which the city was on display, but also sites where it was being talked about, where the modern city as idea was being constructed through discourse.

Coupled with this is the fact that around 1900, immediate public communication was experienced as a new and often fiercely contested phenomenon, particularly in the German-speaking countries. Here, the 1848 uprisings had been concerned with an ongoing struggle to enshrine basic human rights in a constitution. In particular, the revolutionaries were fighting for the right to associate and assemble in public, and the right to free speech, the lack of which had hampered the expansion of immediate public communication in the first half of the nineteenth century. In both Prussia and Austria, however, the 1848 revolutions were followed by a successful counter-revolution. This meant that throughout the remainder of the nineteenth century, and into the twentieth, these basic human rights that would guarantee the functioning of immediate public communication were not taken for granted, but remained a contested area (Klausmann 1998: 233–4), even while, as social historians such as Eley (1992) and Negt and Kluge (1993) have argued, an expansion of discursive space was underway. This situation, coupled with the simultaneous rise of the modern mass media, sparked off intense social, political and philosophical debates about communication, which provided the impetus for later canonical works on language and communication, such as Ludwig Wittgenstein's *Tractatus Logico-philosophicus* (1922), Georg Lukács's *History and Class Consciousness* ([1923] 1972) and Martin Buber's *I and Thou* ([1923] 2004) that have shaped the way communication and language have been studied throughout the twentieth century, in the German-speaking countries and beyond (Peters 1999: 10–22).

Public speaking and the city

In its initial mode of delivery as a public lecture, Simmel's 'Metropolis and Mental Life' was part of a wider phenomenon. Studying this phenomenon entails exploring a number of relationships: between public speaking and the city, between space and speech, and between discourse in space and discourse about space. This is the subject matter of this book, which sets out to contextualise Simmel's ideas on the city and communication, as contained in his writings and exemplified in his actions. The resulting historical sociological account of public speaking in the city draws on two bodies of work: the sociology of the city and the sociology of public speaking. In particular, it seeks to position itself in relation to studies that understand the city as a place of appearance, or a site for performance (Arendt 1958; Sennett 1976, 1991; Habermas 1989; Zukin 1995; Harvey 2003; Blum 2003). Although differing in scope and intent, all these studies assume that public speaking is fundamental to the urban experience, often invoking a long history of public speaking reaching back to Aristotle and the Athenian agora. The present work focuses on the urban experience, or, to use De Certeau's terminology, on the experience of the 'ordinary practitioners of the city' (1988: 93), but it also seeks to demonstrate the connection between this aspect and the space of the city planner or cartographer. This connection between the 'migrational, or metaphorical, city' occupied by 'ordinary practitioners' (93) and the 'Concept-city' of the planner (95) is revealed when we follow Simmel and later thinkers such as Blum (2003), in conceiving the city as an aesthetic, imaginary entity, constructed through discourse, whether primarily textual, verbal or visual. To do so is to think with Michael Warner about the 'poetic' nature of discourse addressed to a public (2002: 114).

This book is about the poetic construction of the modern city through the circulation of knowledge in the form of public speaking, and about the ways in which knowledge relating to the urban experience was modified as it circulated. It contributes to the sociology of knowledge through a study of cultural transfer, and of connections between the circulation of ideas and the circulation of people. In so doing, it also contributes to a debate on the role and status of the public intellectual and the power of the spoken word, demonstrating how in constructing the modern city through speaking in public, Simmel was joined by other members of the intelligentsia, such as the writer, Karl Kraus, and the architect, Adolf Loos. In other words, this study seeks to align itself with a tradition of writing, exemplified by Marshall Berman (1983), David Harvey (2003) and others, that 'show[s] the resonance between cultural symbols, urban space and social power' (Zukin 1995: 269). To reach a full understanding of this 'resonance' entails extending the analysis from the focus on the construction of the modern city through discourse, to a consideration of the influence that the modern urban experience had on the content, form and location of public speaking. This is to draw on the work of theorists such as Henri Lefebvre (1991) and Edward Soja (1989), whose account of the 'socio-spatial dialectic' was based on the idea that social life must be seen as both space-forming and space-contingent (Blau 1999: 13). To grasp this fact is to recognise that while public speaking may be a fundamental part of the urban experience, its form changes according to spatial and temporal location. The present study, then, examines the reciprocal relationship between speech and space, exploring how the imagined city was constructed through public speaking, while also considering how the nature of public speaking changed in response to the new urban experience to which it contributed. The book examines these ideas in four chapters and an epilogue. Each of the four chapters sets out to answer one of a set of questions that, according to Nancy Fraser, constitute a framework for rethinking the public sphere (cited in Triadafilopoulos 1999: 747): the first chapter takes up the question of who participates in public deliberations, the second focuses on what is being talked about, the third turns to an examination of how modern public speaking functions, while the fourth explores the sites where communicative exchange takes place. The resultant 'thick description' of public speaking as an activity reveals the importance of the aesthetic dimension as the point of connection between these aspects, while the epilogue offers a brief reflection on the role of public speaking in the twenty-first century, in the discursive construction of the city to come.

As well as providing a platform from which to begin to reflect on the city of the future, this phenomenology of public speaking in early twentieth century Berlin and Vienna offers a corrective to certain taken-for-granted assumptions about the nature of the modern city. Some of the most fascinating studies of the modern metropolis cast that entity as a visual construction (Cacciari 1993; Frisby 2001; Ward 2001). This view is informed by a reading of contemporary theorists of the city, such as Walter Benjamin (1999: 416–55) and Siegfried Kracauer (1995: 173–85), who presented the figures of the flâneur and the detective, observers of modern life, as archetypal city dwellers. While not wishing to detract from these analyses, this study suggests that sound, appearing here in the guise of the spoken word, also played an important yet underrated role in the culture and construction of the modern metropolis. The seductive power of new communication technology offers one reason for the way that the role of public speaking in the discursive construction of the city has been neglected. Innovative thinkers about communication and modernity such as Kittler (1990, 1999) provide compelling analyses of the way that developments in communications brought sweeping change to the urban experience, but they can blind us to the importance of immediate communication in the modern city, inciting us to fall into a trap similar to that identified by Miles, Borden and Hall: 'To talk of the postmodern city, the post-industrial city or the electronic city is to mythologise a transformation that in reality is far less complete or apparent and which is far more mundane than might be sometimes imagined' (2000: 4). The present work is an attempt to redress the balance, through a phenomenology of public speaking at a point in history when Berlin and Vienna were attempting to transform themselves into world cities. Following Simmel's lecture on the 'The Metropolis and Mental Life', this study contends that the modern world city is as much an experiential and imaginary entity constructed and shaped through speech, as it is a physical one. In a sense, then, it aims to augment our understanding of the modern city by recontextualising Simmel's seminal lecture, in terms of form, content and situation. The first step in this process, and the subject of the first chapter, is a sociological account of the public speaking scene, in which his lecture was embedded.

1
Look Who's Talking

> The form of space is encounter, assembly, simultaneity.
>
> Lefebvre (1991: 101)

In his *Philosophical Investigations*, Ludwig Wittgenstein (1976) developed the concept of the 'language-game', embedded in a distinct 'form of life', offering a model around which to organise this investigation into public speaking, as an activity central to the emerging modern metropolises of Berlin and Vienna in the early twentieth century. It suggests that the investigation proceed in two main, inter-related directions: analysis of the pragmatic rules that are operative in the game (who can speak to whom, and about what?), and an examination of the 'form of life' or situational context in which the language-game is embedded (how is public speaking organised?). What is more, since playing or performing a language-game produces a particular interpretation of the world, thinking about the nature of public speaking in this way will allow us to see how this activity would have contributed to an understanding of urban life. Throughout this chapter, and indeed, in the book as a whole, public speaking is conceived as an activity as well as an event. This means that public speaking is a phenomenon whose temporal and spatial boundaries are entirely fluid, even though each individual event must, of necessity, be limited by both time and space, since each possesses 'occasioned character mark[ing] it as the site whose engagement is punctuated temporally' (Blum 2003: 171). In other words, this chapter describes public speaking as a network of intersecting, yet discrete, language-games.

13

Employing the figure of the network means that we can foreground the role of circulation, both of people and of discourse, in public speaking as an activity. This is to investigate the form of life in which public speaking as a series of language-games is embedded, imagining it in its widest sense, as a game played not only by a speaker and an audience on one particular occasion, but as a series of games where a number of different roles might be assumed by any given individual: where speakers in one situation might be members of the audience elsewhere, and vice versa; where anyone, speaker or member of the audience, might also be responsible for the organisation of the event; where members of the audience may engage in conversation about the event either with each other or with others who did not experience the event in real time; where members of the audience might also be reporters, translating the event into textual form and so facilitating its circulation to a wider urban public; where members of the original audience might, as members of this wider urban public, subsequently encounter the event mediated through text. Other similar scenarios could be added to the above list; the point, however, is to highlight the complex relationship between public speaking and the public, and to seek an alternative to the standard dyadic speaker–audience model of conceptualising the poetic construction of publics and counter-publics through discourse (Warner 2002: 114). This entails understanding the public as the 'social space created by the reflexive *circulation* of discourse' (90, emphasis mine). With its strong emphasis on the figure of circulation, Warner's work on publics and counter-publics provides us with a model for thinking about the way in which public speaking played a central role in the discursive construction of the modern city through the construction of an urban public (or urban publics); as he points out, 'there is no speech or performance addressed to a public that does not try to specify in advance, in countless highly condensed ways, the lifeworld of its circulation' (114).

This chapter begins by demonstrating the ubiquity of public speaking in Berlin and Vienna around 1900 under three main headings: political speaking, with its basis in moral–philosophical discourse; the dissemination of knowledge through the public lecture, where the rational–technical is dominant; and literary or artistic performances, based on aesthetic experience. It focuses on the real existing 'communication communities' (Apel 1980) that could be found in Berlin and Vienna in the early twentieth century, which comprised speakers, audiences, cultural mediators (individuals and institutions) and the media. Presenting a number of different events that can be considered part of public speaking as activity, this section highlights the different forms of being together in the city (or forms of co-presence) that characterise this activity. These include first, the intimacy of 'sociability', which Simmel (1997: 122), in 'The Sociology of Sociability' describes as 'the play form of association'; second, 'association', which people enter into 'for the sake of special needs and interests' (121); and third, 'assemblage', where as in the city crowd described in 'Metropolis and Mental Life', 'bodily proximity' only serves to heighten 'mental distance' (181). While the first section is eclectic in its examples, the following sections focus on Karl Kraus, a prolific public speaker, who exemplifies the public intellectual's social location at the intersection of political, pedagogical and aesthetic discourse. The second section considers in detail the form of life in which Kraus's performances were embedded, drawing inspiration from Alan Blum's work on the urban 'scene', which 'makes concrete and specific [...] the intimacy of the inhabitants of a region of speech and so, in its being done, is a kind of emplacement, a way of making room for its talk' (2003: 178). The final section then offers an investigation into the subject matter of these events. Throughout this chapter, the emphasis is on public speaking as a central urban activity, as a way of both experiencing the modern city and of reflecting upon that experience, and therefore as an integral part of the construction of what Blum (2003) calls the city's 'imaginative structure'.

The world of public speaking

In the early twentieth century, the consumption of public speaking was a sufficiently ubiquitous activity for it to be satirised in an article that appeared in *Kunstwart* (an influential journal for art and cultural politics). The piece presents a fictional dialogue between two women, one identified as an 'Idealist', the other as a 'Sceptic', that offers a satire on the reproduction of 'cultural capital' that is accumulated and transmitted through the language-game of the lecture by both the audience and the speaker (von Beaulieu 1912). The conversation opens with the Idealist reporting that an acquaintance claimed to have attended around a hundred public lectures over the course of the winter. This, the Idealist continues, had put her to shame, but her own attention span was sadly too short to allow her to follow suit. The Sceptic, however, counters that it should be fairly simple to match the said acquaintance, and not too difficult a task to go one better. Surely, the Sceptic suggests, tongue-in-cheek, it would be possible to imagine a day in which one took in

> around coffee-time, a talk about the life of an ichneumon wasp; at afternoon tea, one about Goethe's relationship to Antiquity, or to some other woman; and in the evening, one about the 'Moral Improvement of Waitresses'. In between, there might well be time to fit in one on researching the North Pole, or on the Salome question, or indeed on the problem of marriage.
>
> von Beaulieu (1912: 156)

A cursory glance at any of the daily newspapers published in Berlin and Vienna at the beginning of the twentieth century would reveal that the Sceptic's list of random lecture topics was not far divorced from reality. To take but one example, on 6 February 1914, the listings page in the Viennese daily newspaper, the *Neues Wiener Tagblatt*, contained details of more than 20 separate lectures taking place that evening, covering topics as diverse as 'Legal Aspects of Modern Economic Problems', 'Oscar Wilde' and 'The Will to a World Language'. More evidence for the range and prevalence of public lectures in both Vienna and Berlin in the first decades of the twentieth century can be found in published reports of lectures in daily newspapers such as the Berlin-based *Vossische Zeitung* or the leading Viennese publication, the *Neue Freie Presse*, or in influential cultural journals such as the *Wiener Rundschau* or the *Neue Rundschau*. Further important sources for information on the ubiquity of public speaking at this time are dedicated publications such as *Der Sprecher*, a journal established in Berlin in 1911 for 'reciters, speakers, rhapsodists, elocution and the art of public speaking', or the *Jahrbuch für das deutsche Vortragswesen*, the official journal of the Gesellschaft für die Verbreitung von Volksbildung (Society for the Promotion of Adult Education). This association was set up in Berlin in 1871 as an umbrella outfit that would bring together the vast array of organisations, both socialist and bourgeois, devoted to adult education (Daum 1998: 171–2). Its *Jahrbuch* provided an important service to these organisations by publishing lists of speakers arranged by topic, as well as containing details of lecturers' previous speaking experience, information on whether they spoke with or without notes, and a guide to the fees they would demand. In 1912/13, it listed almost 300 professional speakers, and around the same number of non-professionals, covering a large variety of topics, including psychology and the occult, tourism, wireless telegraphy, dance history, and aspects of globalisation. Speakers ranged from university lecturers based throughout the German-speaking area to popular entertainers, such as 'Mr Vox, the humorous lecture artiste', who offered 'interesting and amusing experiments and explanatory lectures in areas such as ventriloquism, mind-reading, hypnosis, magic and anti-spiritualism' (*Jahrbuch für das deutsche Vortragswesen* 1912/13: 130).

The variety of topics on offer and the sheer number of lectures being held on any given evening would seem to support the Sceptic's claim that in the early twentieth century, an undifferentiated 'fashion for public speaking' could be discerned. This was certainly the view held by cultural critics such as Alfred Auerbach who, writing in the theatre review journal, *Die Schaubühne*, described the contemporary public speaking scene as a 'mish-mash of asserting, maintaining, declaiming, reciting and performing', and concluded that 'the habitually random use of so many different designations demonstrates a general lack of clarity about the nature of the art of public speaking' (Auerbach 1912: 103). Yet returning to the dialogue between the Sceptic and the Idealist, we find the latter arguing that objective criteria for distinguishing between good and bad lectures do exist. She maintains that a good lecture will be characterised first and foremost by the presence of 'personality'. This is a matter upon which both protagonists agree; only when the speaker possesses 'personality', claims the Sceptic, does the lecture 'become a joy, a meaningful event' (von Beaulieu 1912: 157). She then ventures to name three speakers, who, she believes, possess the requisite 'personality' to take an event into the realm of pleasure: Friedrich Naumann, Henry Thode and Maximillian Harden. This choice of speakers offers a way of organising an account of the public speaking scenes in Berlin and Vienna that conceives that activity as a network of intersecting, yet discrete language-games. Each speaker can be regarded as representative of a particular language-game: the politician, Naumann, as the champion of the political speech; the academic art historian, Thode, as a representative of the dissemination of knowledge through the public lecture and the publicist and writer, Harden, as an example of a third category, the literary performance. As we will see, however, there was a significant amount of crossover between these distinct language-games.

Political speech-making

In 'Politics as a Vocation', a lecture delivered in Munich in 1919 to the left-liberal Freistudentischen Bund (League of Free Students), Max Weber distinguished between 'professional politicians' and those for whom politics was an 'occasional occupation' (2004: 39). In Germany, professional politicians, of whom Naumann was one example, blossomed as public speakers in the aftermath of 1848. He and others – including Ferdinand Lasalle, Wilhelm Liebknecht and August Bebel in Berlin, and Viktor Adler, Karl Renner and Karl Lueger in Vienna – were able to make their mark in a new political climate characterised by the introduction of parliamentary debate in Berlin and Vienna, beginning with the short-lived National Assembly that met in the Paulskirche in Frankfurt from May 1848 until May 1849 (Ueding and Steinbrink 1994: 143). The political changes following the 1848 uprisings brought in their wake new possibilities for professional politicians to speak in public. In addition to the bourgeois voluntary associations (Vereine) that played an important role in creating opportunities for political speaking both before and after 1848 (Dann 1984; Judson 1996), the workers' associations established in the latter half of the nineteenth century provided a set of key locations in which professional politicians could address the public. Certain legal restrictions were, however, placed on the activities of such associations at this time. In Austria in the late 1880s, the authorities could justify banning meetings altogether with the catch-all charge of 'endangering public security', although workers' associations were able to circumvent this restriction by citing a law (the *Versammlungsgesetz* of 1867) that allowed events with named guests taking place in associations to go ahead without having to first seek permission from the relevant authorities (Troch 1991: 12–13). Using this loophole, associations linked to the Austrian Social Democratic Party (SDAP) were able to organise meetings attended by up to three thousand people, although they still had to comply with a number of rules and regulations. Most were attended by government officials, who could interrupt speakers at any point, refuse to let them continue, or simply close the meeting (13).

Astute professional politicians also made use of traditional gatherings, large and small, to address their audiences. Folk festivals provided cover for many of the major political rallies held in Berlin and Vienna in the first decades of the twentieth century (Düding 1988; Warneken 1986; Rasky 2005). The most prominent of these were the May Day festivities, first celebrated as a workers' holiday Austria in 1890, when Viktor Adler choreographed a day of action that consisted of a series of public meetings held around the country in the morning, to which, borrowing from the tactics employed by the Chartists in Britain, practised speakers were sent (Troch 1991: 16). While the Social Democrats turned the traditional May Day celebrations into a large-scale platform for political public speaking, politicians from the right often made judicious use of rather more small-scale events. For example, during his time as mayor in Vienna (1897–1910), Karl Lueger attended numerous christenings, weddings and golden weddings, as well as spending time in inns and coffee houses, using these occasions to give impromptu political speeches (Johnston 1972: 66). Professional politicians such as Lueger demonstrated that almost any gathering could be turned into a political meeting; concomitantly, in 'Politics as a Vocation', Weber (2004: 39) argued that anyone addressing a political meeting could be regarded as someone for whom politics had become a vocation, albeit an occasional one. In Berlin and Vienna in the early twentieth century, an expansion of discursive space was taking place, allowing more and more people to discover that, although they were never destined to become professional politicians, politics was still a vocation they could embrace (Eley 1992; Negt and Kluge 1993).

The expansion of discursive space in this period was not merely symbolic; the twentieth century saw political speakers, whether professional politicians or not, take to the streets in their search for a suitable place to make their case. In revolutionary times such as the winter of 1918/1919, this course of action became extremely popular, partly because, as Robert Riemann reported, all available indoor venues were booked up for weeks ahead (and the newspapers were at a loss to provide adequate space to report on the huge number of talks taking place) (1921: 1). That year, as Harry Graf Kessler (1982: 78–9) noted in his diary, Berlin's Schloßplatz came to resemble Speakers' Corner in Hyde Park, with occasional politicians jostling for space with charismatic professional speakers such as Karl Liebknecht. The experience of hearing him speak from the balcony of the occupied Police Headquarters was a profound one for Kessler, who noted on 5 January 1919 that

Liebknecht [...] spoke like a pastor, his words dripping with pathos, slowly and emotionally, turning the phrases into a kind of song.

You couldn't see him as he was speaking from within a darkened room. You could only make out some of what he was saying, and yet the singsong quality of his voice rang out over the silent and intent crowd, reaching far across the square.

Kessler (1982: 91–2)

Public lectures

Like politicians, academics embraced the expansion of discursive space in the early twentieth century. Speakers like Thode, with a background in the humanities, were joined by scientists and social scientists devoted to the popularisation of their subjects, professionals such as doctors and architects keen to enlighten their audiences, and more sensational speakers demonstrating, for example, their personal knowledge of the occult (Daum 1998; Kury 2000). Simmel's 1903 lecture on 'The Metropolis and Mental Life' was not an isolated occurrence, but one of a long series of public engagements spanning many years that allowed him to seek out different audiences for his ideas than would be reached only by his teaching activities. In a lecture given in 1919 on 'Science as a Vocation', his colleague, Weber, sought to formalise the distinction between lecturing as a university teacher and speaking in public, urging the prophet or demagogue to leave the lectern behind and seek a wider audience out on the streets, where he could expect a more critical response since there, the gulf between speaker and addressee was much smaller than in the inherently unequal relationship between university lecturer and student (2004: 20–1).

While not actually taking to the streets, many speakers in the realm of education – some full-time peripatetic lecturers, others attached to a particular education establishment – embarked upon lecture tours throughout the German-speaking world, addressing voluntary associations or appearing in formal institutions for adult education, such as Urania and the Humboldt-Akademie in Berlin, or the Volkshochschule Volksheim in Vienna (Tenbruck 1990; Daum 1998: 87, 113; Filla 1992). Lectures on technical and scientific matters were especially popular at this time, and speakers ranged from well-known scientists of international repute delivering prestigious lectures to professional popularisers bringing science to interested amateurs. The distinction between serious scientists and professional popularisers was, however, not always easy to maintain. For example, during his lifetime, Albert Einstein's lectures became increasingly popular and by the early 1920s, according to the Austrian physicist Philipp Frank, he had become a figure to be conspicuously consumed; his lectures were, apparently, attended by rich American and English ladies in fur coats, who passed the time by subjecting him to a careful appraisal through their opera glasses (cited in Herneck 1976: 83).

Literary and artistic performances

Adult education establishments also played host to literary and artistic performances, including cultural critics, such as Harden, offering acerbic observations, authors reading from their own work and professional reciters performing the work of others, as well as other forms of performance art, including drama, dance, music and variety theatre. Rather more influential in this sphere than education establishments were literary and cultural associations, such as Herwarth Walden's Verein für Kunst (Association for Art). Established in 1904, its first season included evenings devoted to Friedrich Nietzsche and Paul Scheerbart (Pirsch 1985: 374). As revealed in Walden's correspondence, Harden spoke at the Verein für Kunst in 1907 after some persuasion (*Sturm*-Archiv); other writers associated with the Verein's 'artistic evenings' around this time included Hermann Bahr, Maxim Gorki, Heinrich and Thomas Mann, and Rainer Maria Rilke (375). Of these writers, Bahr stands out as a speaker who was also an organiser of similar literary performances in Vienna, demonstrating the way that certain individuals offered points of intersection between 'language-games'. Others playing a leading role in organising literary lectures in Vienna included Hugo Heller, whose bookshop hosted readings by leading authors such as Hermann Hesse and Thomas Mann, and Paul Stefan and Ludwig Ullmann, both of whom were members of the Akademischer Verband für Literatur und Musik in Vienna, a student society established in 1908 to facilitate literary and musical performances (Lunzer 1989: 146–52). Making the most of the freedom accorded to it as a student society, its programmes increasingly came to focus on the controversial, including readings and performances by Karl Kraus and Arthur Schnitzler, as well as by figures from the counter-cultural cabaret scene.

Berlin also boasted similar student-run societies, with connections to the city's burgeoning cabaret scene. One such society was the Neuer Club, which was conceived by its founders, including Kurt

Hiller, Jakob van Hoddis and Erwin Loewensen, as a private organisation that would bring together like-minded young people interested
in philosophy and literature, with the aim of facilitating discussion
in these areas (Hiller 1969: 80; Sheppard 1980–83). Another was the
left-liberal Freistudentischen Bund, whose members included a young
Walter Benjamin and which, as Herwarth Walden assured Karl Kraus
in a letter dated 4 January 1910, was one of the places to be seen on
Berlin's public speaking circuit in the early twentieth century (Avery
2002: 140). Professional cabarets, such as Nachtlicht and Fledermaus
in Vienna, or Max Reinhardt's Schall und Rauch in Berlin also organised performances by literary artistes (Segel 1987; Jelavich 1996), and
'author evenings' were hosted by journals such as Siefgried Jacobsohn's
Die Schaubühne (which later became *Die Weltbühne*), Oskar Julius
Bierbaum's and Julius Meier-Graefe's *Pan*, and Fritz Pfemfert's anar-
chist journal, *Die Aktion*. In the case of the latter, its 'literary evenings' were so successful that from November 1913, it occupied its
own lecture hall, the 'Vortragssaal Aktion' in the Landhausstrasse in
Berlin.

Facilitated by the existence of a network of such cultural associations,
commercial ventures and bohemian artistic groups, literary performers,
like academic lecturers, increasingly embarked upon public lecture
tours throughout the German-speaking world, although there was, it
seems, some tension between the different categories of literary performers on tour. As the writer and performer, Roda Roda remarked in
an article that appeared in *Die Schaubühne*, where once there were
wandering poets, rhapsodists and minnesingers, in the preceding six
or seven years, a group of modern authors had taken to the road,
performing their own texts to express their dissatisfaction with the
work of so-called professional reciters (1913). Not all modern authors
were, however, talented performers; Willy Haas recalls a performance
by Hofmannsthal in Prague in 1910, where the writer was joined on
stage by a dancer:

> The podium proved too confined for sweet Grete Wiesenthal, and
> she got stuck three times. Hofmannsthal read his own poems as
> though he were an army officer reciting poetry by Hofmannsthal,
> without understanding a word of it.
>
> Haas (1957)

Crossover between the spheres

In these brief descriptions of political, educational and literary-aesthetic public speaking, points of connection begin to emerge between the three categories, such as the role that voluntary associations played in facilitating all kinds of public speaking. If we return to Naumann, Thode and Harden, and delve a little deeper into their careers as public speakers, it will become clear that such connections characterised the public lecture scene in Berlin and Vienna in the early twentieth century, undercutting the neat distinctions between categories proposed so far. For example, Naumann combined politics and education to give a series of four lectures in 1910 in Berlin's Philharmonic Hall on German political history (Loew 1985: 8). In the first of these lectures, he drew attention to the importance of the 1848 uprisings – and the speeches given that year in the Paulskirche in Frankfurt – for the development of political culture in Germany. Throughout his life, he remained convinced of the importance of public speaking in political education and so when, together with Wilhelm Heile, he formed the Staatsbürgerschule (National School of Citizenship) in Berlin in 1919 to educate civil servants, it was not surprising that its curriculum included a series of lectures devoted to 'The Art of the Political Speech' (51). Thode, meanwhile, may have been representative of the academic descending from the ivory tower to disseminate his ideas to a wider public, but as the founder of the conservative Werdandi-Bund, an association that stood against 'Parisian decadence' and 'lack of spiritual substance' and for 'wholesome art', he also increasingly engaged in protracted debate on the political aspects of art and ideology in the service of nation-building, demonstrating, in so doing, certain anti-Semitic tendencies (Brühl 1991: 132). Finally, Harden's public speaking career, of which a lecture given in 1898 to the Viennese press association, Concordia, on modern European literature was typical, also crossed boundaries between literary entertainment and politics (*Wiener Rundschau* 1898: 278). This befitted the editor of *Die Zukunft*, a journal combining literature and politics, and the co-founder of the Verein Freie Volksbühne in Berlin, an organisation established to enable the performance of Naturalist dramas that had fallen foul of the censor (Brauneck 1974: 20–8).

These were not isolated examples of interconnections between political speeches, professional lectures and literary performances.

Naumann's forays into educational speaking were part of a larger tradition in which education and politics were closely entwined, and the dissemination of knowledge through public speaking was seen as a way of furthering the population's political education, particularly by the Social Democrats. In Berlin in 1891, Wilhelm Liebknecht founded the Arbeiterbildungsschule, a workers' education establishment that began by offering practical instruction in subjects such as German and arithmetic, but increasingly offered politically oriented education (Urbach 1971: 15). From 1906, the German Social Democratic Party (SPD) also offered intensive political education to a small number of party members in the 'Parteischule' (15). Similar party political schools were also set up in Vienna by the Austrian Social Democrats (SDAP) (Gruber 1991: 92), while a more general form of political education was provided in adult education establishments such as the Volksheim in Ottakring, founded by Ludo Hartmann. Its programme featured lectures by leading left-wing politicians, including Karl Renner, who would become the first chancellor of the First and Second Republics of Austria, and Hans Kelsen, who would later write the constitution of the Republic of Austria (Filla 1992: 88). By the 1920s, both the SPD and the SDAP were organising regular lecture series on political and non-political topics as part of their ongoing commitment to developing working class culture (Urbach 1971; Gruber 1991: 81–113).

Other adult education establishments regarded themselves independent of party politics. In 1912, the *Adreßbuch der deutschen Rednerschaft* (Directory of German Public Speakers) was renamed the *Jahrbuch der deutschen Vortragswesen* (Yearbook for Lecturing Activities in Germany) in an attempt to distinguish lecturers associated with adult education from the 'speakers' ('Redner') that inhabited the world of political agitation (*Jahrbuch für das deutsche Vortragswesen* 1912/13: i). In setting out to provide an alternative to socialist-sponsored adult education, however, apparently non-political organisations in the field of adult education were actually co-opted by particular political agendas. A case in point was the building of the Urania in Vienna in 1910, which enjoyed the support of the Christian Socialist mayor, Karl Lueger (Taschwer 1995: 14–16). During World War I, the Urania in Berlin took on a more overtly political role than had previously been the case, replacing its trademark scientific lectures with patriotic lectures glorifying the 'Fatherland'. Under the banner of geography, lectures were offered on war zones and regions that had been won for Germany, while physics lectures concerned themselves with new developments in modern weaponry (Urania Berlin e.V. 1988: 47). After the war, previously apolitical adult education establishments, such as the Lessing-Hochschule, played host to political speakers including Gustav Stresemann and Theodor Heuss, and leading feminists such as Adele Schreiber and Ilse Riecke (Lewin 1960: 6–8). Meanwhile, the lecturing activity of the Urania had a role to play in foreign policy; in 1909, it was chosen to organise a series of lectures in the German pavilion at the World Exhibition in Brussels (Gesellschaft Urania 1913: 41). These lectures, which were delivered by renowned experts in their fields, gave an overview of the most important aspects of economic and cultural life in Germany, as well as more detailed information on a number of exhibitors, and were sufficiently well received to earn a prize for the Urania.

While political speakers appeared with increasing regularity in previously non-political adult education establishments, some of the writers and artists whose speaking careers had been mainly located in adult education institutions simultaneously began to take up opportunities with political organisations. This was particularly marked after 1918, when writers such as Alfred Polgar, Ernst Toller and Karl Kraus, addressed social democratic associations (*Arbeiterzeitung* 1928; K[ornig] 1929; Csokor 1927; Goldschmidt 1984). In combining literary and political speaking, these writers were drawing on a long tradition of using the theatre as a political platform, that saw, around 1848, actors in Germany being accused of misusing their stage appearances to make inflammatory speeches (Freydank 1988: 260). Later, Harden and others founded the Verein Freie Volksbühne Berlin (an association for popular theatre that had its roots in a social democratic debating club) with the aim of using theatre to construct a counter-public to the dominant bourgeois public sphere (Brauneck 1974: 28). In 1890, author and well-known public speaker Bruno Wille addressed an audience of 2000 at the first meeting of the new association, where he spoke on 'Art for the People' (Freydank 1988: 341; Brauneck 1974: 29–30). According to the association's constitution, one of its main aims was to use public lectures to demonstrate literature's political relevance. This activity attracted the attention of the police, who eventually stopped such lectures taking place and forced the association to remove references to introductory lectures from its constitution (30–6). Meanwhile around the same time in Vienna, the May Day celebrations provided an occasion in which political speaking and popular theatre could unite: they included an annual theatre performance, held in the Prater and starring popular actors such as Hansi Neise and Alexander Girardi, creating a programme that was apparently both entertaining and political (Troch 1991: 133–4).

By 1910, many artists in the German-speaking countries were becoming increasingly politicised, particularly those associated with literary expressionism and with revolutionary political journals such as *Die Aktion*. In such circles, literary performances took on more overtly political and socio-critical overtones (Raabe 1961). During the First World War, however, the mood amongst a number of established writers was more patriotic than critical. Hugo von Hofmannsthal, for example, did his bit for morale by lecturing to German diplomatic circles, joining politicians such as Naumann and academics, such as Georg Simmel, in addressing such audiences (Yates 1992: 170; Loew 1985: 55; Gassen and Landmann 1958: 277). While Hofmannsthal demonstrated his patriotism, other artists used the form of the public lecture as literary performance to demonstrate against the war. As part of a series of lecture evenings held in Berlin, Tilla Durieux read sections of a pacifist novella by Leonhart Frank (Brühl 1991: 82). According to her memoirs, some people were so fired up by this event that they threatened to stage an impromptu street demonstration, but were prevented from doing so by their more level-headed compatriots (Durieux 1971, cited in Brühl 1991: 82).

Durieux's reading took place in Paul Cassirer's art gallery, which had long provided a location in which leading figures from both spheres could mix, reflecting its owner's wide-ranging interests (95). Kessler was another figure at home in both political and artistic circles. His diaries from 1918 onwards provide key insights into the role that public speaking played in Berlin during this period, including accounts of meetings of private debating clubs to which he belonged (a number of which met in the Cassirer's gallery); lectures that he attended, ranging from a memorable recitation of Rilke poetry by Ludwig Hardt, to a lecture on school reform by Gustav Wyneken; and talks that he gave, including a well-received lecture at the Humboldt University, at the invitation of the Sozialistischer Studentenbund, a left-wing student association (Kessler 1982: 18, 117, 235). In particular, he made a number of references to cabaret performances, highlighting another area that bridged literary performance and political speech-making.

As Richard Huelsenbeck maintained in his first provocative 'Dada-Speech' in Germany, delivered on 22 January 1918, cabaret was only one step removed from politics (1982: 56). For many other performers, particularly in the 1920s, cabaret was by definition political, as, for example, in the case of the Austrian Social Democratic Party's 'Political Cabaret' or the 'Jewish-Political Cabaret', established in Vienna in 1925 and 1927, respectively (Pfoser 1980: 65–70; Veigl 1986: 164). As in the war years, however, not all political literary lectures of the interwar period assumed anti-establishment positions. Hofmannsthal, for example, gave a celebrated lecture at the University of Munich on 10 January 1927, at the invitation of the Goethe Society and the Argonauts, on 'Writing as the Spiritual Space of the Nation', which was attended by official representatives of the government and high-up members of the civil service (Hildebrandt 1927: 39). In this lecture, Hofmannsthal outlined his understanding of a coming 'conservative revolution'.

If literature was becoming increasingly politicised in the interwar period, political speaking was also, at times, commodified as entertainment. This is part of the phenomenon that Benjamin described in his 'Work of Art' essay as the 'aestheticizing of politics' (1996–2003: 3, 122). One example might serve to demonstrate how this functioned in the sphere of public speaking. In 1925, a benefit evening devoted to revolutionary rhetoric and its effect on the masses took place in the Philharmonic Hall in Berlin, presenting speeches by iconic figures such as Danton, Robespierre, Pitt, Lenin, Mussolini and Bismarck. Reporting on this event in the weekly literary review, the *Literarische Welt*, Walter Mehring closed his article with the ironic remark: 'The sons of the generation that murdered Luxemburg are going to turn that woman's direct rhetoric into indirect speech. The Philharmonic Hall is the setting for revolutions. The entertainment section continues on the next page' (1925: 50). His critique is clearly aimed at the aestheticisation of revolutionary rhetoric, or, to put it another way, at what he saw as the potential dangers of blurring the boundaries between different forms of public speaking.

Karl Kraus: Public speaking as scene

Like Mehring and others, Karl Kraus was critical of the manipulative potential of rhetoric, but this did not prevent him from becoming a prolific and celebrated performer of the spoken word. During the

1920s, he commanded audiences of up to 2000, at a time in which other writers were scarcely able to scrape together an audience at all (Timms 2005: 410–1). Part of his success was due to the unique character of his public appearances, which embraced music, visual technology and politics, as well as literature. In a nuanced and insightful

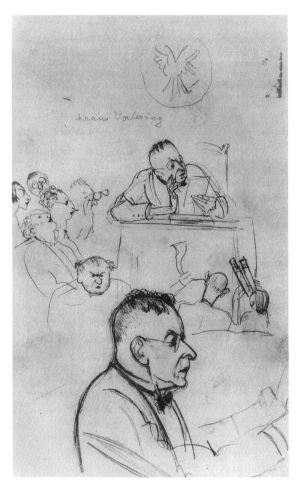

Figure 1.1   Alfred Hagel: Karl Kraus lecturing; *Source*: © Wien Museum

portrait of this controversial figure, first published in the leading German broadsheet, the *Frankfurter Zeitung*, in 1931, Benjamin described him as 'the last citizen [Bürger]' (1996–2003: 2, 454; translation amended).[1] Georg Knepler, Kraus's erstwhile accompanist and author of a comprehensive study of his public performances, took issue with this portrayal, maintaining that Kraus was a man like no other, who situated himself uncompromisingly outside the bourgeois world, as its critic (1984: 181). But this is to misunderstand Benjamin, who recognised the central role that 'the destructive and the critical' played in the development and articulation of Kraus's engagement with the moral intellectual climate of the present, but also, and crucially, saw that the various manifestations of Kraus's destructive persona – comedian, polemicist, madman – with which people were familiar, were actually merely necessary deviations from the central 'civic virtues' that comprised his natural form of engagement with the world (Benjamin 1996–2003: 2, 436, 455). Kraus's work, according to Benjamin, could be understood as a programme, the aim of which was to rediscover a particular sense of 'origin' by 'revers[ing] the development of bourgeois-capitalist affairs to a condition that was never theirs' (454). Benjamin's description of Kraus as 'the last citizen' offers us a clue as to what might be imagined by such a condition; it suggests a connection between Kraus and those residents of the polis (the ancient city-state), who possessed voting rights and could therefore gather together in the agora (the marketplace) to engage in discussion characterised by a 'fiercely agonal spirit' and so constitute the city's powerful public sphere (Arendt 1958: 41). Kraus's authority as a public intellectual, which Benjamin (439) suggests he held onto by the simple but effective method of never disappointing the public, was derived from the possibility of a return to an ideal bourgeois public sphere that, just like its ancient counterpart, would be reliant on the use of undistorted rational language as a tool in the hands of men of integrity.[2] This explains why Kraus's work was, as his contemporary Robert Scheu (1909: 29) suggested, fundamentally a crusade against pseudo-discourse. The critique of the way in which language was (mis)used offered Kraus the philosophical and moral basis from which to engage critically with society.

Kraus's critique may have been predicated on a utopian return to an ideal bourgeois public sphere, but for the most of his life, his status as 'the last citizen' entailed anything but a melancholic retreat from the real existing public sphere of his time. Instead, the destructive force of his work led to an intensive, almost obsessive urge to appear in public, in order to unmask the hypocrisies of contemporary society. He did this as the editor and author of his journal, *Die Fackel* (The Torch), and as a prolific speaker and performer. During his lifetime, he gave 700 public performances, which we know primarily because he was fastidious about keeping a running total in *Die Fackel* of the number of times he took to the lectern.[3] Although he had given public readings as early as 1893, the first of his regular literary performances took place in Berlin on 13 January 1910, at the invitation of Herwarth Walden's Verein für Kunst. It was quickly followed by two further appearances in the city – on 17 January, organised by the left-liberal student society, the Freie Studentenschaft der Universität Berlin, and on 20 January, again organised by the Verein für Kunst. All three events took place in Paul Cassirer's art gallery, and gained much attention from the press, as attested by the reviews reproduced in the *Fackel* (AAC-F 1910 294–95: 30–8). Later in the same year, Kraus gave two performances in Vienna, both of which were organised by the student-run literary society, the Akademischer Verband für Literatur und Musik (AAC-F 1910 300: ii, 303–304: ii). These first public performances saw him mainly reading from his own texts, although he sometimes also read from works by other authors, such as Peter Altenberg (see, for example, AAC-F 1913 370–71: 35). In *performing* his texts, he seemed to have found his medium, describing himself as 'perhaps the first case of a writer who then experiences his writings through play-acting' (Benjamin 1996–2003: 2, 442). He continued giving readings from his work throughout his career, but also, from 1912 onwards, he developed the 'Theater der Dichtung' ('Theatre of Poetry'),[4] in which he staged one-man performances of canonical plays and operettas, including works by Shakespeare, Goethe, Nestroy, Raimund and Offenbach, setting free his 'mimetic genius' (Benjamin 1996–2003: 2, 442). Kraus routinely gave these literary performances a contemporary political twist, by adapting the literary texts and using so-called 'additional rhyming couplets' or 'Zeitstrophen' (topical verse) through which he added his own comments to the texts being performed.[5]

Both forms built on the success of his early performances in Berlin and Vienna (the second lecture in Vienna was organised after the first sold out) and led to Kraus embarking upon extended lecture tours that took him throughout the Austro-Hungarian Empire and into Germany – for example, a tour in October–November 1913 saw him speak in Vienna, Brno, Mährisch-Ostrau, Czernowitz, Trieste, Pola, Graz, Berlin, Dresden and Prague (AAC-F 1913 400–403: 50). Later in his career, he also ventured into Western Europe, appearing in prestigious locations such as the Sorbonne in Paris, where he gave three separate lecture series – in March 1925 (AAC-F 1925 686–90: 36), April 1926 (AAC-F 1926 726–29: 75) and December 1927 (AAC-F 1927 781–86: 75) – all at the invitation of the société pour la propagation des langues éstrangères en France (a body promoting cultural exchange). In the early 1930s, he took advantage of the opportunities offered by technological developments in the field of communication and performed for radio both his own texts and works by Hauptmann, Nestroy, Raimund, Offenbach and Goethe (Knepler 1984: 223–35). In 1934, an amateur film of Kraus performing was produced in Prague, which had its first public airing in the Schwedenkino (a centrally located cinema in Vienna) on 20 April 1934, as part of the celebrations to mark Kraus's sixtieth birthday (Pfäfflin and Dambacher 1999: 511).[6]

By 1934 – a turbulent year in Austria's history, which saw the first armed struggle against fascism in Europe brutally quelled, paving the way for the imposition of the authoritarian Ständesstaat – it seemed as though Kraus was about to retreat from the public sphere.[7] As he explained in a short poem that appeared in *Die Fackel* in 1933 (an issue containing only this poem and the text of the speech that Kraus had given at Adolf Loos's graveside): 'Man frage nicht, was all die Zeit ich machte./Ich bleibe stumm;/und sage nicht warum…[Don't ask about the actions I've been taking/I'll not speak out,/nor say what it's about…]' (AAC-F 1933 888: 4, translated Timms 2005: 494). He actually continued to appear in public until 1936, when he gave his 700th and final performance in the Konzerthaus in Vienna. In a sense, however, committing his performances to vinyl and celluloid, and so constructing a memorial in the form of stored data, symbolised the beginning of the end of the influential urban scene that was brought into life with his early performances in 1910. The end itself was attributable to the world-historical events that ultimately plunged Kraus into deep despair (Viertel 1999: 480). Blum argues that the process of becoming and perishing is typical of the scene, a form of life that plays its part in 'making the city itself a place' (2003: 165). Exploring

Kraus's performances through the prism of Blum's work on urban scenes will allow us to shed new light on the context of his activities as a public intellectual in Vienna, Berlin and elsewhere in the first decades of the twentieth century.

How does Blum define the scene over and above its status as a fluid entity that has an important role to play in the discursive construction of the city? In the *Imaginative Structure of the City*, he devotes a chapter to 'the question of the scene and its status in urban life' (Blum 2003: 165), arguing that the task of those who seek to engage reflectively with this social formation is to construct a 'grammar of the scene, in order to rebuild parameters from its usage' (167). Each scene, he notes, 'resonates with some concerted activity, an activity to a degree specialized, at least differentiated, but not necessarily covert' (166–7). Might public speaking be the kind of activity with which a scene resonates? An initial perusal of Blum's account of the scene's 'grammar' would suggest that this might be the case. Scenes, according to Blum, are occasions for 'seeing and being seen' (171); they are sites in which protagonists can accumulate 'cultural capital' (Bourdieu 1984), which, as the imaginary conversation between the Idealist and the Sceptic cited at the beginning of this chapter suggests, was true of both audience and speaker in the individual public speaking event. Not only that, but scenes are locations that allow strangers to come together; they are places charged with theatricality, 'site[s] of communicative energy' (Blum 2003: 179). In fact, the central activity of the original urban scene – the scene organised through the philosophical exchanges that inspired the circle gathered around Socrates – was speaking in public (176–7).

These general points certainly seem to indicate that we might be justified in talking of 'the public speaking scene', but Blum presents certain qualifications that would suggest that not all instances of public speaking are part of a scene. His argument centres on a detailed phenomenology of the scene, where he shows that features such as providing a meeting place for strangers, theatricality or regularity are not in themselves sufficient to construct a scene. And just because an activity takes place in the city, it does not in itself mean that it is related to an urban scene. He illustrates this point with reference to art, arguing that a city can have art but no art scene (art is only 'practiced privately'), or alternatively, an art scene (which would function to 'stage an encounter between lovers of [art]') but no 'real art'

(Blum 2003: 170). By analogy, we could distinguish between public speaking as urban activity, and public speaking as the central activity of a scene. As we will see, the latter is true of Kraus's appearing in the city, which, as Benjamin noted, is the result of a particular 'programme' (1996–2003: 2, 454). This level of intention is central to the functioning of a scene, which 'accomplishes its work by making a site the occasion of a project' (Blum 2003: 187). And this is not the only indication that Kraus's public performances might be construed as the central activity of an urban scene. Other factors, drawn from Blum's grammar of the scene, include the central tension between the city and the scene figured as 'transgression'; the distinction between strangers and idle onlookers, and related to that, the desire for communality within collective life and the distinctive form of solidarity engendered by the scene; the fusion of art and commodity; and the fact that the scene practices in public something private.

From the outset, Kraus's public performances in Vienna existed in a tense relationship with that city – so much so, in fact, that his first performances there took place behind closed doors, the result of a decade and more of controversy and conflict. As Kraus noted in *Die Fackel* in 1899, since he had begun publishing, he had been the recipient of '236 anonymous letters of abuse, 83 anonymous threatening letters and one physical attack on his person' (AAC-F 1899 9: 23). When the possibility of his appearing in public in Vienna was first mooted, he was understandably apprehensive, and for these first lectures, he took precautions to ensure that his audience would not be hostile, insisting that those requesting tickets should have to provide their full name and that tickets would only be issued to those approved by him (Lunzer 1989: 157–8). A further performance, which was to have taken place in the Bösendorfersaal in December 1910, organised by a professional agency, the Albert Gutmann Konzertdirektion, was cancelled after the owner of the venue refused permission for it to be used for a Kraus performance, citing his fear that Kraus's aggressive attitude towards the Viennese press might mean that his venue was boycotted in the future (AAC-F 1911 326–28: 21–2). In a published excerpt from Hermann Bahr's diary, it was suggested that Kraus had wanted to perform in Vienna, but had been refused use of this particular venue, 'supposedly because there were worries that Kraus was rather unpopular' (Bahr 1911: 81). Bahr noted that there was no love lost between him and Kraus, but suggested that all authors need to stand together for freedom of speech. Kraus, however, rebuffed Bahr's concerns, stating that Bahr was overreacting, as the owner of the venue was not fearful of the reaction of the state, government, police or social order, but of the press (AAC-F 1911 326–28: 19).

Wherever the threat was coming from, these problems, coupled with the fact that restrictions on the audience were deemed necessary at all, demonstrates the tension between Kraus's public speaking activities and the city, showing the 'dangerousness of the scene' to the 'very city it exemplifies' (Blum 2003: 177). This sense of danger was seized upon by the press in its reviews of Kraus's performances, as Kraus demonstrated in *Die Fackel*, where he reproduced a number of press cuttings relating to a performance he gave in Berlin on 10 December 1912 (AAC-F 1913 366-67: 33–7). The resulting collage was constructed to demonstrate the laziness of a form of journalism that had to rely on cliché in its attempt to evoke the atmosphere of a Kraus event. In these excerpts, Kraus was identified variously as the 'The Harden of Vienna', the 'Spinoza of the Leopoldstadt' and the 'Buddha of the Prater'. While the first of these labels was plausibly an attempt to introduce Kraus to a Berlin audience by comparing him to Maximilian Harden, a speaker already well-known in the city, Harden's own controversial reputation means that such a statement also passed judgement on Kraus. This implicit criticism was echoed in epithets such as the 'Spinoza of the Leopoldstadt' and the 'Buddha of the Prater', both of which employ geographical signifiers to locate him on the margins of Viennese society. The Leopoldstadt, Vienna's Second District and part of an island lying between the Danube canal and the Danube itself, was the site of Vienna's Jewish ghetto (Hanak and Widrich 1998), while the Prater, a former royal park gifted to the city of Vienna, figured in the cultural imagination of the early twentieth century as a place of Otherness (Salten 1911). Similarly, anointing Kraus 'Spinoza', the controversial philosopher reviled by many in his lifetime, or 'Buddha', the exotic Eastern philosopher-prophet, served to identify him as an outsider figure. Yet even while styling Kraus as an outsider, such newspaper reports also worked to cement his place in the public sphere by facilitating the 'circulation of discourse' that, as Warner argues, is how a public constitutes itself (2002: 90). At the same time, this commentary on Kraus is typical of the way in which the scene is ascribed an aura of danger, 'through the work of idle onlookers who visit [...] the scene as uncommitted witnesses to the activity' (Blum 2003: 177). To that, we could add: who visit the scene as hostile witnesses.

The distinction between members of the scene and 'idle onlookers' is central to Blum's (2003) phenomenology of the scene, allowing him to argue that the external difference between those who do not belong to the scene and those who do, is greater than any internal distinction between, say, speaker and audience. During a public reading given on New Year's Day 1925, under the title 'Two Hundred Performances and the Viennese Intelligentsia' ('Zwei Hundert Vorlesungen und das geistige Wien'), Kraus complained that the leading Viennese intellectuals of the day chose not to experience his performances of leading authors such as Shakespeare and Nestroy, Goethe and Hauptmann, Raimund and Altenberg – even though, as he pointed out, implying that contemporary Viennese intellectuals could not match up to his chosen authors, members of this putative Viennese intelligentsia would not be personally affected by what they heard in one of his performances (AAC-F 1925 676–78: 59). The challenge issued to the scene by idle onlookers is whether they should be accepted as a gesture of hospitality, or have their status as outsiders confirmed and emphasised (Blum 2003: 168). In 'Two Hundred Lectures', Kraus seemed to suggest that his preferred option would be to offer a gesture of hospitality to the eponymous Viennese intelligentsia. He posited renting a space with private boxes so that people could arrive, stay and leave incognito, and so attend one of his readings without him (or anyone else) actually knowing (AAC-F 1925 676–78: 60). But in denying these onlookers the chance to see and be seen, Kraus was actually seeking to leave intact their status as outsiders.

In the conclusion to 'Two Hundred Lectures', Kraus underlined the distinction between insider and outsider, maintaining that the true Viennese intelligentsia, in contrast to the 'intellectual frauds' that merely styled themselves as such, constituted itself in the audience for his lectures:

> We proudly want to share the suspicion that if there is such a thing as a Viennese intelligentsia at all, then it is gathered in this hall between the table on the podium and the standing room at the back; we want to be proud that we can wrest this name from the grasp of a band of intellectual frauds; we want to be most proud, however, of the fact that if we want to come together, we do not

need their blessing, and if we want to experience the joy of inter-
acting with one another, then we are free to do so without the
presence of those who do not want to hear us, because they are
frightened of being forced to feel.

                                          AAC-F (1925 676–78: 68)

There is, as Timms points out, a sense of community invoked here, a
sense of solidarity between speaker and audience (2005: 410), and
indeed, earlier in the same lecture, Kraus had specified the necessity
of an audience as an integral part of a public reading: '[w]hile the
printed word would come into being and exist even without a reader,
the audience belongs to the performance of text, which would not
exist without its audience, not because the listeners were missing, but
because an essential element was missing' (AAC-F 1925 676–78: 54).

Timms argues that Kraus's attempt to construct a 'true Viennese
cultural community' was characteristic of his work in the 1920s (2005:
411). He also suggests that the success of Kraus's performances – which
regularly filled large halls such as the Middle Hall of the Konzerthaus
with a capacity of almost 900 without recourse to significant prior
advertising – is evidence of the strength of that community. This lack
of advertising is a key element in defining Kraus's public speaking
activities as a scene, since it is characteristic of the scene that it hides
its location from those not in the know (Blum 2003: 167). But in
defining the circle around Kraus as a scene, the question of 'community'
becomes more complex than Timms appears to imagine it to be:

> The scene – never a community in the sense of finality – is a work
> in progress where being with or among others is a constantly
> evolving open question that brings to view the intimacy of social
> life as an unending problem to solve.
>
>   Blum (2003: 188)

This definition of the scene is based on the understanding that for all
its emphasis on communality and solidarity, the scene is inhabited
by strangers, and the disjunction between stranger and intimacy is
a marker of the scene, distinguishing it from other forms of social
organisation such as the association:

> It sounds as if the scene confirms something about the associa-
> tional life of the city, the ways its web of groups, societies, and sects

endow the city with a fraternal spirit, but this images the scene as a Gemeinschaft, whereas, in contrast, it is the mix of Gemeinschaft–Gesellschaft and their impossible reconciliation that makes for the lure and excitement of the scene.

Blum (2003: 176)

Benjamin captures something of this, when he identifies the lecture hall as the place where Kraus is alone with his work (1996–2003: 2, 447). Kraus may have recognised his audience as integral to the performance, but this did nothing to change the fact that they remained strangers to him, as he remained a stranger to them. This suggests that the newspaper reviews that focused on Kraus's role as stranger may not have been wrong, but merely misplaced; their view of Kraus as stranger emphasised his alterity, while the figure of the stranger central to the functioning of the scene is based on the uncanny (Blum 2003: 180–1).

The scene might be a collection of strangers, but this collection is bound together by strength of feeling for a particularly activity, which Blum variously glosses as commitment, love or longing (2003: 168, 170, 176). From the time of Kraus's early performances, the core audiences that he commanded for his literary performances reportedly demonstrated desire in the form of a fanaticism not often seen in the audiences of other speakers. In these early years, Kraus was particularly well received by student societies and his audiences consisted mainly of the young readers of *Die Fackel*, who knew his work well enough to request specific texts as an encore (Bilke 1981: 70). Reporting on 'An Evening with Karl Kraus' organised by the Akademischer Verband für Literatur und Musik in the Beethoven-Saal in Vienna on 6 November 1911, the Danish author, Karin Michaelis, remarked on the youthful nature of the large audience of almost a thousand and, in particular, on the reaction of the women in the audience: 'The hall is full to bursting. It has been filled with youth, a youth that is both beautiful and full of promise. Never before have I seen in one place the magnificent faces of so many young men and so many smouldering young women moved to the point of ecstasy' (AAC-F 1911 336–337: 44). This was not a one-off occurrence; letters received by Kraus indicated that such levels of enthusiasm, often verging on the hysterical, were prevalent in his audiences, particularly amongst the women (Bilke 1981: 72–5). And Kraus was not the only male performer to be received in this way by his female audience. After a successful literary performance held in Vienna's Bösendorfer Saal on 28 March 1897, in which he took to the stage along with Hofmannsthal and Schnitzler, Bahr wrote to his father that, 'the success of our reading was quite peculiar. People, and particularly the girls, acted as though they had gone mad with enthusiasm; there really was a danger [...] of the silly girls trying to cut off locks of our hair' (1971: 404).

The dynamic of female audience admiring male speakers is not surprising, particularly if we consider that attending public lectures was a socially sanctioned activity for the female members of the educated bourgeoisie, as is made clear in von Beaulieu's satire (1912) on 'Education through Public Speaking' discussed at the outset of this chapter. Like shopping (Bowlby 1985), this was an activity that allowed women a place in the public sphere, albeit one still circumscribed by the fact that in Austria and Germany in the early twentieth century, women were not permitted to attend political meetings, far less speak at them (Hausen 1991), while in the non-political realm, certain lectures were closed to women. The advertisement for Simmel's 'Metropolis and Mental Life' that appeared in the daily newspaper, the *Dresdener Anzeiger*, for example, stated that tickets were available 'For Gentlemen' (Frisby 2001: 139). Frisby comments that it is not possible to ascertain whether this meant that women were barred from attending the lecture, but it is not unlikely, since at this time women were often only permitted to attend events organised by associations that were advertised as 'For Ladies' or 'With Ladies'. Some insight into the mindset of the era is provided by a short note that appeared in the official journal of the Austrian architects' association under the title 'Ladies in Technical Associations', maintaining that the main reason for excluding women from meetings of the association is that their hats obscure other people's views (*Zeitschrift des österreichischen Ingenieur- und Architektenvereins* 1906: 238).

Women reacted to being effectively shut out from male-dominated associations by founding their own debating associations and clubs, such as the 'Diskutierklub' and 'Libertas' in Vienna, which provided a stage for female speakers (Projekt Ariadne 2008). Otherwise, with a few notable exceptions such as Bertha von Suttner, recipient of the Nobel Prize for Peace in 1905 and acclaimed public speaker (Cohen 2005), most female speakers were rather limited in their opportunities to appear in public, although adult education did provide one platform for them. When women took up speaking engagements, however, they found an establishment prejudiced against them, as revealed in the attitude of Ewald Geißler (1911: 6), instructor in rhetoric at the University of Halle and author of an influential hand-book of public speaking, who described the female voice as too hesi-tant to be effective in a public forum. This serves to paint a picture of the gendered nature of public speaking at the beginning of the twen-tieth century, characterised by active male speakers and passive, often female audiences. Without wishing to deny this position, applying the logic of the scene suggests that we should be prepared to relativise the conclusion. While women were effectively excluded from much of the associative life in the modern city, many were involved in scenes. Even if this involvement was as member of the audience rather than speaker, we should not ignore the performative and therefore active role of all members of the scene, who are 'performers vis-á-vis an "outside" that is external to [the scene]' (Blum 2003: 171). In the case of Kraus's lectures, the young women that comprised a large section of his audiences were core members of a scene from which representa-tives of the dominant discourse, the putative Viennese intelligentsia were excluded.

Through this logic of inclusion, the scene gives a voice to those who might otherwise remain unheard. To those standing outside the scene – the 'dispersed and uncollected' (Blum 2003: 175) – this may appear threatening. But this is not the only danger associated with the scene; it also poses a threat to its members, which Blum describes as the danger of being exposed to those whom the scene whips into a state of ecstasy. Commentators from the outside recognised this as a problem associated with the scene that gathered around Kraus. By the 1920s, Kraus's lectures were reaching a new generation of young people, but the level of fanaticism remained diminished. One mem-ber of the scene was Elias Canetti, who, in homage to Kraus, gave his autobiographical account of life in Vienna in the 1920s the title, *Die Fackel im Ohr (The Torch in my Ear)*. He experienced Kraus's lec-tures as spiritual events: 'For the past year and a half I had gone to every reading and they filled my spirit as a bible would have done. [...] He [Kraus] was my conscience. He was my strength' (Canetti 1982: 152–3). While Canetti's account of these performances was entirely positive, more critical reviews of these events also drew on the language of spirituality. To give but one example, in a report that first appeared in the Viennese conservative daily newspaper, the *Reichspost*, on 27 May 1913 and was then reprinted in *Die Fackel*, the author used the image of the burning bush to draw an implicit comparison between Kraus and Moses: 'The wondrous embers of this burning bush threaten to consume any attempt at cool, reflective consideration' (AAC-F 1913 376–77: 28). Here, as is made clear earlier in this review, the author is targeting the uncritical response of Kraus's audience, which he describes as being consumed by a 'flaming enthusiasm' (27). Similar accounts of Kraus's audience can be found in a number of other, more favourable, reviews of his literary performances. For example, in *One Way Street*, a unique collection of aphorisms first published in 1928, Walter Benjamin noted: 'Karl Kraus. Nothing more desolating than his followers' – although he did go on to complete the thought by maintaining that there was also 'nothing more godforsaken than his adversaries' (Benjamin 1996–2003: 1, 469).

Benjamin refined this argument in his notes for his full-length essay on Kraus, where he differentiated between the hysterical Kraus admirers, and those on whom his work had a real effect, suggesting that Kraus could have little idea about the true effect of his work, as he could not see past the 'community of hysterics' who made their presence keenly felt at all his public performances (1991: 1092). Yet it was through performing in public that Kraus gained new followers, as even his many critics were moved to suspend their critique of him as critic and satirist, in favour of praising his abilities as a public speaker (Bilke 1981: 70). Outside of Vienna and beyond the circle of his immediate followers, intellectuals such as Benjamin were particularly receptive to the critical power of Kraus's 'Theatre of Poetry' performances. In a letter to Gersholm Sholem, Benjamin declared that he had been tempted to attend one of Kraus's Offenbach performances (1966: 518), while in 'Karl Kraus Reads Offenbach', a review first published in Willy Haas's influential weekly arts publication, *Die literarische Welt* in 1928, Benjamin implicitly likened Kraus's ability to speak through Offenbach and penetrate beyond the surface manifestation of things to Marx's (1977: 231) account of the bourgeoisie stripping away the veil of illusion contained in the *Communist Manifesto*:

> At times they [Offenbach's works] are transformed into a curtain; and like a fairground showman whose wild gestures accompany the entire performance, Karl Kraus tears this curtain aside, exposing

the contents of their and our own chamber of horrors to our gaze. We glimpse Schober and Bekessy; and at its centre point this evening, in honour of our city and this lecture hall, we see Alfred Kerr on a lofty podium.

Benjamin (1996–2003: 2, 111; translation slightly amended)

Benjamin provides us with a memorable account of the performative dimension of Kraus's thought, focusing on how he used destructive language and gesture to turn a nineteenth-century Parisian operetta into a work of direct relevance to Berlin ('in honour of our city') and to the particular occasion on which it was being performed ('in honour of … this lecture hall'). This brings us to the subject matter of the next section, which moves from a description of the circle that gathered around Kraus as a scene to exploring how the city appears as the subject matter of Kraus's performances. This is to think about the way in which the scene not only exemplifies the city, but also facilitates its discursive construction.

Kraus and the city

In a review of a 'Theatre of Poetry' performance that took place in Berlin on 29 April 1922 (AAC-F 1922 595–600: 69), Heinrich Fischer noted: 'When Karl Kraus reads Nestroy more than his mere words comes to life: a city, a milieu, a culture appears' (Fischer 1922: 488). While Fischer's review offers little of Benjamin's sensitivity towards Kraus, his emphasis on the manner in which Kraus is able to bring a particular view of the city to life does connect his perception of Kraus's public performances to that of Benjamin. Both Fischer and Benjamin were struck by the way that everyday city life was an integral component of Kraus's subject matter. Like his contemporaries, Loos and Altenberg, Kraus's view of the city rejects the panoptic in favour of the experience of those whom Michel De Certeau would later describe as 'the 'ordinary practitioners of the city [who] live "down below"'' (1988: 93). This is made clear at the beginning of 'The World of Posters' ('Die Welt der Plakate'), a text that Kraus performed many times, including in his first and his final public appearances. Here he indicates that even as a child, his inclination was to derive his knowledge of life from minute details, and so he found himself drawn to 'street life', listening to the 'noises of the day' (AAC-F 283–84: 19).

Such fleeting impressions were recorded in *Die Fackel*, which 'through 922 issues and thirty-seven years [...] endured in the ephemeral – earning its durability through this endurance' (Cacciari 1993: 146). They were also replayed in his public performances, which were similarly predicated on the relation between 'duration' and 'the ephemeral'.

This method took Kraus in a particular direction. Whether in his 'Theatre of Poetry' performances, or in the readings from his own work, Kraus constantly sought to lay bare aspects of what Siegfried Kracauer (another theorist of modernity fascinated by Offenbach), identified as the 'dark side of modernity' (Frisby 1985: 272). Writing on social space and the city in a piece first published in 1930, Kracauer identified Berlin's Linden Arcade as a place that 'housed the cast off and the disavowed', but as such had its positive side: this 'passageway through the bourgeois world articulated a critique of this world' (1995: 338, 342). Similarly, Kraus focused on prostitution and other manifestations of the urban underbelly, with the aim of revealing the complicity of the middle and the upper classes in these activities. In his ambivalent fascination with the figure of the prostitute and sexual politics in general, Kraus was drawing on an extensive literature, centring on the work of Nietzsche, Weininger and Bachofen, amongst others (Timms 1986: 83–93). These works, in turn, fuelled a particularly prevalent view of the metropolis in the early twentieth century, which saw it as the site of all kinds of sexual 'perversion', and represented it in terms of female sexuality, as Rowe demonstrates persuasively with reference to Berlin (2003). While Kraus's own view of female sexuality may have been skewed, he was ultimately critical of these essentially anti-metropolitan sentimentalities. Beginning in early essays such as 'Morality and Criminality' ('Sittlichkeit und Kriminalität') (AAC-F 1902 115:1–24), Kraus made use of accounts of prostitution in Vienna often gleaned from newspaper reports of current court cases to reveal the glaring hypocrisy of the bourgeoisie for criticising aspects of urban life for which they actually bore responsibility.

In this way, Kraus aimed to expose the hypocrisy of 'public opinion' relating to these subjects, arguing from a standpoint that refused to even recognise its validity, for to his mind, opinions were private matters (Benjamin 1996–2003: 2, 433). As Benjamin recognised, Kraus's initial struggles against 'petty, everyday imitations' turned into a full-scale defence of the private sphere against encroaching forces such as the police, the press, morality and the realm of the conceptual (438). This saw him present the city as a place of corruption, pursuing, in the 1920s, relentless campaigns against authority figures such as Imre Bekessy, the editor-in-chief of the sensationalist newspaper, *Die Stunde*, who was involved in murky dealings such as tax evasion and extortion, or the then Chief of Police, Johann Schober, who Kraus held responsible for the bloody repression of the protest march of 15 July 1927 (Timms 2005: 302–47). Kraus's defence of the private sphere was already prefigured in works such as 'Morality and Criminality' (AAC-F 1902 115: 11). Here, he maintained that the habit of continually creating new laws to limit personal freedom accomplished nothing more than the construction of new areas of immorality ripe for criminalisation. This position would have been extremely reactionary, Benjamin notes, had Kraus's defence not been of a particular form of life: 'the private life that is dismantling itself, openly shaping itself, that of the poor' (Benjamin 1996–2003: 2, 439), to which we could add: the urban poor, in particular. And it is at this point, that the importance of the scene reveals itself. Just as Blum argues that the scene's central function is to 'practice in public something private' (2003: 177), so Benjamin points out that it was Kraus's followers who forced him to give up the anonymity with which he sought to cloak his own life, even while relying on the relentless visibility of the urban poor to make his case against his own class, the bourgeoisie. And, Benjamin comments, 'nothing holds them in check except Kraus's decision to step in person before his threshold and pay homage to the ruins in which he is a "private individual"' (1996–2003: 2, 439).

Kraus's concern with the public nature of the lifeworld of the urban poor, and the hypocrisy of the bourgeoisie's voyeurism in watching this show, but not acting to bring it to an end, led him to donate the proceeds of his performances to particular charitable organisations such as those providing shelters for the homeless or for needy children (Lunzer 1989: 155; Goldschmidt 1984: 233). Later, he also provided funds for political organisations: for example, in 1922, he added three extra dates to a lecture series in Berlin, controversially appearing in aid of those starving in Russia (AAC-F 1922 595–600: 69–70); and in 1928, profits from his performances were used for 'the victims of 15 July and for proletarian political prisoners (Goldschmidt 1984: 236). The retrospective programmes of his performances published in *Die Fackel* provide further information on the range of charities that benefited from Kraus's activities over the years. In *Die Fackel*, Kraus also drew attention to his charitable work and the way it exposed the bourgeoisie's lack of action in a number of texts. In 'Two Hundred Lectures', for example, he pointed out that his 'fellow' writers, such as Felix Salten, criticised him for giving to controversial charitable causes, including the starving Russians (AAC-F 1925 676–678: 64–5).

During the 1920s, Kraus not only spoke *for* the urban poor, but also *to* representatives of that class, giving public readings to Workers' Associations, beginning with an afternoon performance in the Volksheim in Ottakring at the invitation of the Josefstadt branch of the social democratic party (Goldschmidt 1984: 233; AAC-F 1919 508–513: 39). While many of these performances for workers took place in the same central locations that had always housed Kraus's appearances, there were instances where he left these sites behind and spoke in halls in the inner working class suburbs of Ottakring, Mariahilf and Favoriten. These appearances were not without incident; in the published correspondence of *Die Fackel*, two letters dating from 1926, refer to a 'scandalous event' during which a Kraus reading in the Social Democrats' Arbeiterheim in Favoriten was disrupted (Fischer 1962: 234). This skirmish took place at the height of Kraus's crusade against Bekessy during a lecture at which Kraus criticised both Bekessy and the Social Democrats for their complicity in his corrupt dealings. Because of the ferocity of Kraus's attack, a Social Democrat official brought the proceedings to an early finish, to the protest of large sections of the audience (Timms 2005: 320; AAC-F 1926 712–16: 1–18; 35–7). Nevertheless Kraus's public performances for workers provide us with a further fragment of evidence for the productive expansion of discursive space that characterised Berlin and Vienna in the early twentieth century, and which, running counter to Habermas's position on the decline of the public sphere, has been documented by Geoff Eley (1992) and others. According to Goldschmidt, it was these audiences that Kraus found most receptive to his work (1984: 233); after his performance in Ottakring in 1919, Kraus wrote in *Die Fackel* of 'the most grateful audience that I have ever had' (AAC-F 1919 508–513: 40).

As was the case with many of his appearances at that time, a significant number of the texts that Kraus performed in Ottakring in May 1919 were concerned with war. It was through his focus on this subject matter that he signalled his increasingly political stance, itself linked to the politicisation of urban space in the immediate aftermath of the First World War that was seen in cities such as Berlin, Munich and Vienna. Connected to his early admiration for politicians such as Bismarck, who was able to employ aesthetic language in the political sphere (Dallago 1912: 90), but signalling a reversal of emphasis from aesthetics to politics, his performances in the 1920s included readings of a speech by Ferdinand Lasalle, in which he railed against the print media, and of letters by Rosa Luxemburg (Goldschmidt 1984: 234–7; AAC-F 1920 546–550: 5–9). Kraus's anti-war stance gained him new audiences in this period, including the support of previously critical journals, such as *Die Schaubühne* (later *Die Weltbühne*), which then organised, in 1917, his first wartime performance in Berlin (Bilke 1981: 156–7). In 1918, Kraus was subjected to a police investigation after reading in public 'A Kantian and Kant' ('Ein Kantianer und Kant'), an invective against the German Kaiser, and 'For Lamasch' ('Fuer Lammasch'), an article in support of an anti-government peace initiative (AAC-F 1918 474 83–91; Timms 1986: 355). This performance, given on 27 March 1918, also included a reading of 'The Technoromantic Adventure' ('Das technoromantische Abenteuer') (AAC-F 1919 508–513: 98). In this essay, subsequently published in *Die Fackel*, Kraus outlined his view of the two faces of the war: as a technological reality, on the one hand; imbued with a romantic aura, on the other hand (AAC-F 1918 474–83: 41–5). The full threat of a technological reality linked to the economic imperatives of the modern capitalist economy are captured in the rhetorical question:

> Why should it not be possible for technology, which makes today's miracle into tomorrow's commodity, to invent an apparatus which by means of some button, lever or handle would enable a person unfit for military service sitting at a desk in Berlin to blow London to pieces or vice versa?
>
> AAC-F (1918 474–83: 43; translated Timms 1986: 325)

The force of this statement is to show how the city itself could become a central site of war. Kraus then strove to demonstrate that in a sense, this was already the case, encapsulating the miseries of wartime Vienna in a satirical description of the military's demand for recognition when travelling on the city's tram network. In the service of the military, as Kraus demonstrated it to be, the tram network reveals the complicity of all forms of technology in war. As 'reality as symbol', it was representative of the processes of circulation – of people and of commodities – that characterise modernity (AAC-F 474–83: 44). This means that the city is a site in which the triadic relationship between technology, war and capitalism is on show. Implicitly at least, Kraus presents a view of war that would later be expounded by Alexander Kluge (2001: 719). And this is a view that is echoed in Kraus's other important anti-war texts, such as 'Promotional Trips to Hell' ('Reklamefahrten zur Hölle') (AAC-F 1921 577–82: 96–8), which was a staple of his performances throughout the 1920s, and appeared on the programme of his 700th and final public performance in April 1936 (reproduced in Pfäfflin and Dambacher 1999: 357). This was a diatribe against battlefield tourism, based on an advertisement for 'Motoring Tours of the Battlefields' organised by the Swiss newspaper, the *Baseler Nachrichten*. Kraus used the language of the advertisement to provide a barbed indictment of the commodification of war:

> You will recognise that these states have laws that are there specifically to protect the life and even the honour of press-pirates, who make a mockery of death and turn catastrophe into profit and heartily recommend a quick detour to hell as a suitable Autumn excursion.
>
> AAC-F (1921 577–8: 98)

Commodification and the associated lure of advertising was the subject of 'The World of Posters', another essay featuring in his 700th public performance. Published in the *Fackel* in 1909 (AAC-F 283–84: 19–26), and appearing in the following year on the programme for Kraus's first public performances in Walden's Verein für Kunst (AAC-F 294–95: 37), this text criticises the way in which advertisements reduce human beings to consumers. It echoes Simmel's (1997: 174–85) view of urban life put forward in his 1903 lecture on 'Metropolis and Mental Life', but does this through the eyes of a child who imagines that this is how people behave in real life, rather than understanding that the exchanges found in adverts are there only to sell products. In this satire, advertising hoardings dominate the cityscape and indeed, also extend into the countryside. This offers a striking image of the threat of the city encroaching on the country, anticipating a theme that would become important in the 1920s in the work of others, such as Loos, and the conservative cultural critic, Karl Scheffler (Frisby 2001: 268–9). Kraus offers an unapologetically apocalyptic vision of the city in this piece, and this marks the distinction between him and Simmel, whose work depicts metropolitan life as opening up new possibilities, even as it also poses new threats.

In this essay, and others that similarly take the city as their central theme, Kraus offers an impressionistic view of urban life that demonstrates a particular fascination with the increasing importance of visuality in experiencing the city. To use Benjamin's (1996–2003: 4, 19) memorable description of the flâneur, he went 'botanising on the asphalt', presenting the results of his research in visual, as well as textual form. In *Die Fackel*, Kraus reproduced examples of the large-scale posters and small advertisements that dominated the streetscapes at the time (Timms 2005: 127), and as early as 1911, produced a photomontage in the manner of John Heartfield, depicting the editor of the leading Viennese newspaper, *Neue Freie Presse*, in front of the parliament building on the representative Ringstrasse in Vienna (AAC-F 1911 326: insert). He also employed visual material in his performances, making use of slide projection on at least two occasions in Vienna: in his last pre-war appearance on 27 May 1914, and during a reading given in wartime, on 22 January 1917 (Knepler 1984: 183). According to Kraus's introduction to the 1914 slide show, the visual material depicted city dwellers of a certain milieu, including the 'Viennese intelligentsia', engaged in acts of conspicuous consumption on the eve of war (AAC-F 1914 400–403: 46). Kraus describes himself as a kind of recording machine, storing up the sounds and images that he gathered on his journeys through the city and its artefacts, in order to reveal the semblance of his world: 'The aim is not to express or to repeat what is already in existence. The aim is to cite and to photograph. And to recognise the foundations of a century through set phrases and clichés' (AAC-F 1914 400–403: 46). Here, he provides an insight into the method that allowed him to compose telling, if surreal depictions of modern urbanity, such as 'The Vision of Viennese Life' ('Die Vision vom Wiener Leben') (AAC-F 1911 323: 23–4), another piece that often featured in his public readings. Alongside his sharp ear for voices that drew him to popular theatre and operetta (Timms 2005: 393–451), Kraus's discursive construction of the modern city brought visual rhetoric into play, drawing inspiration from the 'science' of physiognomy and the street itself, as Benjamin would later do in influential works on the city such as *One Way Street* and his unfinished *Arcades Project* (1996–2003: 1, 444–88; 1999). Kraus's statement of intent in the introduction to his 1914 slide show finds an echo in Benjamin's programmatic statement of his method: 'Method of this project: literary montage. I needn't say anything. Merely show. [...] the rags, the refuse – these I will not inventory but allow, in the only way possible, to come into their own: by making use of them' (Benjamin 1999: 460).

Benjamin clearly felt an elective affinity with Kraus, based on the similarity of approach in their conceptions of the city. Both were producing works that, as Cacciari remarks of Kraus, were based on 'commentary' rather than 'criticism', where 'the commentary has nothing to do with a Text (the "eternal image"), but rather with mutable landscapes whose contours are unpredictable' (1993: 148). This led both to a fascination with the dream. In his *Arcades Project*, Benjamin famously wrote of the city as the site of the 'dream houses of the collective: arcades, winter gardens, panoramas, factories, wax museums, casinos, railways stations' (1999: 405). In 'Viennese Life as a Dream' ('Der Traum ein Wiener Leben'), Kraus implicitly adds the lecture hall to this list, as his somnambulant passage through the city begins and ends in such a location (AAC-F 1910 307–308: 51–6). He dreamt, he tells us, that the audience for one of his performances was already assembled in anticipation of the event to come, when he realised that he had left his manuscript at home. As we discover through a narrative that employs the stream-of-consciousness techniques that were later to characterise celebrated modernist depictions of city life such as Joyce's (1918) *Ulysses*, he decided to fetch it. This led him to undertake a series of ultimately pointless (since the missing manuscript turns up in his pocket) journeys, travelling by taxi, carriage and tram, punctuated only by a stop at the post office to make a telephone call to Berlin. On his travels, he encountered various figures symbolic of the threatening otherness of the city, including 'modern-day witches' (i.e., prostitutes) in the 'crooked alleyways, in which witches were burned in bygone days' and officials in an underground post office who had just succumbed to decompression sickness, and were being loaded into coffins (AAC-F 1910 307–308: 53). Timms points to the affinity between this nightmare vignette of modern existence and

Kafka's dream parables (1986: 211), but with its emphasis on communication and the circulation of individuals, it could also be read as a literary take on Simmel's account of urban life in 'Metropolis and Mental Life' (1997: 174–85). In its economy, it provides a masterly overview of three broad themes that characterise Kraus's contribution to the discursive construction of the city in his essays and public performances: the city as a rational–technical entity, and the site of commerce and communication; the city as a work of art (constructed from its soundscapes and its visual culture); and the city as the place of encounter with the Other.

The city as site and subject of public speaking

Kraus was perhaps the single most prolific speaker in the German-speaking world in the early twentieth century, but he was part of a larger phenomenon, the existence of which is the condition of possibility that allows us to think about the role of public speaking in constructing an urban public; as Warner points out, it is not the individual speaker that creates a public, but the 'concatenation of speakers and texts through time' (2002: 90). Public speaking certainly played a significant role in urban life in the early twentieth century, contributing to the cultural economy of the city by, for example, providing a focus for urban scenes. More than that, however, public speaking also provided a site for the discussion of the city itself, a place in which the city could be – and was – constructed through discourse. As we have seen, the city in general, and Vienna and Berlin in particular, were important themes of Kraus's public performances. As a speaker, he was not alone in his focus on urban life; a glance at the pages of specialist public speaking journals such as the *Jahrbuch für das deutsche Vortragswesen* and *Der Sprecher* allows us some insight into the ubiquity of the topic. To take but one example gleaned from the latter, a series of talks took place in Munich in 1911, under the title 'The Essence of the Metropolis'. Of the speakers listed, a number have been mentioned in this chapter, including Bahr, who spoke on 'Forms of Life', and Naumann, whose topic was 'The Mechanism' (*Der Sprecher* 1911: 33). Around this time, then, public speaking offered an important forum for the dissemination of ideas about the city and the urban experience, for the construction of the city's 'imaginative structure' (Blum 2003). The city, in other words, was not only the site, but also the subject of public speaking. The next chapter builds on this insight, taking up the three broad themes that revealed themselves in this brief discussion of Karl Kraus as a public intellectual speaking in the city and about the city – the city as rational–technical entity, the city as work of art and the city as place of encounter with the Other – in a discussion of cultural transfer and the circulation of discourse through the lens of a particular group of speakers with a vested interest in the discursive construction of the modern city: architects.

2
Architects and the Urban Public

> The metropolis reveals itself as one of those great historical formations in which opposing streams which enclose life unfold, as well as join one another with equal right.
>
> Simmel (1903)

Peter Behrens, Josef Frank, Adolf Loos, Walter Gropius, Erich Mendelsohn, Hermann Muthesius, Hans Poelzig, Bruno Taut, Otto Wagner: merely listing these names is enough to remind us of the prominence of German-speaking architects in the early twentieth century, but what is it that makes their work so compelling? To a large extent, it is due to the role that these architects played as public intellectuals engaged in the discursive construction of the modern city; their fame is based not only on their architectural output, but also on their ability to talk and write about their work and its physical and social context. They were able to reach out beyond a specialist architectural audience to engage directly with the end-users of their products and ideas, in effect facilitating the construction of an urban public that would enable the circulation of their ideas in discursive space. Adolf Loos was for many years better known for his provocative polemical statements and articles, such as the programmatic modernist lecture 'Ornament and Crime', than for his architecture (1982: 78–88).[1] Otto Wagner's name is synonymous with *Modern Architecture*, a collection of lectures first published in 1896 ([1902] 1988). Hermann Muthesius, another inveterate public speaker, was one of the architects contributing to a lecture series that was part of the 1910 General Municipal Exhibition in Berlin, and in 1926, Hans Poelzig and Peter Behrens were named among the participants in a set of lectures on 'The Architecture of our Times'. These events were held in the State Art Library in Berlin, beginning on 25 January with a talk by the conservative cultural critic, Karl Scheffler, on 'The Future of the Metropolis and the Metropolis of the Future' (*Deutsche Bauzeitung* 1926).[2] Scheffler's lecture emphasised the importance of urbanity – of what he termed the 'spirit of the city' – for contemporary architecture, which must recognise that 'the fate of the metropolis coincides totally with that of the economy, society and culture. The problem of the metropolis is the problem of modern life itself' (Scheffler 1926: 522).

Reflection on the present state and the future possibilities of the modern city was the main point of connection linking these architects belonging to different generations, all of whom radically overstepped the normal boundaries of 'architecture' in their deliberations as public intellectuals on the modern city. Their fame is based on the encounter that characterises their work, on the encounter of architectural discourse with discourse on the city, and on discourse about modern life. Sharing a common interest in defining the nature of modernity and recognising that the city was a prime location of modernity, these leading architects all sought to shape the city both physically and discursively, recognising that participating in the discursive construction of the city was often a necessary prerequisite for contributing to the physical construction of the same. They engaged in debates, in a variety of forms and forums, about the lived experience of the modern city, and contributed to the analysis and diagnosis of the social world in the early twentieth century. Their influence on the form of the modern city was not only practical but also persuasive, addressed to an urban public and so, to follow Warner's line of argument, constitutive of that entity (2002: 114).

Habermas identified the willingness of modernist architects to become involved in wider debates about forms of life in the modern city as the point at which modern architecture began to become overburdened with the expectation that it could set the agenda for social change rather than merely form the backdrop against which such change could take place (1997: 232). At the beginning of the twentieth century, however, it would seem that many architects were not feeling overburdened, but rather distinctly 'under-burdened'. This gave rise to an anxious internal debate in German-speaking architectural circles that was concerned with maintaining the status of the architect in the face of a perceived onslaught from new professions such as engineering.[3] In 'Architecture and the Public', an early lecture on the connections between art, architecture and industry, Muthesius paraphrased Goethe's *Faust* to describe the present as a time in which 'the merchant, the industrialist, the engineer sit at the loom of time' (1907a: 205). One way of coping with the direct challenge this posed, Muthesius suggested, was for architects to become more like engineers, or at least to strive to cooperate with engineers. In 'The Education of the Public in Architecture', he echoed Otto Wagner's (1988: 124) credo that modern architects should be sensitive to the needs of the times, which, Muthesius continued, were synonymous with the needs of the engineer (1907b: 210). Loos, meanwhile, made a similar point in a short article entitled 'Ornament and Education' (first published in the Czech architectural journal, *Wohnungskultur* in 1924) arguing polemically that the modern architect should see himself primarily as a builder, albeit a builder who has learned Latin (Loos [1931] 1982: 177). In all these views, architecture's hope is seen to be its modern technological and functional aspect, which would allow architects to assert their voices in modern rational scientific discourse and so influence those currently shaping the modern world.

Yet this idea, which we could gloss as a move towards the rational-technical in the architects' self-image, is contradicted by a different direction, the pull towards the aesthetic. In works directed towards a general audience, such as his lecture on 'Architecture', first delivered in Berlin in 1910 under the auspices of the Verein für Kunst, Loos seemed to want to downplay the aesthetic dimension, arguing for a sharp distinction to be made between art and architecture, and maintaining that the only forms of architecture that could be regarded as art – since neither has a use value over and above its exhibition value – are the tombstone and the memorial (Loos [1931] 1982: 101). Yet as is so often the case with Loos, this was not his definitive word on the subject. In 'The Old and the New Style in Architecture', first published in 1898, he offered a rather different view of the role of architecture in shaping the future, embodying his ideas in the figure of the 'Über-Architect', a play on the Nietzschean concept of the 'Übermensch' or 'Superman', the epitome of the modern doctrine of 'enlightened individualism' (Loos 1983: 65–7). Crucially, Loos conceived the 'Über-Architect' as an artist and, therefore, as a prophet, whose task was to lead architecture into the future by emancipating modern style from the ornaments of the past, altering the form of utilitarian objects and so effecting social change. The Loosian 'Über-Architect' must take up position at the forefront of the modern, assuming the role of cultural teacher, or trainer (65). Rehearsing ideas put forward not only by Nietzsche, but also by contemporary sociologists such as Max Weber and Georg Simmel, the 'Über-Architect' as artist is representative of a new cultural elite or *Geistesaristokratie* (intellectual aristocracy) and as such, provides a model of cultural attainment towards which the rest of humanity can strive. Loos's call for a new cultural elite provided a point of connection between him and Muthesius (1902: 21), who argued that architects, as prime representatives of the bourgeoisie, had an important role to play in the creation of a new *Geistesaristokratie*. Here he was expanding upon a point made in his 1900 Schinkel Memorial Lecture, 'Architectural Observations on the Current Times', in which he maintained – again, echoing Otto Wagner – that architecture is an art form and, what is more, 'not only an art like all the other arts, but [...] an all-encompassing art, an art of arts, the mother of all forms of fine art' (Muthesius 1900: 146–7).

Muthesius's ideas were reiterated in a talk given by another well-known commentator on contemporary architecture almost two decades later, in the changed socio-political climate of the immediate aftermath of the First World War. Albert Hofmann, the editor of the leading German architectural journal, *Deutsche Bauzeitung*, delivered a lecture to a meeting of German architects in June 1919, in which he reflected on the status of the architect in the modern world, echoing the neo-Kantian tenor of Muthesius's and Loos's arguments. Hofmann argued that modern architects should regard themselves as the genuine heirs of a great German intellectual tradition celebrating the power of the aesthetic (he names Humboldt, Goethe, Schiller, Fichte and Schleiermacher as representatives of that tradition), while also understanding that in revolutionary times, the architect becomes 'more important than any other member of human society; more than others, he contributes to the development of higher forms of life and to more advanced stages of civil society' (Hofmann 1919: 476). He was drawing upon a similar understanding of Social Darwinism as that which influenced Loos's (1983: 65–7) position in his treatise on the future of architecture. In these contributions to the debate on the status of architecture, the emphasis is firmly on the ways in which architecture is extraordinary, on the ways in which architects, as visionaries imbued with the power of the aesthetic, can bring about social change.

There was, however, a third view of architecture in circulation in the early twentieth century, influenced by the English Arts and Crafts Movement. This was the idea that architecture is unique among art forms, in that it is ordinary. According to this conception, put forward by Josef Frank and others, architecture is intimately bound up with everyday life, and so architects belong primarily among the people:

> The only fine art not closed to the public today is architecture, which therefore forms a noteworthy part of our lives. Architecture can be enjoyed immediately, stands on the street and speaks to the people from there, as once philosophy did. Everyone has the feeling of being able to make a personal contribution to architecture since, more than any other art form, it arises from a collective will and collective activity.
>
> Frank (1931: 101)

Similarly, in his 'Work of Art' essay of 1936, Benjamin prized architecture for its very ordinariness, emphasising, like Frank, the relationship between architecture and the collective (1996–2003: 3, 120).

Here, then, are three reactions to the perception that architecture was losing its relevance in the modern world, each related to a different form of discourse. According to the first, architecture is relevant because it is able to assimilate itself to rational-technical discourse on the city; according to the second, it is because it is in the vanguard of avant-garde activity and therefore, in a position to offer a transcendental critique of the city; while according to the third, its relevance to the modern world lies in its ordinariness, which allows it to offer an immanent critique of the city. The first proceeds from a view of architecture as a rational-technical intervention in the social world from outside that world, the second offers itself as an aesthetic commentary on that world as well as a source of possible alternatives, the third is rooted in self-reflexivity and the self-understanding of the social world. Yet these positions are not mutually exclusive, as we realise when we consider that often the same person – Loos, for example – may articulate aspects of all three views. As Cacciari recognises, 'in Loos, one does not find just one form of thought: one finds musical-thoughts, pictorial thoughts, philosophical thoughts – and architectonic thoughts' (1993: 163). In fact, all three perspectives combine in what, following Heidegger, we could describe as the architect's 'Being-in the city', by which we mean the way that the architect both constitutes and is constituted by the city ([1927] 1962). It is precisely the combination of rational, aesthetic-visionary and ordinary discourse that marks the architect's importance in the discursive construction of the modern city, casting him as 'urban hero'. Something of this view can be seen in Hannah Arendt's description of the Greek polis and the central role that architects and lawyers played creating the public sphere. This she defines as 'a space between participants' created by 'action and speech', which can be described as the 'space where I appear to others as others appear to me, where men [...] make their appearance explicitly' (1958: 198).

Reacting to what they saw as the danger of being ignored, architects in the early twentieth century set out to 'make their appearance explicitly' in the modern city. This they claimed as their own, and they were so successful in persuading others of their credentials as urban heroes qualified to talk with authority on this rapidly changing social space, that by 1926, when Poelzig, Behrens and others participated in the 'Architecture of Our Times' lecture series, it seemed self-evident that architects should be talking about changing the world. Presenting a series of case studies, this chapter sets out to explore in greater detail the way in which architects sought to utilise the 'space of appearance' to contribute to the discursive construction of the city in the early twentieth century. The discussion is arranged around the three forms of discourse identified above: the rational-technical, the artistic-visionary and the everyday, relating each to a different view of the city. In the first section, the focus is on the city as a site of technical, political and economic power. It considers the way in which architects drew on their ability to produce and understand representations of space to gain a voice in the hierarchy of power that characterised the modern city. The second section, by contrast, focuses on the city as a work of art, showing how architects engaged with other artists to think about the city in terms of imaginary space and the possibilities it holds. In the final section, the main structuring idea is that of the city as the space in which the Other can be encountered, examining the sometimes tense relationship between architects and the working class, figured spatially as the relationship between the city centre and its suburbs.

This chapter highlights a particular form of cultural transfer, showing how, as was indicated in the previous chapter, discourse circulates by making use of different constellations of speaker and audience, in a wide variety of forms and locations. When we see prominent architects engaging in lecturing activity, this has to be understood as a strategy for using the forms of modernity (circulation) to reinvigorate their influence – for circulating architectural ideas to others and also for being open to ideas from others. In other words, in discussing cultural transfer, this chapter is about changing architectural thought, examining how different ways of seeing and thinking about the world contribute to the discursive construction of the city and indeed, of the (urban) public. As Warner reminds us, these two aspects are intimately related in that the public is 'an ongoing space of encounter for discourse' (2002: 90).

Technical-rational discourse on the city

In 'Concepts and Categories of the City', Weber presents the modern city as a site of production, neatly encapsulating rational-technical discourse on the city as the interplay of industrialisation (including industrial architecture and infrastructure), economics and politics (1978). Many architects striving to gain a voice in constructing the modern city shared this view of the city, and sought to enter into dialogue with industrial engineers and politicians. Yet their enthusiasm was tempered by the fact that the profession also sometimes found itself in conflict with the economic imperatives of the modern city, which resulted in certain architects engaging in discussions with left-wing thinkers and reformers, leading to the architectural associations protesting about the slum conditions of the city around 1900 and, ultimately, to the decentralist politics of an organisation such as the short-lived Arbeitsrat für Kunst (AfK) (Workers' Council for Art). Founded in the turbulent period following the First World War, the AfK espoused a political stance that exposes the limits of thinking about the city as a technical-rational entity.

The first step in architects contributing to the technical-rational discursive construction of the city was for them to set up their own professional associations, in which they could talk freely with their peers. The Architectural Association in Berlin and the Austrian Association of Architects and Engineers date back to 1824 and 1849,

respectively (Stübben 1924: 7; Stoeckl 1899: 1–8). Like other professional associations founded in this period, they were established as a
consequence of the rise in power of the bourgeoisie. Their purpose
was three-fold: first, to create a supportive network of like-minded
individuals that would allow for the productive exchange of architectural ideas; second, to display the credentials of architects as technocrats, as purveyors of scientific discourse, by emphasising close links
to associations of engineers; and third, to raise the profile of the profession, giving it an authoritative voice with which to present itself
to the outside world. These associations set out to achieve their aims
partly through the organisation of lectures and talks, identifying this
as a core activity in their constitutions, and forming standing com-
mittees to oversee their lecture programmes. Both were so committed
to providing ambitious lecture programmes for their members that
when they were in a position to build themselves centrally situated
headquarters, they included not only small-scale meeting rooms, but
also grand halls (*Festsäle*) that could accommodate large audiences
for public speaking (Bürckner 1913: 183; Stoeckl 1899: 45).[4] In this
way, both associations contributed to the physical construction of the
modern city by building spaces for public speaking – urban spaces in
which the city could be discursively constructed.

The discursive construction of the city as a technical-rational entity
by the associations ranged from discussion of technical triumphs, such
as the use of ironwork in the city gasometers, to questions of modern
forms of communication, such as the possibilities afforded by wireless technology, and debates about the appropriate architectural style
for the modern metropolis (*Jahrbuch des österreichischen Ingenieur- und
Architektenvereins* 1912: 111). The titles of the prestigious 'Schinkel
Memorial Lectures', organised by the Architectural Association of Berlin,
offer further insight into the way the city in general, and Berlin, of particular, were constructed through talk (Architekten-Verein zu Berlin 1924:
14–16; Posener 1981). Among those addressing the subject of the mod-
ern metropolis in general were the architect and city planner Joseph
Stübben, who gave the 1895 lecture on 'The Construction of Cities in
History and in the Present'; Albert Hofmann, who lectured on 'The
Metropolis as an Architectural Organism' in 1908; and Paul Wittig,
the director of the Elevated Railway Company (*Hochbahngesellschaft*) in
Berlin, who talked the following year about 'European and American
World-Cities in the Context of Electrical Railways'. A number of

lectures dealing specifically with Berlin also addressed the question of transportation in the city, including James Hobrecht's retrospective lecture on 'The Development of the Transport Situation in Berlin over the Last Fifty Years' in 1893, Richard Petersen's reflections on 'The Responsibilities of the Greater Berlin Partnership Regarding Transport' in 1911 and Erich Giese's recommendations for 'Greater Berlin's Future Suburban Rail Network' in 1919.

In these events, speakers returned again and again to the transport system, a vital part of the architecture of communication in the modern city that both shaped and reflected modern urban life. As Petersen's (1911) lecture made clear, a prime rationale for the development of the transport system was its ability to facilitate the ever faster circulation of individuals and commodities – both within the city, and between Berlin and the 'external world' – that, as Simmel pointed out in 'Metropolis and Mental Life', shaped social life in the modern city (1997: 174–85). Following a rational-scientific impulse to describe and catalogue his research object, Petersen reminded his audience that the modern urban transport system consisted in both fixed elements, such as waterways and industrial areas, and flexible elements, such as people. In the very coexistence of these elements, the transport system reflected the dialectic of stasis and movement that was characteristic of the experience of modern urban life (1911: 237). Finally, Petersen and others conceive the transport system as a complex series of interlocking networks, which then serves as a physical representation of the interaction among social circles that, Simmel argued, defined social life in the modern city (1955: 127–95). By analogy, these lectures on practical aspects of circulation and communication in the city also drew attention to formal aspects of the discursive construction of the city, which took place through the circulation of ideas, or discourse, facilitated by the formation of networks of speakers, audiences and speech sites.

The circulation of speakers had an important role to play in processes of cultural transfer, and in maintaining a view of the architectural profession as an imagined community, with a national and an international dimension. Architects identified as accomplished speakers were in demand to address architectural associations throughout the German-speaking world, delivering versions of the same lecture to a number of audiences in different cities and so binding them together into an imagined community participating in the ongoing encounter with architectural discourse on 'the city' as an abstract entity. Cultural transfer also took place across language boundaries, with architects from other European countries accepting invitations to address the architectural associations in Berlin and Vienna, and in turn, inviting German-speaking architects to talk in a variety of other European countries, as well as venturing further afield to the USA. In addition to selected individuals circulating through a network of associations, there were also opportunities for representatives of the profession to meet and exchange ideas. The late nineteenth and early twentieth centuries saw the development of the international conference as a symbol of the imagined communities of a variety of professions, with architects being no exception. In 1908, the Eighth International Congress of Architects brought delegates from throughout the Western world to Vienna (Österreichischer Ingenieur- und Architekten-Verein 1909). As president of the congress, Otto Wagner gave the opening address, in which he discussed a variety of challenges facing the profession, criticising, in particular, the way in which developers were putting pressure on architects, and so seeking to define and delimit the scope of the architectural profession (Hevesi [1909] 1986: 293–4).

The tenor of Wagner's speech reminds us that the purpose of the architectural associations was based on self-understanding and self-representation. As this discussion of their activities has shown, the associations facilitated the dissemination of knowledge and discussion of aspects of the city among fellow professionals. In so doing, they created a stock of knowledge about the city, but also achieved the social standing that would allow their members to represent themselves as rightful partners in shaping dominant discourse on the city. This led to architects engaging in other forms of discourse on the city, entering into dialogue with city planners and with politicians, among others. This process happened informally, through other professionals encountering architectural discourse, or architects encountering other kinds of discourse, in conversations and chance meetings, in reports of lectures that appeared in the daily press, or in the form of published versions of key lectures. There were, however, also a number of formal opportunities for architects to join with other professionals in the discursive construction of the city as a rational-technical entity.

The architectural associations played a leading role in creating such formal opportunities. In 1907, the Architectural Association of

Berlin joined together with the Union of Architects in Berlin to create a new body, the Architectural Committee for Greater Berlin, which discussed and debated architectural responses to plans for the development of the city (Stübben 1924: 9). This body published its deliberations in a series of memoranda and proposals that were aimed at influencing the decisions of the city's planning authority. Vienna's architectural association set up a similar body, the Committee for the Architectural Development of Vienna, which took it upon itself to pronounce on major projects such as the regulation of the Danube. In early 1910, the committee's call for action on this matter led to the Minister for Public Works (who also happened to be a member of the Association of Engineers and Architects) giving a series of 'extremely noteworthy lectures' on the necessity of regulating the Danube to prevent flooding (Beraneck 1912: 42). These lectures were subsequently published, setting ideas first aired in the confines of the professional association into wider circulation and so addressing them to the urban public. These ideas were later realised, and Beraneck claimed that the association, the site of initial deliberations on the subject, should be credited with bringing about the new regulation of the Danube. This was one example of a professional association using the authority of its position and the status of its individual members to shape dominant discourse on the city, and so to reform the built environment itself.

The case of the proposed and controversial remodelling of the Karlsplatz, which lay on the boundary of Vienna's First District, shows that professional architects were, however, not always successful in shaping dominant discourse on the city (Kassal-Mikula and Benedik 2000: 138, 158–79). Fischer von Ehrlach's baroque church, the Karlskirche, dominated this space, in which Otto Wagner's distinctive modernist entry and exit points to the city railway, and Josef Maria Olbrich's Secession building were erected in the last decade of the nineteenth century. Wagner subsequently proposed designs for further buildings, including a new museum, and put forward plans for the reconfiguration of the square as part of a new avenue leading either westward to the Imperial Palace at Schönbrunn, or extending north to the inner city and east to the Danube canal, all to no avail. The battle over Karlspatz has been often seen as a struggle between tradition and modernity as, for example, in Kraus's satirical take on the conservative architect, Emil Tranquillini, being awarded first prize in a 1913 competition to build a city museum on the square (AAC-F 1913: 378–380: 13–14). Frisby, however, perceptively suggests that what was at stake was not merely New Vienna encroaching, culturally and politically, on Old Vienna but the fact that Wagner's plans 'would have resulted in the flow of urban and commercial capital out of the centre of the city. The *economic* valorization of the first district would have been seriously challenged' (Frisby 2001: 222–4). In other words, what was at stake was the '"game" of valorization of land values and ground rents' (235).

This same 'game' provides us with a further example of architects running counter to dominant economic discourse on the city, in the debate over affordable housing for the ever-expanding working classes. In fact, this issue divided opinion in the architectural associations themselves, to the extent that in Berlin, it caused a rift that led to the founding of a separate Union of Architects in 1891. The central question for this new association was how to provide adequate housing for the working classes and tackle the dire standards of the tenement buildings, the so-called 'Barracks for Rent' ('Mietskaserne'), that had sprung up in Berlin during the rapid expansion of the city in the late nineteenth century. The timing of this initiative was not accidental, but coincided with a significant change in the political landscape of Germany that saw the 'Socialist Law', a piece of legislation passed in 1878 to hold in check the nascent Social Democratic movement, repealed in 1890 (Klausmann 1998: 234). On 5 March 1891, the Union of Architects organised a seminar on the question of housing for the working classes, inviting a number of guests to participate, including representatives from the Ministry of Trade and from other bodies working to improve the lives of the working classes in the city. Three members of the Union of Architects were charged with giving an overview of the current situation from the point of view of the architect. They were asked to address both the 'literary and historical' and the 'practical and commercial' aspects of the problem, pointing to the way in which architectural discourse sought to combine rational-technical and historical-aesthetic considerations (*Deutsche Bauzeitung* 1891: 162–3). Subsequent meetings were held on 9 and 30 April to discuss the questions raised in these lectures. Underlining the commitment to engage a wider urban public in these discussions, certain contributions to the debate – those delivered by Fritsch, Goecke, Goldschmit, Hofmann, Messel and Wieck – were set to be subsequently reworked and published.

The debate carried out in these meetings echoed a larger discussion on city versus country and society versus community that was being played out at the time in philosophical and sociological circles. In his closing lecture, Goecke argued against a simple idealism that saw life in the country as inherently better than life in the city, pointing to the latter's modern 'luxuries', such as artificial light and a sewage system (*Deutsche Bauzeitung* 1891: 241–3). His position was close to that of sociologists such as Simmel and urban theorists such as Scheffler, whose work was predicated on the inevitability of urbanisation and on a recognition of both the positive and the negative aspects of the city as a form of social organisation, and was implicitly critical of thinkers such as Ferdinand Tönnies (1887), who all too readily passed negative judgement on the modern metropolis. Nevertheless, Goecke's conclusion was couched in rather conservative terms, but it was also pragmatic. He and his fellow architects recognised that the state could not cope with the demand for housing and that this being the case, private speculators, who were less interested in living conditions than in their ability to extract profit from buildings, were going to be the architects' most important clients in providing housing for the working classes. This meant that architects had a crucial role to play as mediators between the owners and the users of affordable urban housing, or to put it in another way, between the city as the creator of wealth and seat of the money economy, and the city as home.

These architects recognised that in order to be able to communicate effectively with clients such as the owners of housing for rent, and to influence their decisions, they needed knowledge of other forms of discourse on the city, including ideas emerging from the fields of economics, politics and sociology. To facilitate this, the Architectural Association of Berlin set up a standing committee for education in 1908, which was charged with putting together a lecture programme of invited speakers from different disciplines (Stübben 1924: 9). Speakers in this series included Heinrich Herkner, a social economist, founding member of the proto-sociological Association for Social Politics (Verein für Sozialpolitik) and so-called 'lectern-socialist' (*Kathedersozialist*). In 1910, he lectured on 'The Question of the Working-Classes in its Contemporary Manifestation', situating the modern trade union movement in context, by giving a brief history of the workers' movement in Germany before moving on to a discussion of Marx's contributions to political economy and his influence on present-day thinkers such as Werner Sombart and Karl Kautsky (Herkner 1910: 52). Tailoring his talk to his specialist audience, he concluded this section by refuting the simple teleological argument that economic development would necessarily lead to socialism, and then warning that rejecting Marxism should not mean denying the extreme social problems of the present, including overcrowding in large cities, miserable living conditions and huge growth in real estate prices in the cities.

Lectures such as those of Herkner provided opportunities for different but overlapping social circles in the city to come together, with the speaker being the point of connection. They also provided opportunities for encounters between the different professional discourses on the city: architectural, political, economic and sociological. These kinds of encounter also occurred when architects were asked to speak to other professional associations; Muthesius, for example, gave lectures in 1908 to the Society of Economists (Volkswirtschaftlichen Gesellschaft) on 'Economics and the Arts and Crafts Movement', and to the Verein für Kunst on 'The Unity of Architecture' (1908a, 1908b). Formally, we can understand this function of the lecture with reference to Simmel's description of city life seen from the point of view of the individual, whose identity is circumscribed by the network of social circles to which s/he belongs (1955: 127–95). The potential advantages of an individual providing a point of connection between two disparate social circles, or communicative communities, can be seen in the excitement expressed by Beraneck at the fact that its new president from 1911 was also a member of parliament and so would provide a channel through which discourse on architecture and discourse on politics could flow (1912: 43).

These initiatives provide a clear indication of the architectural associations' desire to play a central role in the discursive construction of the city by seeking to understand people's lived experience of the city. The architectural associations' lecturing activities were predicated on the understanding that, as Scheffler argued, 'the problem of the metropolis is the problem of modern life itself' (1926: 522). He made this point in a lecture delivered in a period in which the problem of the metropolis had intensified due to the miserable living conditions and uncertain political situation at the end of the First World War. The initial response on the part of the architectural associations to the changed socio-political circumstances of the interwar period was to consider engaging more directly in political debate.

According to a report in the *Deutsche Bauzeitung*, in 1919 a series of lectures had to be cancelled by the Architectural Association due to the social and political unrest in the city during that winter (E[iselen] 1919: 265–6). Other lectures continued, but it was felt that questions of a technical and architectural nature were less important than a discussion of status of the profession and of political and economic issues in order to be able to meet the challenges of the changed socio-political climate and make the views of the association on such matters count. Some members of the association were of the opinion that matters should be taken further, arguing for the association to engage directly in political activity. The response to this motion, however, was to form a committee to give the issue further consideration and in the meantime, to expand the remit of the library to take in material from the fields of politics and economics (448).

Other architects were in rather more of a hurry to engage in political activity and by the end of November 1918, when the revolutionary AfK was called into existence, Bruno Taut, Max Taut, Walter Gropius and Erich Mendelsohn had decided to involve themselves in the project. As with the architectural associations in previous decades, the AfK wanted to have a voice in dominant discourse and so sent a deputation for a meeting with the Minister for Culture, Adolf Hoffmann (Whyte 1981: 98). The meeting was a fiasco, as the deputation had no clear political programme to outline, but the AfK contributed to discourse on the shape of the modern city in other ways, such as taking part in ongoing interdisciplinary debates on the contemporary housing crisis. For example, members of the organisation were involved in a conference held on 3 June 1919 to draw attention to the dangers of ignoring the crisis. It gathered together more than 1200 representatives from all the leading organisations in Greater Berlin concerned with housing to meet with representatives from those injured in the war and the homeless (*Deutsche Bauzeitung* 1919b). This coincided with Gropius taking over from Taut as the chairman of the AfK and rejecting Taut's call for artistic revolution to go hand in hand with political revolution, under the leadership of architecture. In turn, this saw the AfK change from being a political interest group aiming for direct political intervention to an avant-garde art association (Whyte 1981: 98).

Nevertheless, the AfK remained of political importance as a hotbed for the discussion of the decentralist politics that helped change the shape of the modern city in the 1920s. While in 1891, the Union of

Architects in Berlin concluded that tenement buildings were the only way forward for housing in the modern city, the changed political climate of the interwar period allowed for different conceptions of affordable housing to be discussed and subsequently realised. The architecture of housing in Berlin and Vienna in the 1920s is the physical representation of a complex debate spanning politics, economics, technical possibilities and spatial practice, to which architects made a significant contribution. This debate resulted in the construction of a number of new forms of social housing, with significant differences between the forms of affordable housing adopted in Berlin and Vienna, respectively (Blau 1999: 6–15). In Berlin, Martin Wagner and others championed exurban estates (*Siedlungen*), constructed on the model of the garden city satellite town and, increasingly, using prefabricated building parts. Meanwhile, in Vienna, two other types of housing for the working classes were being developed: the anti-picturesque urban *Siedlung* that grew 'organically' out of allotment gardening and found its champions in Adolf Loos and Otto Neurath; and the *Hof*, the 'village within the city', that had its roots in the new communal buildings, the 'Workers' Homes' (Arbeiterheime), constructed in the city in the first decade of the twentieth century, and was favoured by the centralist Social Democratic regime in 'Red Vienna'. What these different forms of housing had in common is that they were seen not only as housing, but also as responses to city life, and as ways of coping with processes of circulation.

Public speaking was employed to generate urban discourse that created the conditions to allow for the city to be constructed in a number of different ways; these different forms of housing were representative of different conceptions of urbanity, and connected to different ways of inhabiting the city. In the 1920s, in constellations such as the Settlement Movement, there is evidence of architects seeking to engage with a wider public, thinking about the importance of the popularisation of architecture through public speaking as a key way of influencing and directing urban discourse. This led architects to adopt two main strategies for achieving their objectives: first, certain architects embraced an avant-garde position, based on the idea of the architect as artist, and therefore as a key member of the 'creative elite'; second, others sought to venture out beyond the city centre, leaving the safety of dialogue with fellow professionals and artists, to begin to engage directly with the urban public, not merely through the anonymity of text, but also through face-to-face communication. The following sections discuss these responses in greater detail.

Discourse on the city as an aesthetic entity

As keen as architects were to establish their credentials as profession-als qualified to participate in the construction and governance of the rational-technical modern city, they also sought to ensure their relative autonomy from other professionals, and did so by underlin-ing their self-understanding of the crucial role that art played in the development and maintenance of their profession. This attitude finds clear expression in a manifesto for action, presented at the First Congress of German Architects held on 27 June 1919 and signed by Peter Behrens and others, which proclaimed: 'Capitalism and socia-tion loom large as devastating threats to the individualism of the architect' (*Deutsche Bauzeitung* 1919a: 253–5, 253). This was a call for German architects to unite in defending the role of culture as a pow-erful facet of the nation's wealth from a perceived threat that echoed Otto Wagner's earlier warnings about the dangers posed by develop-ers to the architectural profession (Hevesi [1909] 1986: 253). The 1919 manifesto continued by proclaiming the architect's role as the leader among the arts and urging architects to embrace a common goal in striving to shape people's desire for beauty and to make the 'pulse of the people visible in architecture, the highest of all the art forms' (*Deutsche Bauzeitung* 1919a: 254). As the evocation of Otto Wagner's 1908 opening speech at the Architectural Congress in Vienna suggests, the manifesto was not so much offering a point of departure from previous practice, as reclaiming and formalising an aspect of architecture that was in danger of slipping from sight in the empha-sis on the city as rational-technical entity. Instead, the manifesto is based on a different view of the city – one that Hofmann had under-lined over a decade earlier in his Schinkel Memorial Lecture on 'The Metropolis as an Architectural Organism' (1908).

Hofmann focused on urban development in his illustrated lecture, talking briefly about Rome, Paris and London, before going into some detail on the restructuring of Vienna, and then highlighting a number of aspects of contemporary American city planning. He ended his lec-ture by focusing on Berlin, outlining his hopes that the city would not pass up the opportunity to produce a new urban plan with artistic integrity that would be worthy of Berlin's status as a world city. In his conclusion, he returned to the problem announced in the title of his lecture, attempting to reconcile the different ways of viewing the city that characterised discourse on urban planning in the early twentieth century. This form of discourse is often described in terms of a tension between two opposing positions that can be labelled in a number of ways: tradition and modernity, culture and civilisation, square and street, organic and artificial. Hofmann's intervention in the debate can be read as an attempt to press art into service as a mediator between these opposing conceptions of city development, both of which often claimed to be defending the city's artistic integrity. By implication, the element linking these positions was encapsulated in the idea of the city as a work of art, as a place conceived and viewed as such, and also as a place in which discourse on the city as an aesthetic entity was constructed.

Of course, Hofmann was addressing his remarks on the city as an aesthetic entity to a closed architectural audience, which was also the case with the manifesto proclaiming the architect as artist signed by Behrens and others. Similarly, when Loos introduced the Nietzschean idea of the 'Über-Architect' to explain his view of architecture as art and the architect as artist, he did so in an article published in a specialist architectural journal, *Der Architekt* (Loos 1983: 65–7). Loos, however, sought to match his words with action, entering into dialogue with artists from other fields, in order to develop a new discourse on the city as an aesthetic entity that ran counter to the dominant view of the official architectural associations in the late nineteenth and early twentieth centuries, which saw their aesthetic mission in protecting a received ideal of beauty encapsulated in historicist architecture. In pursuit of this mission, the Viennese Association of Architects and Engineers created its Committee for the Architectural Development of Vienna, which styled itself as a 'higher authority that usually was able to effectively maintain and enhance the beauty of Vienna's architectural image' (Beraneck 1912: 42). In contrast, Loos and others availed themselves of a number of different communicative opportunities in contributing to the discursive construction of the city as an aesthetic entity. Their experience demonstrates a move away from the professional architectural association to other, often less formal communicative locations and communities, including literary and aesthetic associations such as the Verein für Kunst in Berlin or the Akademischer

Verein in Vienna, educational organisations such as the Bauhaus, private salons, and informal regular meetings (*Stammtische*) in coffee houses and other similar establishments.

In pursuing an alternative conception of the city as an aesthetic entity, Loos initially allied himself with Otto Wagner and others, identifying with their interest in developing an aesthetic response that would do justice to the new rational-technical city. Soon, however, his encounters with other artists and art forms led him to a response that ran counter to the demands of that city. This new response could be termed an 'aesthetic of disruption'. According to this view, the city might still be understood as a work of art, but in an age where, as Benjamin argued in his 'Work of Art' essay, artists of all fields were calling into question the nature of the work of art itself (1996–2003: 3). In this period, the modern city was a prime site of artistic production, but artistic practice often sought to undermine the ideas and assumptions underpinning its very existence. In the visual arts, for example, expressionist artists such as Ludwig Meidner and Ernst Ludwig Kirchner explored the sense of fragmentation and alienation they associated with life in the big city, while George Grosz produced a series of works that depicted the loss of individuality (Rowe 2003: 130–82). Similar themes and anxieties relating to the dark side of modernity surfaced in later aesthetic movements such as Neue Sachlichkeit; in paintings such as Otto Dix's *Big City Triptych* (1927–28), artists laid bare the human cost of economic rationalisation and modern capitalism. All these responses to the city were part of what Andrew Benjamin has glossed as the 'modernist metaphysics of disruption' (2000: 170). When talking in artistic circles, architects such as Loos abandoned the defensive aesthetic strategy of the official architectural associations, embracing instead the possibilities offered by engaging with this response and its associated critique of the rational-technical city, which, in some cases, also resulted in imagining the construction of a different kind of urban environment.

In an essay on the cultural critic Eduard Fuchs, Benjamin argued for the importance of destruction, stating that it is 'the destructive moment which authenticates both dialectical thought and the experience of the dialectical thinker' (1996–2003: 3, 268). Whenever Benjamin referred to Loos – in his essay on Karl Kraus and in the notes for this essay, as well as in 'Erfahrung und Armut' and *One-Way Street* – it was to focus on the destructive moment of Loos's critique, and to identify him as an archetypal 'destructive character' (Benjamin 1996–2003: 2, 434, 456; 1991: 1111–2; 1974: 216; 1996–2003: 1, 469). Loos's 'aesthetic of disruption', upon which Benjamin's assessment drew, was sketched out in a set of key lectures developed around 1910 and given a number of times in key venues in Vienna and Berlin, including 'Ornament and Crime', delivered on 21 January 1910 in Vienna at an event organised by the Academic Association for Literature and Music; 'On Architecture', given in the Architektenhaus in Berlin on 8 December 1910 under the auspices of the Verein für Kunst, at the invitation of Herwarth Walden; and 'My House on the Michaelerplatz' held in the 2000-seat Sophiensaal in Vienna on 11 December 1911, again under the organisation of the Academic Association for Literature and Music.[5] A similar thematic was reiterated in later lectures, such as the series of talks Loos gave at the Sorbonne in 1926, under the programmatic title 'The Man with the Modern Nerves'.

These lectures were aimed at an audience of artists and intellectuals, as confirmed by the existence of an undated fragment of a letter to Herwarth Walden, in which Loos suggests that certain intellectuals – 'the economists (Sombart), philosophers (Simmel) and psychiatrists' – be invited to attend his first lecture in Berlin (*Sturm*-Archiv). What is more, his lectures were often organised by associations that themselves courted controversy, celebrating the modernist aesthetic of disruption. For example, the Academic Association for Literature and Music organised the premiere of Arnold Schoenberg's *First Chamber Symphony* in Vienna in 1907, which provoked one of the most notorious scandals in Viennese concert history, in the course of which Gustav Mahler came very close to having a fistfight (Arnold Schoenberg Center 2003). In line with the worldview of their organisers and audiences, Loos's lectures themselves were often controversial in nature, playing on an element of disruption, as was the case at a lecture held in Vienna in 1927 on the Arts and Crafts organisation, the Wiener Werkstätte, during which 'the crowd went berserk, applauded, hissed and protested' (Ermers [1927] 1985: 92).

This element of disruption was not merely a function of reception, but was also inherent in the subject matter of Loos's lectures. Perhaps the most perceptive analysis of Loos's take on the 'aesthetic of disruption' and its role in the discursive construction of the metropolis is provided by Cacciari. Offering a Heideggerian reading of Loos's work, he argues that anti-ornamentalism is for Loos the overall tendency, the 'destiny' of Rationalisierung, of capitalist Zivilisation. The concept of ornament in Loos hence goes well beyond the façade – it boils down to a concern for the ends of construction, production, and communication.

Cacciari (1993: 104)

Loos assigns different roles to different people, but the role of the architect as artist is to lead and to teach, and in so doing, to grasp the possibilities offered by 'Nihilismus'. As Cacciari notes, this is not Loos's only response to the modern condition, but it is the response that he offers to an audience of artists. According to this view, it is incumbent upon the artist to grasp the nature of the modern city and to seek to communicate 'the endless contradiction between the thought-out space of calculation, the equivalence of the exteriors, and the possibility of place, the hope of a place' (Cacciari 1993: 172). Cacciari sees Loos's architecture as the epitome of this aim, but it can also be discerned in his lectures delivered primarily to audiences of artists and intellectuals.

Largely missing from Loos's later work is any kind of utopian perspective; as Benjamin suggested in his notes on Kraus, in Loos's thought by the 1920s, 'the constructive has been completely degraded' and along with it, 'the creative impulse' (Benjamin 1991: 1111). Other architects, however, who similarly drew upon the influence of the 'modernist metaphysics of disruption' in order to participate in the discursive construction of the modern city, exhibited more utopian tendencies. Of those belonging to this category, perhaps the most well known were Bruno Taut and Gropius, both of whom were strongly influenced by the work of the archtetypal artist-visionary Paul Scheerbart, identified by Benjamin (1996–2003: 3, 33) 'Paris, City of the Nineteenth Century' as a utopian thinker in the mode of Charles Fourier. Scheerbart's critique of the rational-technical city, like that of Taut and Gropius (Whyte 2003), is characterised by a spiritual dimension that is, for the most part, absent from Loos's thinking.

Just as Walden gave Loos a platform from which to address the Berlin avant-garde art scene, so he was instrumental in providing Scheerbart with a space to present his ideas to a sympathetic audience, initially in the form of an evening dedicated to his work organised by the Verein für Kunst in 1904, in its first season of events (Ikelaar 1996: 42). It was through Walden and the *Sturm*-circle (the group of writers, artists and others, who gathered at his Stammtisch in the Café des Westens) that Bruno Taut made Scheerbart's acquaintance in 1913 (Ikelaar 1996: 48). Their intensive communication over the next year led not only to the publication of *Glass Architecture* (Scheerbart 1972), but also to the construction of Taut's Glass House, dedicated to Scheerbart, which was a focal point of the German Werkbund exhibition in Cologne in 1914 (Bletter 1981: 33; James-Chakraborty 2000: 48–50). After 1918, Scheerbart's ideas, contained in a number of short prose texts, as well as *Glass Architecture*, informed discussions about the nature and work of the AfK, continued to exert an influence on Taut's work and can be traced in the language of Gropius's opening manifesto of the Bauhaus, together with his inaugural address to students in the school (Bletter 1975, 1981).

In literary performances, coffee house conversations and writings, Scheerbart carried the idea of the destruction of the metropolis to a more radical conclusion than Loos, who ultimately found the destructive ideal permeating so much of his later work too radical to embrace fully. In contrast, Scheerbart clearly called for the dissolution of the metropolis in its existing form, linking this to the contemporary political and social situation, and the threat of a new kind of war, a war that would be waged from the air (1909a). He argued that a possible way of dealing with this threat would be to eliminate peacefully its central target, the densely populated urban area, relocating city dwellers to decentralised garden cities. In 'The Development of the City', he wrote of his conviction that the modern metropolis would prove unsustainable, staging his critique in a fictional account of a congress of psychiatrists (in other words, utilising a fictionalised public-speaking situation to make his point) (1910a). In direct contrast to the positive technocratic arguments that dominated the discussion of the metropolis in professional architectural and engineering circles, Scheerbart's piece drew on contemporary discourse on nervous complaints and the metropolis to make the case for an alternative model of urbanity, based on a proliferation of suburbs and an unobstrusive transport system. In *Glass Architecture*, he became more precise about the nature of these new forms of settlement, whose realisation was dependent on the dissolution of the existing modern metropolis, providing a rather straightforward account of the future advantages of glass architecture, which lie in the moral rather than the technical or economic spheres.

Building on earlier fictional work, in which he had mooted the idea of the mobile or transportable city, as well as the floating city (Scheerbart 1909b, 1910, 1912), and in line with his modernist credentials, he focused on the flexibility and fluidity of glass architecture. He also demonstrated an affinity with Nietzsche in extolling the aesthetic possibilities of using coloured glass and light as ways of heightening sensory perception and highlighting the importance of bodily affect (Blondel 1991). In particular, the form of the gothic cathedral was invoked as demonstrative of the potential of glass architecture to transform the perception, both psychological and physical, of the built environment (Bletter 1975: 89).

Taut and colleagues took up these ideas after the First World War, disseminating them in a variety of forms, including the 'Crystal Chain' letters (which could be conceived as a *Stammtisch* at a distance), lectures, publications and architectural performance (Whyte 1985). The latter found its expression in a work conceived by Taut (1920a) under the title *Der Weltbaumeister* ('The master world builder'). Although not staged in Taut's lifetime, this work of performance art in 57 pieces is important as an example of the varied forms of communication that offered themselves to architects who understood themselves as artists, taking seriously the new possibilities opening up to architecture in its engagement with avant-garde art. It was not an isolated example of the communication of architectural ideas through theatre; this had, for example, been a stated aim of Peter Behrens'1900 Darmstadt production, *Feste des Lebens und der Kunst* (Celebration of life and art) (Anderson 2000). Of particular relevance to our argument, however, is the way in which Taut's production sought to communicate his understanding of Scheerbart's vision for the city of the future that would only be realisable after the dissolution of the existing metropolis.

The new city imagined by Taut and others follows Scheerbart in two main ways: first, in revisiting tradition and according central importance to the Gothic cathedral; and second, in emphasising the importance of a city permeated by nature. In the sketches for *Der Weltbaumeister* (Taut 1920a), in publications such as *Die Stadtkrone* (The city crown) (Taut 1919) and *Die Auflösung der Städte* (The dissolution of the cities) (Taut 1920b), and in lectures delivered under the auspices of the AfK, Taut constantly made reference to these elements. Perhaps the most telling representation of this view of the new city is contained in the final sketches of *Der Weltbaumeister* (Taut 1920a), which present the central feature of this city, the crystal building (*Kristallhaus*).

First the exterior is seen, illuminated, and bathed in red evening light. Then the building opens to reveal its 'inner wonder' in the form of illuminated cascades and fountains, and sparkling glass against a dark red background. The building is in a state of flux; all of its elements move and flow, it sparkles and flashes in a rainbow of colours resolving into violet light. The final scene shows the building completely opened up to allow the interpenetration of interior and exterior: stars shine through the crystal panes unifying architecture, night and universe. At this point, underlining a sense of finality and perfection, the music sustains an 'impossibly long' tone, while all movement is arrested.

In this example of architectural discourse engaging with art, architecture itself takes up the central role of the speaker, using visual language as its preferred mode of communication. Others, however, translated Scheerbart's ideas into more straightforward linguistic form, as was the case with Gropius who, in his address to students at the Bauhaus in June 1919 on the occasion of the school's first exhibition, prophesied the creation of a 'grand, universal, overarching, spiritual and religious idea, which must finally find its crystalline expression in a grand Gesamtkunstwerk'. He went on, 'And this grand Gesamtkunstwerk, this cathedral of the future, will then shine its light upon the most mundane aspects of everyday life' (Gropius 1987: 74). In the typescript of this lecture that can be found in the State Archive in Weimar, the words 'geistig-religiöse Idee' ('spiritual and religious idea') are underlined, highlighting the fact that the new city espoused by Scheerbart, Taut, Gropius and others was based above all on the belief in a new form of spirituality (Gropius 1919).

This emphasis on the spiritual dimension was not, however, shared by all progressive architects participating in the discursive construction of the metropolis through dialogue with artists and intellectuals in the early years of the Weimar Republic. Although initially aligned with the AfK, Mendelsohn soon moved to distance himself from its metaphysical leanings (James 1997: 44). Alongside a lecture delivered to the AfK in 1919 on 'The Problem of a New Architecture' (Mendelsohn 1930), he conceived a series of eight illustrated talks on architecture for a private audience that consisted of intellectuals

Öffnen - Entfalten des Baus - Bewegen und Fliessen aller seiner Elemente -
Blitzen und Funkeln - - alle Farben - in violett werdendem Schein - ~-

Völlige Entfaltung - ~ Sterne durchschimmern die Kristalltafeln - - ~ Architektur -
- Nacht - Weltall - - eine Einheit - - - - - -
Keine Bewegung mehr - das Bild steht still - - - DIE MUSIK SCHWEBT AUF EINEM UN-
ENDLICH LANGEN TON - - - - -

Figure 2.1 Final scenes from *Der Weltbaumeister; Source*: Taut 1920a

and industrialists and gathered in the Molly Philippson's salon in Berlin (Mendelsohn 1919a, 1919b; Heinze-Greenberg and Stephan 2000: 14–44). The point of these lectures, according to Mendelsohn, was to prepare the ground for the challenges of a new era, underlining the fact that architecture was a unique art form that could not afford to deny its relationship with industry and the economic (38–44). His rhetoric, however, was at times similar to that of Scheerbart. His first lecture, on 'The Laws of Development of Art, Sculpture, Painting, Ironwork: The Present State and Urgency of Our Task', begins with a description of the present as a time of revolution and ends with the moral injunction that 'these evenings are designed to accomplish no more than to open up a space for the unchangeable laws that will have to come into force again, if we are to call ourselves free and honest people' (Mendelsohn in Heinze-Greenberg and Stefan 2000: 20). In the fourth lecture in the series, Mendelsohn turned his attention to the city. Like Scheerbart, Taut and Gropius, his concern was with the city as the locus of community; unlike them, however, he emphasised the importance of the everyday over the monumental, of the physical over the metaphysical, arguing that 'the backyards of a city, rather than its representative spaces are the true measure of its value and its art' (Mendelsohn in Heinze-Greenberg 2000: 23).

In addressing his remarks on the relationship between architecture and art to an audience that included industrialists and others in a position to make concrete changes to the built environment of the city, Mendelsohn was pointing away from a preoccupation with architecture as art, towards a more differentiated conception of the role of architecture and art in the discursive construction of the modern city. To the extent that they outline possibilities for the future, the tenor of his lectures is similar to that of those given in the same period by Taut, Gropius and others. Yet Mendelsohn also emphasised the practical dimension of his lectures and here, there are connections to Loos's thought. The latter, of course, invoked the idea of the 'Über-Architect' and engaged in dialogue with artists, only then to argue that architecture is not primarily an art form, but has a direct effect on everyday life (Loos [1931] 1982: 101). This puts the onus on architects to recognise and embrace this aspect of their profession, which many did through implementing programmes of education and popularisation.

Discourse on the city as a place for encountering the other

In the preceding sections, the emphasis was on architects seeking dialogue with other groups with whom they felt an affinity. In this final section, the net is cast wider, to show how architects sought to communicate directly with a non-specialist, non-professional urban public, and indeed, to construct a public that would be sensitised to architectural issues and questions about the built environment of the city. They did this partly by building on the sense of the architect as cultural leader that was developed through their engagement with the other arts, but also by developing the idea that architecture is ordinary. The preceding sections centred on rational-technical and aesthetic perceptions of space, respectively; this section shows how in engaging in the discursive construction of the modern city, architects also engaged with the idea of the city as a place for encountering the Other. As we will see in the case studies examined in this section, that encounter was only really there to facilitate knowledge that would undermine the status of the other as Other. In other words, the point of aesthetic education in the architectural sphere as argued for and practised in the early part of the twentieth century was not to understand strangers as strangers, but to encourage strangers to become selves, enacting a form of Kantian cosmopolitanism.

In his Schinkel Memorial Lecture, on 'Architectural Observations on Current Times: A View from the Turn of the Century', Muthesius (1900) argued that it was important for architects to reach out and speak directly to the urban public, since the architects' lack of social status and influence was related to the wider public's total lack of interest in architecture and architectural matters. From this point on, he made it his business to popularise architecture and to attempt to persuade others to do the same. In 'Architecture and the Public', he suggested that alongside publishing texts in daily newspapers and magazines aimed at a general readership, the most effective way to reach a wider audience would be for architects to give public lectures. He went on to suggest that the time was now ripe for such activities since 'lately, and most pleasingly, associations that have as their aim the cultivation of culture, and that seek to realise this aim through organising lecture series, have been expressing their desire to hear talks about architecture' (Muthesius 1907a: 213–4). In remarks such as these, Muthesius was contributing to the discursive construction of the city as a location of public appearance, drawing on his own experiences of life in London, where he worked as technical attaché in the German Embassy between 1896 and 1904 (Hubrich 1981: 31–4). The subject of his first official report in this capacity was William Morris, another populariser who placed great faith in the force of the spoken word (Read 2000: 120).

The Seventh International Congress of Architects was held in London in 1906. Muthesius addressed the meeting on the subject of 'The Education of the Public in Architecture', arguing that there was a need to educate both architects and the public about modern buildings (Hubrich 1981: 73).[6] He went on to argue for the importance of strategies of popularisation, maintaining that architects could not afford to rely on historical architectural objects to speak for them. The need for popularisation through education was also a theme taken up by Hofmann (1901), in an article reflecting on the status of architecture as part of the artistic public sphere. The catalyst for this article was an announcement by the Austrian Emperor Franz Josef that he was to open up the arts to his subjects, making art collections easily accessible in the capital cities of all the lands of the Austro-Hungarian Empire, and ensuring that architecture was accorded the same status as the other arts. Hofmann argued that this signified a radical change in public perceptions of architecture, which, until this point, had at best played a supporting role in the artistic public sphere. He then drew a number of conclusions relating to the situation in the German Empire, which had no public architecture museum. When architecture did feature in art exhibitions, argued Hofmann, it was all too frequently pushed into a corner. He picked out two city sites in particular that he saw as playing a central role in architectural education: the exhibition and the museum.

Just under a decade after Hofmann published his call for the popularisation of architecture in Germany, the General Municipal Exhibition in Berlin opened on 1 May 1910. The opening ceremony included an address by the architect Otto March, chair of the joint committee of members of the Union of Architects in Berlin and the Architectural Association in Berlin that organised the exhibition. March noted the existence of a general interest in questions of urban planning, and suggested that the challenge of the metropolis in the future would be to combine socially acceptable housing with the monumentality of the representative city. Education, he argued, would be needed to change people's sense of what it meant to live in a metropolis, and to change their sense of the aesthetics of the city. In talking of awakening people's 'slumbering sense of art' March (1910: 145) reiterated a point that Otto Wagner had made in his lectures on architecture more than a decade earlier, where he noted that the public's attitude to artistic style was characterised by 'indifference, even dullness' ([1902] 1988: 77). Wagner, however, had articulated his hope that making use of its 'extraordinary sensitivity' to fashion, the public could be educated into a different attitude towards architecture.

In the General Municipal Exhibition, popular education was provided formally through two series of public lectures designed to provide an introduction into the different specialist areas covered by the exhibition (*Deutsche Bauzeitung* 1910a). The first set of lectures, delivered between 1 and 21 May, included reflections on both rational-technical and aesthetic aspects of the city: Goecke opened the series with a lecture on the expectations associated with the competition to create a new city plan for Greater Berlin; Friedrich Krause, the architect and city planner, who oversaw the construction of the north–south rail axis in Berlin, talked about transport; Rudolf Eberstadt, an economist who worked on the 'housing question' in Berlin, provided a comparative overview of working-class housing in Germany and in England; and Fritz Stahl, art historian and art editor of the daily newspaper, the *Berliner Tageblatt*, talked about 'The City as a Work of Art' (*Deutsche Bauzeitung* 1910b). Similarly, the second set of lectures provided a combination of the political, the comparative and the aesthetic, with individual contributions including Muthesius talking about 'The Garden City Movement'; Werner Hegemann, a city planner and architectural historian who trained in Berlin before moving to the USA and directing the first city planning exhibition in Boston in 1909, providing insight into city planning in the USA; Felix Genzmer, professor of urban planning at the Technical University in Berlin, lecturing on 'Interior Design and City Planning'; and Hermann Jansen, the architect who took joint first prize in the competition to create a new city plan for Berlin, talking about his vision for the shape of the city in the future, which was based on trying to reconcile two opposing needs of the city-dweller – the need to dwell and the need to be mobile.

These lectures played an important role in the exhibition, as Hegemann made clear in his concluding report of the event. He noted

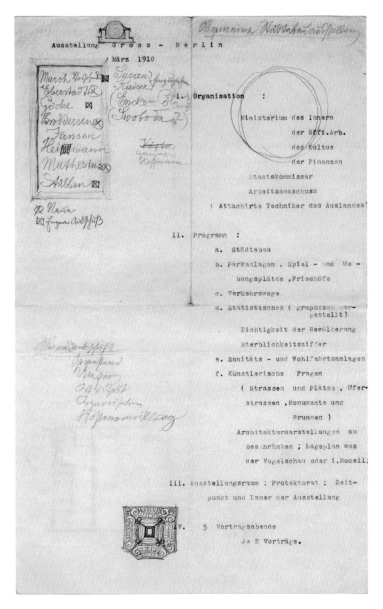

Figure 2.2   Information about the 1910 General Municipal Exhibition in Berlin, with handwritten notes listing speakers by Muthesius; *Source*: Werkbundarchiv Museum der Dinge Berlin, Estate Hermann Muthesius, Notizen

that the exhibition's central achievement was in sensitising the urban public to questions of city planning, serving in particular to demythologise the city in its current state, and to counter the received wisdom that the poor actually wanted to live in narrow, dirty streets. According to his report, the exhibition and related events such as guided tours and lectures were in fact embraced with enthusiasm by the working class. Out of a total of 65,000 visitors, 13,500 were members of a trade union, while the exhibition played a central role in the management of the building society, 'Ideal' (set up in 1907 to promote affordable housing in the working-class district of Rixdorf). In turn, this society mounted an exhibition about its housing project, attracting some 28,000 visitors, who demonstrated their interest in their enthusiastic responses to the exhibition and to the accompanying lectures. Hegemann concluded by stating that the risks of the miserable living conditions in the big cities needed to be countered with a tireless programme of education about the extent of the danger, and ways in which it could be overcome (Hegemann 1911: 87–90). Echoing Muthesius's lecture on 'Architecture and the Public' (1907a), Hegemann suggested that this would require making use of the written word in the form of newspaper articles and flyers, while also pressing the spoken word into service in exhibitions and museums, in lecture series in adult education establishments, and in other popular talks and meetings (1911: 90).

After the success of the first German Municipal Exhibition in Dresden in 1903, other German cities were keen to host similar events. In 1913, the city of Leipzig was home to the International Exhibition of Building, and in line with Hegemann's suggestions, it set out to develop an ambitious academic programme that would go some way to providing a systematic engagement with questions of urban planning (Langen 1916: 3). The result of this co-ordinated programme was a comprehensive collection of material which, it was decided, should endure in the form of a 'mobile museum' (*Wandermuseum*) long after the exhibition had run its course. The project, which was directed by Gustav Langen, drew on the work of a number of academic associates, including leading Berlin-based architects and city planners such as Jansen, Muthesius, Petersen and Stübben. Other prominent architects were invited to be part of an advisory board, including the theorist and pedagogue Paul Schultze-Naumburg, and Fritz Schumacher, city planner and founding member of the German Werkbund (Langen n.d.: 3–4).

In a short story entitled 'Transportable Cities', Scheerbart had imagined a new kind of mobile city that could be carried on three lorries and erected in under an hour (1909b). Although not a 'mobile city' in the Scheerbartian sense, the 'mobile museum', designed to be stored and moved from town to town in a single furniture van, could be described as the 'mobile idea of a city'. Its remit was to exhibit in German cities, and abroad, educating the public at large and awakening interest in central questions relating to city planning, by juxtaposing local issues and examples with more general concerns. As Langen argued in a speech given at the official opening of the museum's vist to Karlsruhe in November 1913, a common vision for the beautiful cities of the future could only be realised by setting out to educate the population as a whole. And what better way to do that, he continued, than to 'travel the length and breadth of the country, armed with word and image'. This was achieved by providing tours through the exhibition, which could be arranged in either German or English, and organising related events in the city hosting the exhibition, such as a series of lectures. The latter proved particularly successful in Karlsruhe, where Langen and others addressed audiences so large that the spacious conference room in the town hall was full to overflowing (Langen n.d.: 5–13).

Langen's 'mobile museum' was not an isolated case, but rather an example of the way that architects and other professionals set out to construct pedagogical aids and spaces that would allow them to engage in the education of a public sensitised to architectural issues. One related venture was the creation of the Museum for Social and Economic Affairs (Gesellschafts- und Wirtschaftsmuseum) in Vienna under the direction of Otto Neurath, a philosopher, sociologist and political economist, with strong interests in urban planning, who sought to facilitate the dissemination of social and economic knowledge to a broad public (Nemeth and Stadler 1996). Like the 'mobile museum', the Museum for Social and Economic Affairs grew out of the desire to provide a more permanent home for material initially gathered together for a temporary exhibition – in this case, the 5th Exhibition of Allotments, Affordable Housing and Domestic Architecture which took place in Vienna in 1923 on the square in front of the Town Hall. Neurath used the exhibited material as the foundation for a 'Museum for Settlement and Urban Planning' (Museum für Siedlungs- und Städtebau), which, a year later, developed into the Museum for Social and Economic Affairs, and for which Josef Frank created permanent exhibition space in the Town Hall (Welzig 1998: 83). Neurath's museum played a major role in the popularisation of city planning issues in Vienna, as well as exhibiting in other cities, including Berlin in 1929. This may, in turn, have had an influence on ambitious plans for an extended ten-year Architecture Exhibition, which was to open in 1930 (*Deutsche Bauzeitung* 1927b). Two years later, the *Deutsche Bauzeitung* reported that the exhibition would open in 1931, a year later than initially planned, and that themes had been agreed upon for the first five years of its existence. During the active months, May to October, the plan was to hold conferences, congresses, lectures and educational courses at the exhibition site, which was to be constructed according to plans drawn up by Poelzig and Martin Wagner (*Deutsche Bauzeitung* 1929).

The educational remit assumed by these exhibitions and museums served to complement the expanding offerings in the field of formal adult education from across the political spectrum. Towards the end of the first decade of the twentieth century, a number of speakers qualified to address issues relating to architecture and urban development began to advertise their services in the *Adreßbuch der deutschen Rednerschaft*. Initially, these speakers tended to be associated with left-wing political movements, as was the case with Hans Kampffmeyer, then the General Secretary of the German Garden City Society, or Adolf Damaschke, the editor of *Bodenreform* (a critical land reform journal). Kampffmeyer was listed as offering illustrated lectures on subjects such as 'Garden City and Lifestyle' and 'What Should be Borne in Mind when Furnishing a Flat' (*Adreßbuch der deutschen Rednerschaft* 1908/09: 54). In the same year, Damaschke's entry included the following lecture titles: 'New Theoretical Approaches to the Social Problem', 'Land Reform as Reconciliation between Socialism and Individualism' and 'The Housing Crisis and Ways Towards Self-Help' (26). A year later, these offerings had been supplemented by more general lectures on the theme of modern architecture, such as Ernst Cohn-Wiener's offerings: 'Introduction to Understanding Architecture', 'Alfred Messel's Importance for Modern Architecture' and 'Artistic Culture Now' (*Adreßbuch der deutschen Rednerschaft* 1909/1910: 23). In later years, other speakers advertising lectures on similar topics included Gustav Langen, Ludwig Lesser, and the art and architecture critic Adolf Behne. Additionally, from 1910/11, the Society for the Promotion of Adult Education was able to hire out to its members ready-to-view slide shows complete with lecture notes relating to aspects of architecture in Berlin.

While adult education establishments such as the Urania and the Humboldt-Akademie in Berlin, or the Volkshochschule Volksheim in Vienna initially provided locations in which discourse on architecture and urban planning could be disseminated to a wide public, in the changed political climate of the 1920s, they were supplemented by two other kinds of organisation. On the one hand, specialist institutions such as the Freie Deutsche Akademie des Städtebaus (Free German Academy of Urban Planning) were established in order to provide much-needed knowledge and expertise in this area to a new audience. This body, founded in 1922, aimed to bring knowledge of the most important aspects of city planning and affordable housing to the public at large (*Deutsche Bauzeitung* 1922: 286). The academy initially met on the first Thursday of every month, and in the first year of its existence, guests included Albert Hofmann, and Bruno and Max Taut (*Deutsche Bauzeitung* 1923: 111). On the other hand, centrally located associations such as this had their counterpart in the suburbs, in organisations associated with the Settlers' Movement (*Siedlungsbewegung*) and the Garden City Movement. These movements, which had their roots in the early twentieth century, but which increased in strength and influence in the 1920s, united architects, politicians and the working classes in discussing the provision of low-cost housing in metropolitan areas and mooting alternatives to the living conditions typical of the existing city. In Vienna, one such space was the 'Settlers' School' organised by the Austrian Association for Settlers and Allotment Gardeners. In 1921, it offered courses such as 'The Garden City Movement' (Hans Kampffmeyer), 'Furnishing the Settlement House' (Grete Lihotsky), 'The Settlement House as Educator' (Adolf Loos), 'Economic Aspects of the Settlement Movement' (Otto Neurath) and 'Building Economically' (Josef Frank) (Novy and Förster 1991: 38). Taken at face value, these lectures may be regarded as having been progressive in content and intent, and yet, like many similar initiatives, their net effect was, to paraphrase Warner, to counter the threat to the dominant urban public posed by a particular counterpublic (2002).

In order to explain this statement, we can turn to a lecture given by Loos in Stuttgart in 1926 on 'The Modern Settlement'.[7] He argued that human labour could be divided into two parts – destruction and reconstruction – describing the work of the settlers as essentially destructive, and adding, 'and the greater the contribution of destruction is, indeed if human work only consists in destruction, then it is truly human, natural and noble work' (Loos [1931] 1982: 183–206, 184). This, as Benjamin commented in his essay on Kraus, is the radical side of Loos's thought (1996–2003: 2, 456), in which the settlers are presented as a counterpublic that defines itself by 'such distinctively embodied performances' that it cannot be easily brought back into general circulation (Warner 2002: 103). The settlers described in Loos's lecture were fighting on two fronts; with their gaze turned outwards, their role was to extend the city boundaries through a process of urbanisation, but with their gaze turned inwards, their work and value system threatened to destroy the existing city centre (Stewart 2000: 164). As Loos commented in 'The Day of the Settler', written on the occasion of 30,000 settlers marching in protest into Vienna's city centre on 3 April 1921, this section of the urban proletariat could be considered to have already completed a 'velvet revolution' against the barrack-like confinement of the factory (Loos [1931] 1982: 161). In his lecture on the modern settlement, he sounded a note of caution from his position as a member of the dominant social group:

> Those like me, who want to avert revolutions, those who are evolutionists, should constantly bear the following in mind: Owning a garden will inevitably have a provocative effect on the individual and those who fail to recognise and act on it will be responsible for every future revolution or every war.
>
> Loos ([1931] 1982: 186)

Loos's role, and that of his fellow educators, was to recognise and contain the revolutionary potential of destructive work – the 'distinctive performance' of the settlers – organising them in such a way that their lot was improved while existing social structures were maintained. In other words, Loos and others, intent on granting the settler status as a citizen, concentrated their lectures on advising how to live rather than exploring the revolutionary potential of living differently.

From the beginning of the twentieth century onwards, much of the lecturing activity of architects to a general audience – whether located in the city centre or the outer suburbs – consisted in the dissemination of information about modern architecture, with a focus on advising people how to live or, to put it in another way, in the dissemination of information that would enable those possessing it to become part of the discursive community that comprised the dominant urban public. There are, however, a few examples of speakers who recognised that advising people how to live might include encouraging them to enter into dialogue about architecture and the city, rather than passively consuming information offered by the experts. One of the foremost speakers in this category was Damaschke, who combined a career arguing for reforming land ownership laws in both written and spoken form with publishing and lecturing on the art of speaking in public. In 1911, he first published a manual entitled *The Popular Art of Speaking in Public*, which enjoyed great success, and encouraged him to also include a special section in his bimonthly journal, *Bodenreform*, on 'German Public Speaking' (Damaschke 1912: iv). Damaschke recognised the importance of not only informing the urban working classes about modern architecture and contemporary urban planning, but also giving them a voice that would essentially undermine that counterpublic's conflict with what Warner describes as 'the norms that constitute the dominant culture as a public' (2002: 112). By inculcating the norms of modern public speaking as understood by the dominant culture into the working classes as they began to take advantage of the expansion of discursive space offered in the early twentieth century, Damaschke and others sought to 'lasso…back into general circulation' a particular counterpublic (Warner 2002: 103), countering its threat to destroy the city in its present form. But what were these norms? That is the subject of the third chapter, which takes up the complex question of the form of public discourse in this period.

3
Appearing in Public

> Public speaking reveals its secrets in all that it com-
> municates through the realm of the visual [...] and
> through the imponderables of the speaker himself.
>
> Simmel (1908)

Damaschke (1912) opened his treatise on the 'Popular Art of Public
Speaking' in a somewhat counter-intuitive fashion, by putting forward
the now familiar argument that the spoken word lost its aura with
Gutenberg's invention of the printing press in the mid-fifteenth century. This is the stuff of a narrative that later gained popularity, prin-
cipally through the works of Marshall McLuhan (1962) and Walter
Ong (1958, 1967, 1982), both of whom sought to explore and criticise
aspects of the 'Gutenberg Galaxy', a term that McLuhan coined to
encompass the constellation of changes in communication between
humans experienced in European society in the wake of the introduction of the movable type. Damaschke's work, of course, predates
these accounts and does not share their emphasis on history. He was
writing in direct response to a fundamental shift in oral culture in the
late nineteenth century, which is described persuasively in Gert
Ueding and Bernd Steinbrink's overview of the history of rhetoric in the
German-speaking countries as a narrative of *both* decline *and* durability
through change (1994: 134–56).

The idea of rhetoric's decline in the nineteenth century was
mooted as early as 1812, in a celebrated series of lectures given in
Vienna by the economist and theorist, Adam Müller ([1812] 1967).
In his 'Twelve Talks about Eloquence and its Decline in Germany',

he laid the blame for the perceived decline on three related conditions: first, the emphasis on writing and the self-satisfied attitude of German literature; second, the absence of an educated and appreciative public able to listen productively; and third, the lack of a republican tradition (Ueding and Steinbrink 1994: 136–7). Almost a century later, a similar thematic was taken up in an article on 'The Art of Speaking' published in *Kunstwart*, which opened with the following anecdote:

> A lady friend recently told me that she never tired of listening to a Frenchman. A Frenchman? Yes, a common or garden Parisian of the most humble sort. He spoke so beautifully, just in conversation, that she greatly enjoyed listening to this delightful language, even though she only understood the half of it.
>
> K. (1909: 340–1)

The author goes on to ponder why the French appear naturally predisposed to talk in public, while the Germans struggle, citing as evidence for the latter, the fact that a Prussian member of parliament had recently demanded that universities provide their students with more practical training in pronunciation to make up for existing deficiencies in this area. The author of the piece doubts whether this measure would have the desired effect, arguing that the problem is too deep-seated to be eradicated by simply 'training the tongue'. He suggests that the problem is a cultural one; the pervasiveness of the written word means that as soon as people begin to speak in public, they abandon the concise language that would be the stuff of private conversation, replacing it with 'bad newspaper speak' (341). Writing in *Der Sprecher*, a specialist public-speaking journal, Eduard Engel made a related point, arguing that while the English and the French are able to speak from the lecture platform as though they were in the middle of noble society, the Germans all too often speak as though they were reading aloud: 'The basic style of German formal public speaking is that of the professor at the lectern reading from notes' (1911: 25). Similarly, Loos broached the idea of an apparently unbridgeable chasm between written and spoken language, and the concomitant tyranny of the written word in the epilogue to *Ins Leere gesprochen* (*Spoken into the Void*). The main target of his criticism is orthography, specifically the German custom of capitalising all nouns, and the piece reads in part as an apologia for the spoken word.

His typically polemical conclusion, however, is damning for the public-speaking scene in the German-speaking countries: 'The writer is unable to speak, the speaker cannot write. And the German, it turns out, can do neither' (Loos [1921] 1981: 205).

This rather pessimistic comment situates Loos's thought in the wider sociocultural landscape of the early twentieth century, a period in which the problem of communication with others loomed large. At this time, as Kittler argues, the mechanisation of writing through the invention of the typewriter brought about the detachment of the act of writing from subjectivity (1999: 183–263). Echoing Simmel's diagnosis of modernity as the time in which objective culture surged ahead of its subjective counterpart (1990: 463), Kittler points out the crucial link between the history of the typewriter and Nietzsche's 'notion of inscription', which, he argues, 'designates the turning point at which communications technologies can no longer be related back to humans. Instead, the former have formed the latter' (Kittler 1999: 211, 229). This was but one facet of the rise of new media technology around the year 1900, which resulted in 'the ordinary, purposeful use of language – so-called communication with others – [being] excluded' (229). Approaching the problem from a slightly different angle, Peters comments that at the beginning of the twentieth century, 'the problem of communication becomes not only one of getting messages across the waste expanses traversed by the telegraph wires of the interference-prone "ether" of radio transmission, but one of making contact with the person sitting next to you' (1999: 178). In *Wittgenstein's Vienna*, Janik and Toulmin argue that by 1900, all major fields of thought and art faced a set of linked problems: 'problems of communication, authenticity and symbolic expression' (1973: 119). This, they claim persuasively, set the stage for a wide-ranging cultural and philosophical critique of language and representation, which drew in particular on Ernst Mach's work on 'sense impressions', on the Kantian analysis of representation and on Kierkegaard's 'anti-intellectualist approach to moral and aesthetic issues'. This critique found apologists in such diverse figures as Loos, Fritz Mauthner and, of course, Wittgenstein whose *Tractatus*, sought to demonstrate the importance of separating 'reason from fantasy [...] straightforward descriptive language from "indirect communication"' (Janik and Toulmin 1973: 198).

The 'language scepticism' seen in the work of Mauthner and others was informed by a sense of loss, corresponding, perhaps, to the idea of rhetoric's decline (1901–03). Yet as Ueding and Steinbrink show, the late nineteenth century witnessed not only the decline of oral communication, but also its ability to endure (1994: 134–56). Just as writing underwent a fundamental change with the introduction of the typewriter, but did not disappear, so too oral culture took on new forms in the sociocultural climate of the early twentieth century. This climate was influenced by new technologies, including the invention of storage devices for archiving speech, such as film and the gramophone (Kittler 1999), but also by socio-political and legal struggles around two basic rights: the right to free speech and the right to associate in public (Klausmann 1998: 233–4). The site of the latter was, of course, the political sphere and it was there, according to Damaschke, that the spoken word demonstrated its durability most clearly, as it continued to play a leading role in influencing public opinion. In fact, he argued, in this arena the art of public speaking was actually rapidly increasing in importance, and he regarded this a matter for concern, since 'throughout history, serious voices [Tacitus, Montaigne and Thomas Carlyle] saw such developments as a sign of rhetoric's degeneration and decline' (Damaschke 1912: 9). Ultimately, however, Damaschke rejected the pessimism of his assembled experts, to present his claim that in the hands of honest and independent thinkers and activists, the art of public speaking could be a useful tool. The implication here is that a new form of public speaking was necessary that would reject the overblown grandeur so often typical of self-representation through speech. This move had its correlate in the style of the city: just as the grand architectural gestures of the ascendant liberal bourgeoisie in the nineteenth century such as Vienna's monumental *Ringstrasse* were replaced by the more playful architecture of the Secession or the more restrained architecture of Loos and his pupils, so the pathos, pomp and bombast of late nineteenth century rhetoric gave way to a pared-down, yet complex style of public speaking around the beginning of the next century. This chapter sets out to describe this new style, which developed in response to questions of how best to appear in public in a modern urban world shaped, in part, by the development of new forms of communication technology and an attendant 'language crisis', and concomitantly, of how best to communicate knowledge of that world. It offers insight into the forms of communication employed in the discursive construction of the metropolis, focusing on two aspects in particular: the interplay of dissemination and dialogue, and the role of the aesthetics of appearing. These are explored with reference to the public-speaking activities of Simmel and Loos, which were linked, formally as well as thematically, to the modern city.

Dissemination and dialogue

Damaschke's (1912) public-speaking manual may have had a unique selling point in its orientation towards the newly enfranchised working class, but it was by no means an isolated example of work discussing the formal aspects of appearing and speaking in public in the early twentieth century. Reports of lectures appearing in newspapers and journals frequently commented upon style as well as substance, and alongside such reports, many leading cultural journals, such as *Kunstwart* or *Der neue Rundschau*, carried articles on public speaking. While some of these were clearly the work of the professional critic concerned with the aesthetics of the communicative event, others were written with a rather more pedagogical bent, connecting them to another form of writing on public speaking – the instruction manual. Finally, alongside these written works, self-reflexive lectures on public speaking were also being given, often as part of the training provision offered by universities or adult education establishments. The latter's directory of public speaking, the *Jahrbuch für das deutsche Vortragswesen*, lists a number of speakers, including Damaschke, prepared to talk about speaking in public.

Particularly, the more pedagogically oriented publications often sought to codify a specific form of current practice in the field of public speaking, generally with reference to a traditional schematic rhetorical education. Handbooks such as Geißler's *Rhetorik* (1914) are also, however, clearly of their own time, moulding a rhetorical heritage to the needs of the first decades of the twentieth century, to a time that the philosopher Karl Jaspers described in his controversial political work, *Man in the Modern Age*, as the 'era of advanced technique' (1933: 46). This was an age, Jaspers maintained, in which positivism was the dominant 'attitude of mind' (47). And positivism, he posited, drawing on his philosophical interest in social and linguistic intercourse between human beings, tended to establish 'a sort of "universal language"' or 'conventional ethic of association' (50). In 'Metropolis and Mental Life', Simmel had already identified a tendency towards uniformity in modern urban life (1997: 178–9). Writing in the early 1930s in direct response to the mass political movements of the time, Jaspers's contribution was to extend this observation to the field of communication and association.

One method of ensuring a certain level of uniformity, over and above the publication of prescriptive instruction manuals on how to speak in public, was a service provided by the German Social Democratic Party (SPD), whose education wing (the *Zentralbildungsausschuß*) lent out sets of slides together with a ready-made set of lecture notes to local party associations. According to the notes that accompanied a lecture prepared by Adolf Behne (1915) on 'The Art Treasures in the Eastern War Zone' (designed as part of a series to provoke discussion on the First World War), this form of lending out lectures was designed to save local associations money, by making the professional speaker redundant. All that the association had to provide was a 'comrade who was able to read the accompanying text clearly, with the requisite intonation and attention to detail' (Behne 1915: 2) and, implicitly, without deviating from the approved text. This initiative was not unique to the SPD; the Society for the Promotion of Adult Education offered a similar service, suggesting in the foreword to the 1914/15 edition of the *Jahrbuch für das deutsche Vortragswesen*, that associations finding themselves with insufficient funds to invite talented speakers should consider making use of the Society's lending service, which included slide series, films and even a mobile cinema.

The view of public speaking underlying these initiatives conceives it as a medium for the dissemination of information and, therefore, for retaining control of that information. This is close to the critical account of the lecture that Adorno later put forward in his theoretical treatise on the essay, 'The Essay as Form', where he suggested that the domination of the scientific world view and its corresponding use of discursive logic effected a fundamental change in the nature of the lecture, which lost its grounding in dialogical communication, becoming merely a vehicle for imparting knowledge and, concomitantly, for controlling that knowledge (1991: 22). His dissatisfaction with this form of communication led him to prize the written word in the form of the essay as the most appropriate medium for cultural critique and critical social theory; other theorists similarly rejecting the discursive logic of the lecture, remained true to the spoken word, looking to the 'ordinary language' of 'everyday conversation' for a viable alternative.

Moritz Lazarus ([1879] 1986), a philosopher and proto-sociologist, whose Berlin salon was frequented by intellectuals and writers such as Wilhelm Dilthey and Theodor Fontane, raised the possibility of conversation offering an alternative to the homogenising tendencies of the lecture in a lecture given in 1876 in Berlin's Singakademie. This was a lecture (delivered almost a century before Goffman (1969) took up his sociological work in a similar field) about *ordinary* language,

> about conversations in the most simple, narrowly-defined sense of the word, not about dialogue that has been produced artificially in literary form for the benefit of poetry or science – it is about real conversations as they are had by ordinary people on a daily, indeed hourly, basis.
>
> Lazarus (1986: 5)

Yet the fact that he was talking about ordinary language did not prevent him from making claims about the extraordinary potential of conversation: 'the words of the conversation are the key that opens the heart, the tie that binds souls together and the light that enables minds to illuminate one another, allowing them to see' (45). The irony of extolling the virtues of conversation in a lecture were not lost on him; closing his reflections by pointing out the merits of Socratic dialogue, he left his audience to ponder how much richer an experience they would have had, had he been able to communicate with them as individuals in private conversation (46). Lazarus was not alone in making such observations. For example, in an extended discussion piece on 'Sociability and Intellectual Culture' written for the *Neue Rundschau*, Karl Joël (1913) made a strong case for the rediscovery of the 'feminine' culture of conversation and bourgeois sociability to combat the sense of alienation that characterised the dominant philosophical discourse of the late nineteenth century, exemplified by Nietzsche.

Linking these accounts is a sense of faith in ordinary language and private conversation that was not shared by many others writing about language at the time. Franz Kafka, for example, was less convinced of the straightforward ability of 'ordinary language' to offer a valid alternative to the ravages of the modern world; as Peters remarks, the presentation of new communication technology such as the telephone in *The Castle* 'foregrounds potentials for schizophrenia, paranoia, dissimulation, and eavesdropping that lurk in everyday speech' (1999: 205). Kraus, meanwhile, railed against the unconscious use of ordinary metaphor as cliché, which, he argued, meant that speakers never fully realised what they were saying. If they did, he suggested, 'if they saw and felt the full impact of the verbal reality that inheres in their words and has only to be uncovered to make its effect, then they would [...] speak differently, and indeed live differently' (Stern 1966: 78).

If neither the ordinary language of private conversation nor the discursive logic of the formal lecture was felt to be in itself an adequate form of communication in the modern world, then what style was the forward-looking public speaker to adopt? In Vienna, it fell to Hermann Bahr to propose a way of moving beyond the binary opposition between monologue and conversation, dissemination and dialogue, masculine and feminine. Writing on the subject of 'decadence', Bahr put forward the then current Parisian craze for the 'Conferénce' as a form that sought to combine monological speech and conversation, describing it as

> delicate, coquette, and yet, unconsciously and without noticing, making the objective personal [...]. It's neither sermon, nor lecture, nor chat and yet takes a little from all three. One sits as though at the fireside, but also as though at the lectern.
>
> Bahr (1897: 1)

The foremost exponent of this new style of public speaking, according to Bahr, was the symbolist writer and poet, Comte Robert de Montesquiou-Fezensac, towards whom 'all the apostles of tomorrow thronged' to hear him talk on subjects 'faraway, foreign and in demand' thrilled by his 'dark, intense voice, slightly tinged with the language of Gascony' and his 'carefree, quiet and casual' style of delivery (2). Other theorists subsequently provided support for Bahr's observations. Max Dessoir (philosopher, renowned speaker, and author of *The Speech as Art Form* (1940)) published an article on 'Speeches and Conversations' in the leading Viennese weekly newspaper, *Die Zeit*, in which he contrasted the traditional form of public speaking (the monological speech based on declamation) with a modern style of speaking that had its basis in conversation and dissemination (1902).

The importance of combining dissemination and conversation also formed a cornerstone of Damaschke's *Popular Art of Public Speaking*, in which he maintained that 'the lively talk has to be a kind of exchange of ideas, just like a conversation, and so from this it derives its rules' (1912: 72).

Bahr, Dessoir and Damaschke were all calling for a form of public speaking that would insist upon a dialectical relationship between dissemination and dialogue, two forms of communication that, as Peters argues, have long been regarded as diametrical opposites in the Western rhetorical tradition (1999: 33–62). Throughout the twentieth century, thinkers such as Adorno, Bakhtin and Habermas cast their lot with dialogue, to the detriment of dissemination, perpetuating the age-old ideological divide between these two forms. Peters, however, suggests that this view may be due for revision, concluding a chapter on the relative merits of dialogue and dissemination with the remark that 'dissemination is not wreckage; it is our lot' (1999: 62). At the beginning of the twentieth century, speakers were not ready to ditch dissemination altogether, but neither were they satisfied with a rhetorical style that ignored the dialogical. Rather, they called for an approach that would encompass both, combining the dissemination of rational-technical discourse with the dialogue typical of ordinary discourse to construct a form of public speaking located in the realm of the aesthetic. In heralding a new form of public speaking fit for the new century, both Bahr and Damaschke invoked the conversation, but they did so, tellingly, using the conditional. Bahr (1897: 1) argued that the 'Conferéncier' should sit '*as though* at the fireside, but also *as though* at the lectern', while Damaschke (1912: 72) maintained that modern speaking should be '*just like* a conversation' (my emphases). These formations imply that the modern public speaker is a *performer*, who speaks as though simultaneously appearing in two apparently mutually exclusive locations: the fireside and the lectern. The former stands for ordinary discourse and the latter for rational-technical, while the idea of performance foregrounds the importance of aesthetic appearing. This combination of rational-technical, aesthetic-visionary and ordinary discourse cast the architect as 'urban hero' poised to play a leading role in the discursive construction of the modern city. The ideal public speaker, combining dissemination and dialogue, is also poised to take on this mantle. Comprehending the simultaneity of dissemination, or rational-technical language, and dialogue, or conversation, is to recognise the 'performative dimension of public speaking' that is crucial to grasping how publics are constructed (Warner 2002: 114). To understand how this dimension operated, we need to turn to an analysis of the 'aesthetics of appearing' (Seel 2005).

The aesthetics of appearing: Performing dissemination and dialogue

Arendt's description of the public sphere accords a central role to performance, which she glosses as the *act* of appearing; the public sphere is, 'the space where I appear to others as others appear to me, where men exist not merely like other living or inanimate things, but *make their appearance explicitly*' (Arendt 1958: 198; my emphasis). The kind of appearing that she has in mind here is similar to what Seel later labelled 'artistic appearing', which, he argues, must be distinguished analytically from two other categories of 'aesthetic appearing' identified in his work: 'mere appearing' and 'atmospheric appearing' (2005: 91–7). The 'mere appearing' of an object is perceived when 'we let the object be, purely in its sensuous appearing [...] what counts here is nothing but perceiving the momentary simultaneity of what is sensuously perceivable' (91–2). 'Atmospheric appearing', meanwhile, refers to the way in which an object can affect the character of its setting, and concomitantly, the way in which that character 'becomes intuitable in these objects' (92). As one example of this kind of appearing, Seel makes us consider how 'a certain architecture can modify the expression of a city' (92). This point will be taken up in the next chapter, which sets out to investigate the city as a collection of speech sites, looking at how these sites influenced the character of contemporary public speaking, as well as how they were influenced by it. Before proceeding in this direction, however, this chapter investigates public speaking in general, and the role of the speaker, in particular, in terms of 'artistic appearing', a form of appearing in which 'an encounter with presented presence takes place' (98). In introducing the concept of 'presence', Seel demonstrates a certain affinity with Hans Ulrich Gumbrecht's *The Production of Presence*, in which the latter argues that the humanities and arts have been guilty of 'bracketing out presence', and ultimately presents a playdoyer for 'a relation to the things of the world that could oscillate between presence effects and meaning effects' (Gumbrecht 2004: xv). Seel, too, is interested in thinking about the relationship between presence and meaning, which, he argues, are inextricably linked in the work of art. For him, artworks are special in that they are 'formations of an *articulating* appearing' that 'need to be *understood* in their performative intent' (Seel 2005: 96). This sense of 'intent' is what he means by 'presented presence' (98), and indeed, what Arendt is thinking of when she defines the public sphere as the space where 'men [...] make their appearance *explicitly*' (my emphasis) (1958: 198).

How does all this relate to the present investigation of the form of public speaking around 1900? Writing in 1898, Robert Scheu diagnosed the strength of the successful lecture in terms of appearing, explaining that certain speakers have the ability to impress an audience in an instant, to hold people in thrall from the moment the first word has been uttered. Like 'love at first sight', he argued, this is only explicable if we accept that a person's whole personality can be contained in a single gesture or sentence, and this, in turn, relies on

> the great secret of 'making an appearance' [*des Auftretens*]. Which is, by the way, a glorious word that already expresses all of that: for in the very moment that the speaker first appears or emerges, his full presence is made manifest.
>
> Scheu (1898: 266)

Seel, however, is at pains to point out that the production of presence is in itself not sufficient to label a given aesthetic event as 'art'. To do so, a further requirement must be met; the aesthetic event in question must invite its audience to engage in 'imaginative projections and reflections about the game of their lives' (2005: 137). In Scheu's view, the 'artistic lecture' – implicitly opposed to the academic lecture rooted only in discursive logic – does exactly this, through its form of presentation, which demands a continual openness to paradox (1898: 265). Understanding this kind of lecture, Scheu insists, means paying attention to more than a straightforward narrative; it entails perceiving and understanding pragmatics (linguistic effects of language in use) and gesture. These are aspects of performing in public that are taken up in theoretical and practical works on the subject. Warner notes the importance of pragmatics – including 'the effects of speech genres, idioms, stylistic markers, address, temporality, mise-en-scène, citational field, interlocutory protocols, lexicon' – in understanding any kind of 'discourse as poetic world-making' (2002: 114). Damaschke, meanwhile, placed great emphasis on the effects of gesture and corporeal communication, citing the case of the politician, August Bebel, who recalled, in 1903, how distracting he had found it when the celebrated speaker Ferdinand Lasalle had stuck a finger in the armhole of his waistcoat during a speech given some forty years earlier. Damaschke comments that 'forty eventful years were not enough to wipe the memory of this uncomfortable position' (1912: 83). The force of pragmatics and gestures – the way that they produce 'presence effects' and 'meaning effects' in a form of presentation constantly open to paradox, a form of 'artistic appearing' – can only be appreciated fully through paying the presentation the kind of intense attention that Seel (2005: 96) labels 'lingering sensuous perception'.

By emphasising the importance of 'artistic appearing' in understanding and producing public speaking, Scheu was situating his article in the context of a form of thinking prevalent around 1900, which saw celebrated writers such as Hofmannsthal react to 'language scepticism' by positing 'indirect communication' as a plausible alternative, as part of a general turn towards the 'body' in German modernist literature (Schiffermüller 2001), which in turn was indebted to the centrality of physiognomic perception and expression in the work of philosophers such as Mach and Nietzsche. In *Thus Spake Zarathustra*, Nietzsche presented his philosophical position as an embodied narrative utilising dance, acrobatics and other forms of movement ([1883–85] 1969). In other words, it is not only what Zarathustra says that is important, but also the manner in which he says it (Mattenklott 1983: 143). Indeed, according to Blondel, Nietzsche's philosophy conceives the body as 'a *relation of forces* of the *assimilated* signs [...] an *interpretative space*', which enables the articulation and perception of things that may not be expressible through language (1991: 238). In his fictional 'Letter of Lord Chandos', Hofmannsthal wrote: 'I have lost completely the ability to speak or to think of anything coherently' (1991: 48). Convinced that language was no longer adequate to express matters of (philosophical) importance, he turned instead to performance, and specifically to the medium of the theatrical *Gesamtkunstwerk*, which he produced in collaboration with Max Reinhardt, Richard Strauss and others (Yates 1992). Kraus had nothing but disdain for Hofmannsthal's spectacular theatre, and yet, as we have seen, he too knew of the power of performance, packaging his moral lectures in the form of operetta and popular theatre. Indeed, as a speaker, Kraus appears to have been the very epitome of Scheu's description of the manifestation of presence in the act of making an appearance. Writing in *Der Sturm* after Kraus's first performance in Vienna in May 1910, Mirko Jelusic noted that '[t]he hall was overflowing as Kraus stepped up to the podium [...]. His expression, both facial and vocal, is cool, mocking, superior. And before Kraus begins to speak, you know that his voice will be clear and sharp' (cited in AAC-F 1910 303–304: 38).

Kraus's talent for appearing in public was nurtured, it seems, without the aid of formal training; others seeking to emulate his success sought instruction in the art of speaking in public. Alongside the courses offered by universities and adult education establishments, Walden's prodigious art school, the Kunstschule *Der Sturm*, established in 1916, provided specialist training in this area, aimed at those who saw public speaking primarily as an art form (Pirsch 1985: 383–7). Indebted to *Der Sturm*'s uncompromising commitment to expressionist art, the Kunstschule's take on speaking in public was rather different to that of more traditional institutions, even if there was some overlap in their concepts of the ideal student – according to an advertising brochure, the department of the Kunstschule devoted to rhetoric, recitation and drama was to be open to 'lay people' such as 'teachers, lawyers, public speakers, army officers and men of the cloth' (Pirsch 1985: 383). The man tasked with establishing and running the department was the actor and celebrated reciter, Rudolf Blümner, who also had strong theoretical interests in speech and movement, and argued vociferously for the status of the speaker as an artist-creator in his or her own right. In a number of articles published in *Der Sturm* and elsewhere, he maintained that the act of performing a text (*das Vortragen*) – regardless of whether or not the author and performer were the one and the same person – was not merely the interpretation of an already existing work of art, but actually entailed the creation of a new entity. Blümner's work demonstrates an affinity with Seel's writing on the 'aesthetics of appearing', since he suggests that the new work of art comes about through the speaker exercising what

Seel would later call 'performative intent', and so engaging in 'artistic appearing' (2005: 96).

Blümner's theoretical take was based on a distinction between two kinds of public speaking, between 'reading aloud' (*vorlesen*) and 'performing a text' (*vortragen*), and on the idea that only the latter would enable the development of a modern form of speaking. This emphasis on 'performing a text' offers a point of connection with Damaschke's criticism of speakers who contented themselves with reading out a manuscript instead of performing (1912: 70). While Blümner and Damaschke, both talented speakers in their own right, were convinced of the centrality of performance to successful modern public speaking, other apologists for public speaking, such as Dessoir, were rather more cautious about putting their faith so wholeheartedly in performance. Writing on the difference between modern and traditional public speaking, and aligning himself with the former, Dessoir declared: 'When we speak, we do not want to put ourselves on show, but rather to subordinate ourselves to the subject of our deliberations' (1902: 198). He may appear to offer an uncompromising indictment of performance over substance, but a careful reading of his article suggests that although he is clearly arguing against what we could call 'the performance of performance', he is actively promoting the modernity of a different kind of performance, which we could call the 'performance of non-performance'. In his view – and this is strikingly similar to Bahr's (1897) account of the task of the 'Conferéncier' – modern public speaking depends on the public performance of intimacy and informality. In other words, the 'peformative intent' of the modern public speaker, which is necessary for artistic appearing, is to perform intimacy in public. Blum recognises the force of such 'performative intent' when he describes the scene as 'the place for bringing to view the affiliations which bind people as a collective of co-speakers as if they are dwelling in nearness to one another, as if together they incarnate a structure of mutual recognition' (2003: 178). His use of the conditional, 'as if', here points to the performative aspect of the scene. To put this in another way, the very condition of possibility of modern public speaking depends on the kind of paradox to which, Scheu argued, the public speech as work of art had to be continually open (1898: 265). It depends on a form of public speaking that in performing intimacy, encompasses both dissemination and dialogue. As we will see, this was a form of public speaking practised by Simmel.

Georg Simmel: The public performance of intimacy

As private lecturer and later, untenured professor at the University of Berlin hoping to be appointed to a permanent position, Simmel's task was to prove himself by attracting students to his courses. By all accounts, he was rather successful in this; the majority of the essays contained in a commemorative collection put together to mark the 100th anniversary of his birth, are written by his former students, many of whom focus on his talents as a lecturer (Gassen and Landmann 1958). Simmel's correspondence with Heinrich Rickert, published in the same collection, documents the popularity of Simmel's lecture courses. In a letter dated 27 January 1900, Simmel wrote: 'For my part, I have occasion to be satisfied with both work and my students, at least quantitatively speaking. I have around 315 students in my three courses' (99). Simmel's talents as a speaker also brought forth invitations for him to speak in public in Berlin, Vienna and other cities throughout Europe. According to his son, Simmel 'greatly loved this activity of a "wandering priest". He found it exciting; on the return journey he was sometimes already at work on his next lecture' (Simmel, H. 1976: 258). It was in this context, of course, that he gave his lecture on 'The Metropolis and Mental Life' in Dresden in 1903, but there are many other instances of him addressing a variety of different publics, including, during the First World War, German troops. Simmel later related an anecdote about a group of soldiers who left his lecture on 'Goethe and Love' disappointed to have heard a philosophical discussion of love rather than a graphic description of Goethe's amorous conquests (Gassen and Landmann 1958: 277).[1]

Simmel's written work was notoriously dense and complicated; his lectures, according to contemporary reports, were much more accessible, which may begin to account for his popularity as a speaker. Emil Ludwig, for example, maintained that 'the complexity of [Simmel's] writing style [...] is unravelled when the speaker unravels the sentence' (Gassen and Landmann 1958: 154), while Paul Fechter suggested that the way in which Simmel appeared to his audience also aided understanding.

> One watched while the figure on the lecture platform became the medium of an intellectual process, whose passion was not

only realized in words, but also in gestures, movements, actions. When Simmel wanted to reveal to his audience the very kernel of a thought, an idea, he did not just formulate it; in a manner of speaking, he held it aloft. His fingers stretched outwards and upwards and then closed again, his whole body turned under the force of his uplifted hand, in which the problem was resting.

Gassen and Landmann (1958: 160)

This brief account suggests that Simmel's audiences reached understanding through more than mere words. To use Gumbrecht's terms, both 'meaning effects' and 'presence effects' were brought into play in the course of these lectures, which were, primarily, 'aesthetic events' (2004). Simmel made use of pragmatics and gesture, offering those he was addressing a 'capacity for recognition which [was] enhanced through the sharing of narratives which are fully embodied' (Frank, A. 1991: 89). The notion of the embodied narrative, of course, played an important role in Nietzsche's philosophy; similarly, it was central to Simmel's theoretical accounts of physiognomy, of the body as an interpretative location. In developing his theory of physiognomy, Simmel set out to study gestures and movement styles in order to explain how immediate intersubjective understanding, or face-to-face communication functioned (Moynahan 1996: 44). Tellingly, for someone engaging in the public performance of intimacy, his theoretical concern with physiognomy was grounded in his conception of the body as the site of representation of thoughts and emotions, and so played a central role in his ground-breaking work on the sociology of emotions and intimacy (Nedelmann 1983).

Simmel's theory of physiognomy was, however, not without its weaknesses. In his *Arcades Project*, Walter Benjamin offered a critique of the 'phantasmagoria of the *flâneur*', which he glosses as the belief that the profession, background and character of a person can be read from the face (1999: 429). He suggested that although Simmel's 'Sociology of the Senses' may have ultimately managed to avoid this form of vulgar physiognomy, it nevertheless demonstrated a certain affinity with it (Benjamin 1999: 433–4). In Benjamin's own work on corporeality, in which he was keen to overcome the problems of vulgar physiognomy, he emphasised the body's status as a site of representation and framed this idea with reference to his interest in the multiple connections between language, perception and the body

(Weigel 1992: 58). This led him, in 'Problems of Socio-Linguistics', to turn his attention to the continuing importance of the mimetic dimension of language (Benjamin 1972: 452–80). Rejecting the simple, but popular schema that described the ontogenetic and phylogenetic development of language in terms of a move from mimesis to semiosis, Benjamin posited the simultaneity of the mimetic and semiotic dimensions of language. He found evidence for this view in the work of theorists such as Heinz Werner and Rudolf Leonhard whose 'linguistic physiognomy [...] crosses the threshold to the idea of the mimetic in language' (Benjamin 1972: 478).

Something of what Benjamin means by 'the mimetic in language' and its relevance to a discussion of public speaking can be gleaned from a brief consideration of Rudolf Blümner's concept of 'the absolute art of speaking' (*absolute Sprechkunst*), which he outlined in a series of articles published in *Der Sturm* and elsewhere (see Blümner 1907, 1926/27; Pirsch 1985: 586–99). Blümner suggests that performing expressionist lyric poetry, with its illogical, 'art logical' connections between words, allows the speaker to concentrate on rhythm, although even here, the speaker's autonomy is compromised by the fact that the words are provided for him (591). The most extreme form of 'the absolute art of speaking', therefore, would entail the complete elimination of the word, as in the work of the Dadaists, whose performance art, as Blümner pointed out, systematically rejected the syntactic and semantic characteristics of language. Successful public speaking may not have been able, or indeed have wanted to deny the semiotic dimension of language entirely, which is the ultimate aim of Blümner's theory, yet rather less avant-garde writers on rhetoric also found themselves arguing for the importance of mimesis. Geißler, for example, argued that 'the children of the scientific and technical age' tended to use language as a tool, but that it could and should be used more extensively as it contains healing powers that can mitigate the one-sidedness of the scientific age with its overemphasis on logic and reason (1911: 5). Drawing on ideas such as these, modern public speaking as practised by Simmel and others made extensive use of the mimetic dimension of language to aid the performance of intimacy. It did this through employing what Colin Sample calls 'the physiognomic dimension of language' (1996: 117).

Sample puts forward a theory of aesthetic language which holds that the sensual and conceptual domains are intertwined in the Kantian

'aesthetic idea', and argues that aesthetic language in particular continues to make extensive use of the mimetic function: 'by seeking to
present its meaning iconically [mimetic dimension] instead of refer-
ring to it arbitrarily [semiotic dimension], aesthetic language presents
"aesthetic ideas" that lend sensuous life to verbal language' (Sample
1996: 114–15). He develops a framework through which the physiognomic dimension of language connects it to the felt context of a
sensual human being in the world, focusing on the three main ways
in which the body can present and perceive physiognomic aspects in
a given communicative situation: vocalisation, kinesis and facial
expression. These three categories structure the following discussion
of Simmel's lectures as 'aesthetic events', which demonstrates that in
modern public speaking based on the performance of intimacy,
rational-technical and aesthetic language combine in the interaction
of the mimetic and semiotic dimensions of language.

In 'The Art of the Body', Julius Bab (1906) took existing theories of
acting to task for failing to conceive of the body as anything other than
a purely optical object, and so neglecting important 'bodily functions' that play a role in physiognomic perception. Foremost in his
list of other 'bodily functions' was the human voice, the importance
of which for perception Simmel took up the following year in his
'Sociology of the Senses' (1997: 109–20). He maintained that the correspondence between speech sound and its meaning forms a bridge
through which one gains knowledge of the other. This correspondence leads 'us into the human subject as its mood and emotion and
out to the object as knowledge of it' (111). Distinguishing between
the human and the non-human object, he maintained that while
sensory perception and recognition of the non-human object are two
distinct processes, in the case of a person, emotional value and instinc-
tive knowledge of 'sense impressions' (a term brought into circulation by Ernst Mach) together form the foundation of a relationship
to another person.

Simmel's analysis of the interaction between the sound of the
voice and the meaning of that sound found an echo in the works of
Goffman (1981) and Hans Georg Gadamer (1993), both of whom
wrote specifically about public speaking. In a sociological analysis
of a variety of 'forms of talk', Goffman argued that the main difference between the producer of a written text and the speaker is that
the speaker is not only the author of a text, but also the 'animator'

(the lecturer vocalises the text) and the 'principal' (the lecturer appears to believe personally in what is being said) (1981: 167). In his meditations on 'Voice and Language', Gadamer made a similar point, maintaining that a particular strength of the lecture is the sense of closeness that is created when the originator of an idea gives voice to that same idea, which in turn is linked to the unity of meaning and sound characteristic of poetic language (1993: 278). In terms of public speaking as 'artistic appearing', the perceived connection between 'meaning' and 'sound' is an important factor in the public performance of intimacy.

When describing Simmel's 'real greatness' on the lecture platform, Nikolas Spykman singled out his 'beautiful voice' and his 'elegant diction' (Gassen and Landmann 1958: 186). Not all those who attended Simmel's lectures were so impressed by his manner of speaking, however. In independent pieces, both Ludwig and Richard Kroner describe his voice as 'laborious' (Gassen and Landmann 1958: 155, 228), with Ludwig complaining about Simmel's 'high sharp voice' which 'revealed acoustically how much presence he lacked', in comparison to more charismatic speakers such as Werner Sombart (155). Kroner's reservations about Simmel's voice, however, did not prevent him from recognising the intimate connection between meaning and sound in Simmel's public performances:

> His voice, apparently slightly laborious, his language and his manner of delivery were incomparable, indeed utterly original. His voice circumlocuted the object, encircling it, holding its note, vibrating and then rising a little, intoning strangely and finally wrapping itself in the object, boring into it; his voice precisely matched his form of thought, this process of winding, slowly unwinding, turning and suddenly grasping, only to break off in decisive fashion. Simmel 'simmeled' everything he concerned himself with. He gave things his imprint, so that they assumed and expressed his incomparable spirit, but at the same time illuminated their own essence and truth.
>
> Gassen and Landmann (1958: 228)

Kroner draws attention to the combination of the ideal and the sensuous at play in Simmel's work, suggesting that these lectures were indeed vehicles for 'aesthetic ideas'. As such, they were couched in aesthetic language, with its particular emphasis on the mimetic dimension of language, picking up on the importance of aspects such as rhythm, which was, of course, central to Blümner's conception of the 'absolute art of speaking' (1907, 1926/27). Kurt Gassen focused on this dimension of Simmel's use of vocalisation, arguing that the key to understanding his lectures was to follow the tone of the lecture from word to word. Having described in detail the rhythm, tempo and musical intonation, Gassen concluded that 'this kind of language, this way of speaking is that of the poet' (Gassen and Landmann 1958: 301).

In likening Simmel's use of language to poetry, Gassen recognised an essential component of Simmel's lecturing style, which was modelled on the writer and cultural critic, Stefan George (Gassen and Landmann 1958: 297–8). Like Bahr in Vienna, George was a prominent figure in the arts and public-speaking scenes in Berlin, appearing in important Berlin salons and gathering around him a coterie of young poets known as the 'George-Circle'. It was not only George's style of delivery that influenced Simmel, but also his appearance. In particular, George's habit of dressing only in black, priest-like garb fascinated Simmel and, according to Kurt Singer, he took to adopting this form of attire for his own performances (Gassen and Landmann 1958: 297–8). His concern with the way he looked when at the lectern suggests that he took seriously the idea of public speaking as the embodiment of text. This is borne out in Ferdinand Bruckner's reports of Simmel's lectures, which suggest that seeing him in action was as important as listening to what he had to say (Gassen and Landmann 1958: 147). Simmel's 'Sociology of the Senses' provides a theoretical explanation for Bruckner's impression, based on the notion of an essential difference between the ear and the eye in terms of perception.

> The most extreme sociological contrast between the eye and the ear lies in the fact that the latter only offers us a revelation of the human being within the temporal form and the former only the lasting element of the person's nature, the precipitation of their past in the substantial form of their features, so that, as it were, we see the succession of their life in simultaneity before us.
>
> Simmel (1997: 113–14)

Simmel argues that while the spoken word contains objective meaning that could be transmitted in a different way, the look cannot be substituted and so binds people together in a unity. Directly suspended in the event and its function, the look comprises a more direct and less differentiated connection than sound, focusing on similarities between people rather than what distinguishes them one from another. To illustrate this point, he turns his attention to the students in an auditorium listening to a lecture who 'somehow feel themselves to be a unity' because they 'see each other during the communalizing process but cannot speak' (117). This point is, of course, directly related to the one he had made earlier in 'Metropolis and Mental Life', where he suggested that the sense of alienation rife in urban life was a direct effect of seeing others without being able to address them directly, much less engage them in conversation: 'the reciprocal reserve and indifference [...] are never felt more strongly by the individual [...] than in the thickest crowd of the big city. This is because the body proximity and narrowness of space makes the mental distance only the more visible' (Simmel 1997: 181).

In the 'Sociology of the Senses', Simmel maintains that the 'division of labour' between the senses, according to which the ear is associated with perception of the fleeting ('the wealth of divergent moods of individuals') and the eye, with the enduring, is tempered by the fact that people have a much greater ability to recall what has been heard than what has been seen (1997: 117). The reports that we have of Simmel as a lecturer, however, stand in direct contradiction to this claim, focusing on the visual rather than the aural effects of his performances. Claiming that 'he thought visibly', that he was a person who 'philosophized with his whole body', that he 'thought with his whole body' or that 'he represented the concepts in the flesh', many of these impressions provide vivid descriptions of Simmel's use of his body as he spoke (Gassen and Landmann 1958: 147, 161, 163, 193). These accounts afford us insight into the central role of kinesis in verbal communication, which, according to Sample, provides a 'sensual expressive background dimension' that exists concurrently with the semiotic dimension of language (1996: 118).

Many descriptions of Simmel lecturing mention that the intensity of his thought was expressed in his body, emphasising, for example, the way that he would raise his arm, point his fingers and twist his body as he spoke. Other reports centre on Simmel's 'strange appearance', maintaining that his manner of lecturing was 'just as ugly and as fascinating as he himself was' (Gassen and Landmann 1958: 156).

Figure 3.1   Georg Simmel at the lectern, 1906; *Source*: Böhringer and Gründer 1976

The repetition of adjectives such as 'ugly', 'gaunt', 'twisted' and 'awkward' suggests that reactions to Simmel's physical appearance were as ambivalent as those to his voice. Just as his voice appears to have attracted sections of his audience, while leaving others aghast, so his 'grotesque' body image fascinated and repulsed his students in equal measure.

While these reports of Simmel's use of voice and the body demonstrate a certain lack of consistency in detailing the immediate impression of his manner of appearing, they are almost unanimous in emphasising the effectiveness of his use of vocalisation and kinesis in communicating the objective content of his lectures, all the while giving the sense that each lecture was being created for the first time in the presence of the audience. To express this, many reports utilise metaphors of birth to describe the perceived intimacy of the experience of witnessing Simmel's performance of his thought processes. Margarete Susman, for example, maintained that 'Simmel's lectures were extraordinary: he spoke in a lively fashion, completely without notes, as if every single thought was being born just at the moment in which it was being articulated' (Gassen and Landmann 1958: 279), while Georg Hermann remembers that 'you had the feeling that you were witnessing the birth of his [Simmel's] thoughts when he spoke' (163). Such accounts centre on the productivity of the speaker and the role that physiognomic expression played in delivering the illusion of creativity. In so doing, they confirm Ludwig's account of the 'genius of the body', which likens the public speaker to the acrobat (*Körperkünstler*), the star of variety theatre, since both perform the production of presence (1912: 1589–90). And this is akin to Seel's observations about 'aesthetic appearing' being tied to 'presented presence' (2005: 98).

During the course of his lectures, Simmel appeared to speak and act spontaneously, and yet, as Fechter reveals, this was often an elaborate performance. Fechter recalls attending a public lecture given by Simmel in Berlin around 1912 on the problem of style in the Arts and Crafts Movement. During the lecture, Fechter took extensive notes, which he wrote up as a newspaper article the following day. Before he could submit the article for publication, however, an older colleague recognised the title of the lecture and produced his account of a talk given by Simmel two years previously under the same title. On comparison, the two articles demonstrated such striking similarity that Fechter concluded:

> without relying on a manuscript, Simmel had delivered the same lecture as before; he had mastered the sound of the words, and using the sound of the words, he had conjured up for his audience the

same performance of the process of thinking which had accompanied his first lecture, perhaps even with the same gestures.

Gassen and Landmann (1958: 161)

According to Goffman, one of the central distinctions between the written text and the lecture as the embodiment of text is grounded in the uniqueness of the lecture as performance (1981). This, he argues (with a nod to Emile Durkheim), is an important aspect of the ritual character of performance, which uses the sense of uniqueness of the occasion to afford 'supplicants preferential contact with an entity held to be of value', heightening the sense of intimacy between speaker and audience (Goffman 1981: 187). In the case of Simmel's public speaking, it would appear that the uniqueness of the lecture as performance was itself part of the performance and, therefore, an elaborate illusion. Most reports of Simmel's lecturing activity mention the perceived spontaneity of his performances, documenting how successful he was in maintaining the illusion. Yet if we turn to an examination of Simmel's use of facial expression – Sample's final category of the physiognomic dimension of aesthetic language – then we would see how Simmel's lectures as performance undercut the sense of 'preferential contact' with the speaker that the illusion of uniqueness might seem to guarantee.

Since both vocalisation and kinesis figure so prominently in the descriptions of Simmel as a public speaker, it is all the more striking that scant attention is paid to his use of facial expression, but his own work suggests a possible reason for this ostensibly curious omission. In 'The Aesthetic Significance of the Face', Simmel concludes that the face, standing in for appearance, represents the process of simultaneously concealing and revealing the self that, he argues, characterises modern existence (1995: 42). While the public speaker's use of vocalisation and kinesis are both grounded in the sense of closeness that, Gadamer argues, is created when an idea is voiced by its originator (1993), the dialectic of concealing and revealing linked to facial expression adds a certain complexity; distance is brought into the equation. In his 'Sociology of the Senses', Simmel points out the essential reciprocity of the look that serves to bind people together (1997: 115), but it would appear that this was an aspect missing from his lecture performances. Although he was gazed upon, he did not reciprocate, and so knowingly detached himself from his audience. Susman's comment that she saw Simmel's eyes for the first time at the end of his lecture course, in a one-to-one situation, illustrates the distance that Simmel created in the space of his lectures (Gassen and Landmann 1958: 279). This sense of aloofness found expression in Ludwig's contribution, in which he suggested that although Simmel's lectures were dialogical in nature, this involved Simmel engaging in dialogue with himself, rather than with his audience (155).

In a letter to Rickert (dated 15 August 1898), Simmel confirmed that he preferred distancing himself from his audience, and complained that he found the brightly coloured clothing of the many women who attended his lectures distracting: '[s]ince I don't really speak to the audience, but to myself, I like it best when the auditorium is as colourless and indifferent as possible' (Gassen and Landmann 1958: 96). Simmel, of course, clad himself in black à la Stefan George while lecturing, embodying his own theoretical stance on fashion according to which 'the individual appearance never *clashes* with the general style, but always *stands out* from it' (Simmel 1997: 191). In this passage from his 'Philosophy of Fashion' and elsewhere in his writings, Simmel focuses on fashion's twin impulses: towards individuation, on the one hand, and homogenisation, on the other. This, in turn, is related to his conception of the 'aesthetic significance of the face' that both reveals and conceals the self.

In the hands of the public speaker, these simultaneous processes of revelation and concealment play on the interaction between proximity and distance. The introduction of the 'Conférence' brought about a corresponding theoretical emphasis on the importance of dialogical communication and calls for a new form of public speaking that would build on the sense of intimacy between audience and speaker created through a close relationship between meaning and sound. Simmel's lectures, while characterised by the performance of intimacy, also reserved the right to preserve the element of dissemination through constructing a certain distance between speaker and audience. As we will see in the following chapter, this distance was achieved partly through the spatial relations of public speaking, which tended to see the active speaker positioned above and in front of the passive audience. But this was not the only method of achieving distance associated with modern public speaking. Earlier in this chapter, the 'technical reproducibility' of the lecturing process through the provision of ready-to-view slide shows was discussed. Requiring only to be 'animated', these shows called into question the necessity of an identity between speaker and text, between sound and meaning, and so disrupted the sense of an unmediated relationship between the speaker, as the originator and articulator of an idea, and his or her audience.

Distance could also be attained in a more subtle fashion, through the speaker refusing to reciprocate the gaze of the audience. This too served to disrupt the sense of the relationship between a speaker and a public being akin to the dyadic relationship between author and reader, revealing instead the actual 'constitutive circularity' of publics (Warner 2002: 115). In their disruptive capacity, Simmel's lectures could be understood as an embodied critique of the performance of intimacy, which serves to complicate Blum's account of 'theatricality' and its place in the 'urban scene'. According to Blum, 'performance challenges self-containment and in so doing, saturates the scene with an aura of danger [...] performance makes it impossible to sustain the invisibility of the body, making the unseen seer someone to be seen' (2003: 174). In contrast, a close analysis of Simmel's style of public speaking suggests that it was possible for the unseen seer – a role that was central to Simmel's work as an urban sociologist keen to maintain a certain distance between himself and the urban masses – to remain essentially unseen, while also, and simultaneously, putting himself self-consciously on display.

Understanding the force of this aspect of Simmel's form of presentation entails being open to paradox, which, of course, was an essential element in Scheu's (1898: 265) description of the lecture as a work of art. It was also an important stylistic feature of Simmel's essays and lectures, which nearly all commence and conclude with antinomies, 'Metropolis and Mental Life' being a case in point (Frisby 2001: 143). The ultimate aim of Simmel's performance of paradox was not to privilege concealment over revelation, distance over closeness, but to hold them in balance. Ernst Cassirer recognised this impulse in modern public speaking in general, arguing that

> distance is posited [in the spatial relationship between speaker and listener] but by this very positing it is in a sense surpassed. In the intuitive space acquired with the help of language the factors of separateness and juxtaposition, of absolute discreteness and

absolute equilibrium, may be said to counterbalance one another, to stand in a kind of ideal equilibrium.

Cassirer (1957: 152)

This kind of 'ideal equilibrium' offers an alternative to Simmel's pessimistic diagnosis of modernity, which 'culminates in the tragedy of culture, in the inevitable conflict and ever-widening gap between subjective and objective culture' (Frisby 1985: 104). In his later works, Simmel does not hold out any hope of achieving an 'ideal equilibrium', but in his style of public speaking that possibility was at least mooted, even as the ongoing struggle between subjective and objective culture was being played out in his performances. In this way, his style of public speaking mimicked the metropolis, whose function, as Simmel noted in the conclusion of his lecture on 'Metropolis and Mental Life' was 'to provide the arena for this struggle and its reconciliation' (1997: 185). In other words, there would seem to be a clear and discernable link between the modern city and the form of public speaking practised there. To explore this connection further, I now want to turn to a brief discussion of Loos, another celebrated public speaker engaged in the discursive construction of the modern city, who, like Simmel, self-consciously employed the performance of intimacy as a tool to demonstrate his take on the nature of urban life.

Adolf Loos: Performing (in) the metropolis

Loos was an enthusiastic and prolific public speaker travelling throughout Europe like a 'preaching mendicant' to deliver his message about the true nature of modernity (Friedell 1985: 77). Perhaps the best representation of this aspect of Loos's multifaceted career was on an advertisement for a series of lectures about modern architecture that he gave in Prague and Brno in 1925. The poster highlighted his mobility as a speaker, describing him as a 'citizen of the world, with permanent residency in an express train shuttling between London, Paris, Vienna, Brno and Prague' (Stewart 2000: 25). Often Loos spoke to huge audiences; in 1925, he gave a series of lectures at the Sorbonne on 'The Man with the Modern Nerves', attracting such interest that he could only be accommodated in the largest available lecture theatre, the 'salle Descartes' with a capacity of nine hundred (M[arilaun] [1926] 1988: 7), while in 1910 in Vienna, his lecture 'My House on the Michaelerplatz' reportedly sold out the 2000-seat Sophiensaal (Wymetal [1911] 1988: 74). Yet despite the mass appeal of his performances, Loos was, by all accounts, another example of a modern speaker working in the paradigm of the performance of intimacy. Reviewing on a talk on 'The Technical, Artistic and Cultural Meaning of Thrift', which Loos gave in Vienna in 1922, the *Neue Freie Presse*'s critic commented that

> [i]t is always a compelling social event, when Adolf Loos engages the public in conversation about contemporary everyday matters. His way of appearing on stage as a Conferéncier could hardly be described differently. 'Lecture' ['Vortrag'] is a much too weighty word to express the playful carefree spirit of his art of conversation, which has as little in common with planned structure and rhetoric as it does with schoolmasterly self-importance. It is the art of improvisation, full of brilliant wit.
>
> L. K. (1922: 1)

The extent to which Loos's public speaking was based on 'the art of improvisation' should not, however, be overestimated. Full manuscripts exist for certain lectures, such as 'My House on the Michaelerplatz', given in Vienna in 1911 (Rukschcio 1985), while there is evidence to suggest that reading aloud from the work of others formed part of Loos's performances, such as a letter from Kraus to Sidonie Nadherny von Borutin, which mentions that Loos closed one of his lectures by reading aloud Kraus's open letter, 'Beauty in the Service of the Salesman' (Kraus 1974: 213), or an unpublished poem by Peter Altenberg entitled 'Lecture Evening', which begins 'AL [Adolf Loos] read aloud "Tulips" by PA [Peter Altenberg]' (n.d.). All this goes to suggest that, like Simmel, Loos often merely *performed* improvisation, as part of a more general performance of intimacy. This is further borne out by recent detailed accounts of Loos's 'colourful, even ornamental style' of language and the highly constructed literary nature of his published essays, many of which began life as public lectures (Maciuika 2000: 76; Scheichl 2002).

In performing intimacy, Loos, even more so than Simmel, relied on the effects of the 'communicative body' to construct what Gumbrecht (2004) calls 'presence effects', as described in this excerpt from an undated newspaper cutting.

In a truly amusing manner, he portrayed the man of the previous century, describing how the position of his feet distinguishes him clearly from the man of our own century. He demonstrated how Old Fritz's army marched past with feet rigidly pointing outwards. He then illustrated the way that modern men walk, showing that their toes always point straight ahead.... Perched on the edge of his chair, Herr Loos imitated the diffident underling, highlighting the curious fact that people always believe they are showing their opposite number deep respect and deference when they make themselves as uncomfortable as possible in their seats.

Loos (n.d.)

In Berlin in 1926, Loos reportedly gave a talk entitled 'Between the Charleston and the Black Bottom'. During the course of this event, held in the fashionably bohemian Café des Westens, he illustrated his take on the new dance crazes in Paris with a demonstration of the most important steps, accompanied by some of the 'most beautiful women' from his audience (Dolbin 1926: 11). Both these examples suggest that Loos's lectures at times verged on cabaret, an art form that strove to tear down the Cartesian fourth wall between performer and spectator, demanding dialogue as well as dissemination. Characterised by rapid turnover and a continuous search for the new, cabaret can be understood as an archetypal site of modernity, reflecting the continuous flux and circulation typical of the structure of the metropolis (Nenno 1997).

Like the cabaret performances to which they were related, Loos's lectures were linked thematically and formally to the metropolis. Beginning his public-speaking career towards the end of the first decade of the twentieth century, with a series of lectures in Berlin and Vienna, Loos used the form primarily to reflect on modern urban life: in 'Architecture', he contrasted the experience of life in modern Berlin and Vienna with country life ([1931] 1982: 90–104); in 'Ornament and Crime', the increased tempo of modern life and the nature of work in the metropolis are analysed (78–88); while in 'On Walking, Standing, Sitting, Eating and Drinking', the unique nature of the cultural forms connected with the modern bourgeoisie city was discussed (1983: 176).[2] Amongst his most prominent lectures on the modern metropolis was one given in Vienna's Sophiensaal on 11 December 1911, in defence of his controversial Haus am Michaelerplatz, a commission for the Viennese firm of tailors, Goldmann and Salatsch, situated directly opposite Fischer von Ehrlach's Imperial Palace (Hofburg). With its plain upper façade, the Haus am Michaelerplatz appeared to rebuke the palace for its ostentatious use of ornament, and in so doing, brought considerable furore in its wake (Czech and Mistelbauer 1989). That furore has come to be regarded as 'the culmination and fiercest stage in the controversy over modern architecture which had been going on [in Vienna] since 1896 when Otto Wagner was appointed professor at the academy and shocked the architectural profession with his inauguration speech' (Topp 2004: 140). Loos's lecture was designed to allow him participate in this debate on modern architecture that played a considerable role in the discursive construction of the modern city. He did so, according to contemporary reports, with considerable aplomb.

> In the succinct and highly expressive form of a public lecture about his 'House on the Michaelerplatz' that made the case both for the defence and the prosecution at one and the same time, this controversial architect has allowed his talents as a public speaker to burst onto the scene once more.
>
> Wymetal ([1911] 1988: 74)

Over and above the thematic connection to the urban environments in which they were delivered, Loos's lectures also demonstrated a formal link to the city, suggesting a reciprocal influence between the form of the city and the form of public speaking that flourished there, and contributing to the discursive construction of that particular phenomenon. In *Soul and Form*, an extended essay on the essay, Georg Lukács ([1911] 1974) pointed out that the essentially fragmentary nature of the form makes it the ideal vehicle for expressing the fragmentary nature of modernity itself, arguing that a meaningful analysis of the totality of modern life could only be approached through an examination of the particular. This view of the essay was later taken up by Adorno, who described its structure as comprising a collection of interlocking arguments in which 'thought does not progress in a single direction; instead, the moments are interwoven as in a carpet' (1991: 53). He could not have hoped for a better illustration of this structure than Loos's lecture on 'Ornament and Crime', in which the argument is constructed from a number of interlocking remarks and conjectures, drawing correspondences between Socrates, Voltaire and Beethoven, the tattooed people of Papua New Guinea, Goethe's use of language and the uniform of the Austro-Hungarian infantry ([1931] 1982: 78–88).

These seemingly incongruent threads are brought together in a masterly example of the way in which the form of Loos's cultural criticism reflects the form of its own subject matter, modern urban life. Loos's lectures and essays may, as Amanshauser points out, refuse to advance a single coherent theory, but this is actually one of its strengths rather than, as Amanshauser would have it, a weakness (1985: 209). The structure of modern metropolitan life itself is reflected in the way that Loos's lectures weave disparate elements into a network-like structure that never loses sight of its basis in paradox, underlining their status as examples of 'artistic lectures' as defined by Scheu (1898). As Simmel points out in 'The Metropolis and Mental Life', dissociation was one of the central pillars of urban life: '[w]hat appears in the metropolitan style of life directly as dissociation is in reality only one of its elemental forms of socialization' (1997: 180). Another central pillar was the nature of the network of social structures, which Simmel described as the 'interconnection of social circles' (1955: 127–95). The central paradox upon which Loos's texts are structured, meanwhile, is redolent of his own lived experience of early twentieth century metropolitan existence that involved being 'torn between modernity and antiquity, modernism and traditionalism, [...] heterogeneity and homogeneity, display and disguise' (Stewart 2000: 169). In form as well as content, Loos's lecture performances were vehicles for translating his individual lived experience (*Erlebnis*) of the metropolis into collectively secured experience (*Erfahrung*).

Public speaking as 'Poetic World-Making'

Blum maintains that cities are key sites for the production of new norms (2003: 18). This exploration of the new norms of public speaking developing in Berlin and Vienna in the early twentieth century gives weight to such a proposition, which can be seen most clearly in the formal connection between public speaking and the city, illustrated here with reference to Loos's public-speaking activities. At its best, modern public speaking was a complex entity, encompassing both dialogue and dissemination to perform intimacy, while simultaneously

Figure 3.2 Poster advertising Loos's 1913 lecture, 'Ornament and Crime';
Source: © Wien Museum

embodying a critique of this kind of performance. Both Loos and Simmel were engaged in such complex performances of the Self in the modern city, performances that were shaped by the experience of urban life, and based on aesthetic appearing and its linguistic corre-late, aesthetic language, which combined to structure and perform the modern city itself. The city, then, was not only the site for the production of new norms of public speaking, but also the result of the operation of these norms. As we saw in Chapter 1, Warner argues that every speech or performance addressed to a public tries to specify in advance the lifeworld of its circulations, through both content and form (2002: 114). While Chapter 2 demonstrated the way in which the content of architects' lectures served to construct a particular urban public and therefore, a particular view of the city, this chapter has shown that the form of public utterances also contrib-utes to the construction of the city as 'poetic world-making' (114). Warner highlights the importance of both content (what) and form (how) in the construction of publics, but his focus on text means that he can largely ignore physical space (where). An investigation into speaking in public, however, that is sensitive to the effects of the co-presence of bodies, cannot do likewise. This being the case, the final chapter sets out to locate the voices, considering the effect of 'atmos-pheric appearing' through an analysis of a collection of speech sites (Seel 2005: 92).

4
Locating the Voices

> All productive activity is defined [...] by the incessant
> to-and-fro between temporality (succession, concate-
> nation) and spatiality (simultaneity, synchronicity).
>
> Lefebvre (1991: 71)

> An entirely new proportion between permanence
> and transience not only predominates in the [...]
> structure, but also in the aesthetic criteria.
>
> Simmel (1898)

In his *Popular Art of Public Speaking*, Damaschke noted that space had
a key role to play in the success or otherwise of oral communication,
before bemoaning the paucity of theoretical work that would explain
why certain spaces were better suited to public speaking than others
(1912: 88). This was something of an overstatement – at the time
Damaschke was writing, Simmel, for example, was providing some
insight into the link between proxemics and public speaking in
'Sociology of the Senses' (1997: 109–20). Yet it was not until the later
twentieth century that the social sciences really began to address the
question of how space and speech interact, in the wake of the 'spatial
turn' that saw social scientists begin to examine the effects of space
on social interaction and vice versa. Goffman (1963), in particular,
developed an interest in the relation between speech and space,
expanding upon Simmel's initial investigations to examine how architectural arrangements construct, and are constructed by specific types
of co-presence. While both Simmel and Goffman offer formal and

generalised approaches to the relation between speech and space, Alan Read provides a fascinating historical analysis of one particular 'speech site', Kelmscott House in London, which was once home to William Morris, 'an uneasy but inveterate public speaker'. He argues that in this place, 'a history of orality reveals something more than oral history, a location where locution might be amplified in order to discern an ethics of speech for an emerging metropolis' (Read 2000: 120–1).

Read's major contribution to our understanding of the speech/space relation lies in the correspondences he posits between location, speech and the emerging metropolis. Listening to the voices of key figures such as Kraus, Loos and Simmel has afforded us insight into the discursive construction of the city as an 'imagined structure' (Blum 2003). The next step in this phenomenology of public speaking is to locate these voices, tracing the relation between the imagined city and the built environment – the site and the product of the imagined city. This relationship is complex, involving negotiations with a number of different conceptions of space: first, 'representations of space', the 'conceptualised space' that is the realm of architects as planners and social engineers; second, 'representational space', space that is experienced through narrative, whether everyday or artistic, of the present or of the past; and third, 'spatial practice', which 'propounds and presupposes' a given society's view of space (Lefebvre 1991: 38–9). To put this in another way, technocrats use acts of the imagination to control and produce physical spaces, while artists and inhabitants appropriate such spaces through processes of imagining and performing. All this, in turn, is circumscribed by 'spatial practice', which is at once limiting and productive; it provides the idea of a shared sense of space that is necessary for architects to plan and artists to describe, and simultaneously constructs and refines that sense of space. Spatial practice, then, is the key concept here and this, Lefebvre argues, can be 'revealed through the deciphering of space' (1991: 38). This chapter sets out to do just that, assembling a collection of speech sites and subjecting them to an analysis that considers evidence from the planning perspective as well as the perspective of the artist or inhabitant, and looking for correspondences between these different sites, while remaining sensitive to their unique character. In so doing, the aim is to address the question of 'atmospheric appearing', considering the way in which an object can affect the character of its setting and concomitantly, the way in which that character 'becomes intuitable in these objects' (Seel 2005: 92). The complexity of this undertaking lies in the fact that speech sites are simultaneously objects set in the emerging metropolis and settings for public speaking as an activity.

What are the speech sites that will be under investigation here, as both objects and settings? A number of different locations for public speaking have already been mentioned in the preceding chapters, including prime examples of bourgeois representative architecture such as the Konzerthaus in Vienna, more intimate spaces such as Paul Cassirer's salon and art gallery or the Café des Westens in Berlin, and open-air sites such as the Prater in Vienna or the Schloßplatz in Berlin. None of these locations are monumental sites designed to house and represent public speaking to the exclusion of all other activities; instead, public speaking is just one of the activities that take place there. In other words, these locations function as speech sites through the 'occasioning of space', a process that transforms space into a place (Blum 2003: 187). Speech sites, then, are constituted by the event of speaking in public; they have a temporal as well as a spatial dimension. Cacciari pointed out the tension between durability and the ephemeral that characterised Kraus's work (1993: 146). That tension, often expressed in terms of stasis and mobility, extends to the locations in which Kraus and others appeared in public, and is often related to the tension between dialogue and dissemination that characterised the form of public speaking in the modern city. It is also reflected in the method underlying this chapter, which casts the author as collector, bringing together an eclectic selection of urban spaces in a new constellation, portraying the emerging metropolis as a network of speech sites. The resulting taxonomy of speech sites is presented in broad linear order, moving from what might be categorised as the 'more public' spaces to those that might be classified as 'more private' public spaces, considering in turn, streets, squares and parks; coffee houses; great halls and other public halls; theatres, cabarets and broadcasting houses; educational establishments and, finally, salons. This is but one possible way of ordering the collection, but one that facilitates a particular interpretation, affording us further insight into the relations that Read (2000) posits between speech, location and the emerging metropolis at the beginning of the twentieth century.

The street, the square and the park: Stasis and motion

Although neither Berlin nor Vienna was subjected to the major destruction that characterised Haussmann's reshaping of Paris in the mid-nineteenth century, the restructuring and expansion of both cities around 1900 was influenced by Parisian fashions setting in motion a major debate in German city planning circles on the relative merits of streets and squares (Ladd 1990: 113; Frisby 2002: 16). Typifying the two poles of this debate, Otto Wagner developed the idea of the primacy of the street as an 'artery of motion' (Schorske 1981: 100), while Camillo Sitte emphasised the importance of the square as the central feature of an ideal city based on the 'organic' medieval city ([1889] 1985). These two distinct spatial formations promoted different forms of communication. As a facilitator of circulation, the street supported transparency and communication at a distance, but simultaneously reduced personal contact to an exchange of glances. While the forms of communication facilitated by the street seems to reduce social interaction to the reifying gaze, Sitte's ideal of the medieval square, an enclosed, static space, promoted speaking and listening, as well as seeing and being seen.

The rapid industrialisation that characterised both Berlin and Vienna in the early twentieth century allowed the street to achieve dominance over the square as the primary spatial formation of the modern metropolis. City planners and others, however, soon recognised that to make these cities liveable, it would be necessary to provide spaces in which city dwellers could temporarily escape the relentless circulation of metropolitan modernity. Existing green spaces were appropriated for this purpose, and new parks were built, including Friedrichshain, and Treptower Park in Berlin, and the Türkenschanzpark in Vienna. In the early twentieth century, many of these parks underwent further development as a result of pressure from the Public Park Movement, an important urban phenomenon with its roots in the USA and Sweden.

One of the most influential apologists of the Public Park Movement in the German-speaking world was Ludwig Lesser, whose definitive work on the subject was the result of a long engagement with these ideas dating back to 1906. His aim was to create new green spaces within the urban environment that were designed not just to be strolled through, but to be areas in which 'the masses and all social classes' could play and rest. He sought to effect a change in park design, shifting the emphasis from the idea of movement through space, to the idea of being in space. This change is best exemplified by his desire to subordinate pathways through parks to objects devoted to allowing people to dwell in parks, including pavilions, playgrounds and benches. In terms of the street-versus-square debate, his conception of the ideal park was based on the unstructured meandering in space typical of the square, rather than the controlled linear movement through space facilitated by the street. Yet he also sought to provide spaces that would provide a means of escape from the polyphony of voices characteristic of social interaction in the square, arguing that benches should be carefully positioned to allow users of the park to enjoy moments of intimacy or solitude, cultivating a solipsistic gaze upon nature (Lesser 1927: 6–38).

Underlying these representations of space was the idea that shaping elements of the city could influence the way in which people inhabited the city and engaged in social interaction. Examining streets, squares and parks in Berlin and Vienna from the point of view of representational spaces and spatial practice, however, presents a rather different picture of the communicative aspects of these spaces. While planners conceived public parks as meeting places, they were not designed as spaces to be used for public speaking. The closest that Lesser comes to this is in his description of pavilions and open-air stages, providing focal points around which large groups of people could gather together to listen to music or experience theatre productions (1927: 63–70). In the early twentieth century, however, parks, streets and squares began to be appropriated as locations of protest, and as meeting places in which public speaking came to have an important role to play.

The May Day demonstrations first held in the Prater in Vienna in 1890, and the 'Suffrage Stroll' ('Wahlrechtspaziergang'), which took place in the Tiergarten in Berlin in 1910, are prime examples of the appropriation of parks for political protest. The May Day demonstrations were symbolic occasions in which the workers peacefully and legally occupied all areas of the Prater, temporarily flouting the geographical and social boundaries that symbolised the highly stratified nature of Viennese society at the end of the nineteenth century. Although certain restrictions were applied to the form of protest, official permission was granted for these events (Fricke 1990: 278). This was not the case in Berlin two decades later, when the German Social Democratic Party (SPD) organised a 'Suffrage Stroll', in protest of the Prussian three-class system of suffrage. The SPD had originally applied for permission to hold an electoral rally on 6 March, but this was denied. Party officials then announced that instead of a rally, a 'Suffrage Stroll' would take place in Treptower Park. The Police President, Traugott von Jagow, countered by declaring that this too would require official permission, which he was not prepared to grant. The SPD signalled its intention to go ahead with the protest regardless, but at the last minute, secretly switched the venue from Treptower Park to the Tiergarten, outwitting the police, who were waiting in large numbers in Treptower Park. By the time the police arrived in the Tiergarten, the SPD demonstration was over (Warneken 1986: 42–3).

In these examples, workers protested by moving through centrally located parks that were symbolic of the old order, temporarily transgressing existing social boundaries. The 'Suffrage Stroll' marked the first time that a workers' movement had managed to turn the centre of Berlin into the forum for a mass demonstration (Warneken 1986: 43). Neither in Vienna in 1890 nor in Berlin in 1910, however, did these demonstrations lead to the former royal playgrounds being identified as speech sites in the way that, following the Chartist demonstrations of 1855, Speakers' Corner was formed in Hyde Park (Roberts 2001: 320). During the May Day celebrations and the Suffrage Stroll, the parks were used as spaces in which to assemble and move through, rather than in which to assemble and dwell. Only a matter of weeks after the Suffrage Stroll, however, a number of Berlin's parks became *de facto* speech sites. On 10 April 1910, the SPD and the bourgeois Democratic Union (DV) joined forces and organised simultaneous rallies in Humboldthain, Friedrichshain and Treptower Park. In each location, multiple temporary platforms were erected, marking an important stage in the transformation of public parks into speech sites. These demonstrations took place before the advent of the microphone, and enabling as many of those present at a mass rally as possible to actually hear the speeches presented a major logistical problem. Newspaper reports of the event suggested that the chosen format was far from perfect.

> The speakers then commenced their often futile attempts to render themselves understandable to the crowd. An icy wind ripped the

words out of their mouths, so that only those standing next to them could follow their arguments. There were ten platforms in the [Treptower] park, and most of the crowd heard only a mish-mash of fragments ringing out from all sides.

Warneken (1986: 50)

In order to impose a sense of unity and imagined community on such a spatially diverse event, and demonstrating the way that public speaking involved the 'occasioning of space' (Blum 2003: 187), tim-ing played a central role in ensuring that all the rallies followed the same format. At 1pm, a trumpet signal marked the beginning of the event in each of the parks. This was followed by a number of long speeches, all of which had to end by 2pm, at which point the same resolution was read out from each of the platforms, following a sec-ond trumpet signal (Warneken 1986: 49–52).

Using parks as speech sites did not fundamentally challenge the dominant conceptions of this type of urban space, which was primarily designed to provide temporary respite from manifestations of metro-politan modernity. According to the Haussmann-influenced view of the city, the prime function of streets was to facilitate the circulation of people and commodities, which would be disrupted by their trans-formation into speech sites. Berlin's Police President underlined this view of the street when he had the following notice posted around the city in 1910: 'The "right to occupy the streets" is being announced. Streets exist solely to facilitate circulation. Resistance to the authority of the State will lead to firearms being employed. Let the curious be warned' (cited in Warneken 1986: 35). At a number of points in the early twentieth century protestors defied this warning to take tempo-rary possession of streets in the centres of Berlin and Vienna, in order to express their views on aspects of modern urban life.

The majority of political protests, whether spontaneous or orga-nised, that took place in the first decades of the twentieth century were communicative events that combined movement through space and assembling in space to disrupt the rhythm of city life. Protests organ-ised by the Social Democrats in Berlin followed the pattern of groups of demonstrators assembling in squares located in the suburbs, then parading through the city from these squares to a central meeting place, where formal speeches would be made (Ehls 1997: 43). At these rallies, the dominant form of communication was the dissemination of political ideas and positions, but viewed as a whole, the communicative event comprised both dissemination and dialogue, as the march to and from the rally afforded protestors time and space for anticipating and discussing the speeches. In providing sites for organised political protest, streets, squares and parks enabled circulation and assembling, facilitating a form of public speaking that entailed both dissemination and dialogue, albeit with each taking place in distinct spatial and temporal locations.

Less formal events provided a slightly different picture, as is suggested in the following description taken from Kessler's diary entry of 24 December 1918, describing the temporary transformation of the Schloßplatz in Berlin into a speech site:

> In the crowd, Spartacus agitators are holding mini public meetings; you go to challenge them, but end up listening to them. A tall, fanatical fellow [...] bitter with rage, his eyes flashing with malice, is shouting down a gentleman who is trying to reason with him [...]. Another man, older and rag-taggle, a kind of vagabond, is preaching reason, arguing that if both sides were a little more reasonable, consensus could be reached. Every speaker has his own audience. These small conventicles, where the discussion is at times fanatical, at times subdued, remind me of Hyde Park on Sunday evenings.
>
> Kessler (1982: 78–9)

Here, the square emerges as a place that could offer space to a number of speakers simultaneously, functioning as a microcosm of the view of the city as a network of language-games. Dissemination and dialogue were not banished to separate spatio-temporal locations; rather the event, as it unfolded in this space, involved a constant back and forth between these forms.

Other voices, however, poured doubt on the possibility of streets and squares functioning as speech sites in the modern city. In 'Screams on the Street', first published in 1930, Kracauer sought to differentiate between the streets of proletarian suburbs such as Neukölln and Wedding, which seemed to be 'streets for parades' and the streets of Berlin's west end, which were without the history invested in other parts of the metropolis, and so devoid of an important dimension of representational space. In these western streets, a sense of anomie dominated: '[h]ere no one expects anything from anyone else. Uncertain, they extend themselves, without content and empty' (Kracauer 1964: 29, translated by Frisby 1985: 142). His view of the square, offered in 'Two Surfaces' (first published in 1926) was equally melancholic: 'the force of the quadrant', he stated, served only to emphasise the solitude of the individual caught in its midst (Kracauer 1964: 26). Squares, he suggests, are spaces for dissembling, not assembling.

The coffee house: Dissemination and dialogue

The new cafés that sprang up in Berlin and Vienna around 1900, although not designed primarily to house formal public speaking, were inflected by their historical importance as spaces that facilitated communication (Mannheim 1956; Habermas 1989). At the beginning of the twentieth century, however, the coffee-house tradition underwent certain changes. Critics argued that there was a qualitative difference between traditional establishments and the new cafés under construction, which led Hans Schliepmann to suggest that analysing Berlin's new cafés would shed light on the city's upward trajectory to the ranks of metropolis (Güttler 1980: 53). At this time, the city was expanding rapidly in a westerly direction, and the construction of a colony of villas in the suburb of Grünewald was the impetus needed to begin to develop the Kurfürstendamm, later to become one of Berlin's most important leisure locations (Schwenk 1998: 158–9), and so the epitome of the empty streets of the west in which Kracauer discerned a sense of terror related to non-communication. One of the first new buildings on this street was the unprepossessing coffee house soon to become known as the 'Café des Westens' ('Café of the West'). The retrospective literary advertising brochure, *Twenty Years of the Café des Westens*, published by the owner of the café, Ernst Pauly, begins with a snapshot of that part of the Kurfürstendamm just before the café was opened.

> The Kurfürstendamm was without form, and void. A two-storey villa stood at the corner of the Fasanenstrasse, forming a bulwark against the allotments and real estate speculation.[...] All over this miserable wasteland[...] there were gaping stretches of undeveloped land. Here and there, a sign planted between discarded tin cans and rubbish proclaimed: 'Plot of Land For Sale'.
>
> Pauly (1913/14: 3)

Neues Romanisches Haus. Café. Architekt: FRANZ SCHWECHTEN in Berlin.

Figure 4.1 Interior of the Romanisches Café. Architect: Franz Schwechten: *Berliner Architekturwelt* IV (1901/02)

The Café des Westens, located on the ground floor of a five-storey apartment building erected in 1894/5 on 'this miserable wasteland', was of little architectural interest. In a survey of Berlin's cafés, Hans Ostwald (1905: 33) noted dismissively that the interior of Café des Westens was designed in a 'laughable misunderstanding of Rococo style'. Yet it was one of Berlin's modern coffee houses, deriving its modernity not from its architecture, but from its geographical location and from its clientele. By 1905, it had become a well-known haunt of bohemian circles, including the scenes that formed around central figures such as Walden and Pfemfert. 'Megalomania Café', as it was dubbed by Ostwald (1905: 33), continued to function as a prime speech site at least into the 1920s, when Ernst Blaß described it as 'an unparliamentary parliament' where 'even the fearful learned to speak up' (1928: 269).

The Rococo interior of Café des Westens was a product of the late nineteenth century trend for historicist architecture (Schwarzer 1995), as was the Romanisches Café (see Figure 4.1), another new coffee house that appeared in western Berlin at that time and subsequently became a well-known speech site. In this case, however, the chosen architectural style did reflect something of the status of the café as speech site. The café occupied the ground floor of a building designed by Franz Schwechten as part of an ensemble known as the 'Romanesque Forum', which was built between 1890 and 1906, with the Kaiser Wilhelm Memorial Church at its centre (*Berliner Architekturwelt* 1901/02; Zietz and Rüdenburg 1999: 60). A prominent architectural feature of the building in which the Romanisches Café was located was a series of large windows felt to be reminiscent of the style of the arcade (Güttler 1980: 54). Both the forum and the arcade were architectural forms that historically symbolised public communication. In describing itself as a 'forum', Schwechten's composition recalls the chief public square in ancient Rome, a space for public speaking. Meanwhile, in the Middle Ages and into the Renaissance, the presence of an open arcade signified a building open to the public (Burckhardt [1867] 1985: 149).[1]

In the Romanisches Café, however, the arches of the arcade were not open, but glazed; as Simmel pointed out in 'Bridge and Door', while windows give the impression of connecting interior with exterior, actually, 'the teleological emotion with respect to the window is directed almost exclusively from inside to outside: it is there for looking out, not for looking in' (1997: 173). The form of communication symbolised by the arcade-like glazed front of the Romanisches Café was exclusive and one-directional, undercutting the historic sense of the coffee house as an original site of democratic discussion signified by referencing the Roman forum. The way that space was used in the Romanisches Café, dividing the interior into two distinct areas and so erecting spatial barriers to communication, also served to call into question the ideal view of the coffee house. On the left was the so-called 'pool for swimmers', containing twenty tables reserved for those who had already made a name for themselves. To the right was the 'pool for non-swimmers'. Here, young hopefuls frequented the sixty or seventy tables, on the chance of being noticed and invited to enter the inner circle of the communication community. Meanwhile, tourists were steered to the outer glass terrace (Schebera 1988: 33), from which they could look out at the street, but not into the inner sanctum.

While Schwechten's Romanisches Café was a speech site that questioned the nature of such sites in the modern city, Loos's remodelled

Café Museum in Vienna set out to reflect on the nature of communication itself. Situated just off the Ringstrasse, more or less next to
Olbrich's new Secession building, the Café Museum provided Loos
with the ideal opportunity to produce a 'high-profile demonstration
piece on the issue of modernity' (Gronberg 2001: 23). What he produced was a modern café that sought to re-inscribe a particular tradition of oral culture, in a city that was in the process of reinventing
itself as a site of modern communication technology, as seen in displays of the 1898 Imperial Jubilee Exhibition. The Café Museum
provided a counterbalance to the exhibition; while the exhibition fore-
grounded the technologisation of discourse, Loos's coffee house was
designed around the idea of the embodiment of discourse. He was
seeking to remain true to his belief that the corporeal experience of
space was more important than its representation, as he stated in a
talk on 'Architecture' – first delivered in Berlin in 1910 – in which he
invoked the Café Museum in order to explain why his works were seldom to be found in the pages of architectural journals. This was because,
he argued, gazing at a photograph does not have the same effect as
experiencing a building's presence, which was how architectural work
was judged before the dominance of mediated communication (Loos
[1931] 1982: 96–7).[2] His works, constructed according to a set of principles that he would later articulate in his *Raumplan* theory (glossed as
'thinking in space'), were designed to be experienced in three dimensions rather than consumed as two-dimensional images (Jara 1995).

As a space designed around the idea of the embodiment of discourse, the Café Museum, Loos claimed in a talk given at the
Schwarzwaldschule in Vienna, referenced the tradition of the 'old
Viennese Biedermeier coffeehouse' (Rukschcio and Schachel 1982: 67).
Some art critics agreed with this account of Loos's work. Wilhelm
Schölermann, for example, maintained that for Loos, 'tradition is everything' ([1889] 1985: 9). Others, however, perceived the Café Museum as
an entirely modern creation. Ludwig Hevesi provided a detailed description of the café's interior, with its matt-green velour wallpaper, plain
white ceiling, dark mahogany furniture, mirrors, polished brass, cheap
thonet-style chairs in beech and sofas in green velvet, as a precursor
to arguing that although Loos was a 'Non-Secessionist', he was not
'an enemy of the Viennese Secession, but [...] something different, since
in the final analysis both are modern' ([1899] 1985: 11–2; [1899]
1988: 12).

Hevesi's description of the Café Museum as 'nihilistic', offers a way of reconciling these apparently conflicting perceptions ([1899] 1988: 12). In his lecture on 'Architecture', Loos appeared to take issue with this characterisation, noting that although his fellow architects had labelled his work 'Café Nihilism', it was still standing years later (Loos [1931] 1982: 96). This was, however, an interesting rhetorical strategy on Loos's part. On the one hand, he seemed to be disassociating himself from the description of his work as 'nihilistic', but on the other hand, by repeating the phrase 'Café Nihilism' in a new context, he was actively contributing to the nascent mythologisation of his work. Loos's apparent ambivalence towards the term has been taken up by Cacciari, who has devoted much time to exploring what 'nihilism' signifies in Loosian discourse, arguing that 'in philosophical terms, the problem that presents itself in Loos is that of the possibility and meaning of dwelling in the age of Nietzschean nihilism fulfilled' (1993: 199). Loos's answer to this problem, according to Cacciari, is to call into question the 'project of fulfilled nihilism, and its architecture' (201). In the case of the Café Museum, Cacciari locates Loos's resistance to this 'project' in his composition of an interior based on the contradiction between tradition, signified by the place of the old Viennese Biedermeier café, and modernity, characterised by processes of '*Entortung*' (removing place from space) and '*Mobilmachung*' (setting the circulation of individuals into motion). Essentially, Cacciari sees in the Café Museum a 'dialectic of the interior', in which Loos demonstrates 'the endless contradiction between the thought-out space of calculation, the equivalence of exteriors, and the possibility of place, the hope of a place' (172).

Cacciari's concept of the 'dialectic of the interior' gives us a sense of the complexity of the Café Museum. Other than functioning as a visual and material critique of the modes of mediated communication on show at the 1898 Imperial Jubilee Exhibition, the building offered a commentary on the nature of immediate communication in the modern city, and its relationship to space. In the second half of the nineteenth century, the grand architectural gestures of the liberal bourgeoisie, the heirs of the pre-1848 voluntary associations, were increasingly directed towards the creation of private spaces for the dissemination of knowledge and ideas, and the creation of an urban public around a particular speaker. Loos's Café Museum, 'an open-plan space designed for intellectual communication'

(Rukschcio and Schachel 1982: 67) demonstrated an understanding of the dominance of a form of oral culture that centred on the representational value of the speaker around whom a public assembled. The mass-produced thonet-style chairs with which he furnished the Café Museum were lightweight and portable, allowing the room to be easily transformed from traditional coffee house to the form of the 'Synoptikon', where the audience's gaze is directed towards the speaker.

As well as offering the possibility of configuring a temporary space for representational public speaking, however, the Café Museum also signified a different kind of immediate communication. It did this by invoking the tradition of the Viennese Biedermeier café as a location in which a public could create itself through sociability, as opposed to association or assemblage, but emphasised the modernity of this kind of communication by creating a new kind of space in which to house it. Apart from the main L-shaped room, the Café Museum also included a smaller, more intimate space, the 'Gibson Room' that Loos had decorated with images of modern woman by the American artist, Charles Dana Gibson (Gronberg 2001: 24–5). The Gibson Room – 'a little piece of American modernity appended to the larger space of the Café Museum [...] a richly coloured and textured [space] identified with [...] ephemerality [...]' (29, 31) – was configured to facilitate the kind of sociability that Simmel described in his 'Sociology of Sociability' as 'the play form of association' (1997: 122). As a whole, the Café Museum was a space that enabled oscillation between sociability, based on 'conversational proximity', and association, based on 'visual proximity' (Simmel 1997: 117). In designing a modern space that, paradoxically, set out to re-inscribe a tradition of oral culture in the city, Loos provided the spatial correlate of the modern form of public speaking based on both dissemination and dialogue.

The grand hall: Permanence and transience

From the mid-nineteenth century onwards, a large number of multi-purpose grand halls were constructed in Berlin and Vienna as part of the bourgeois remodelling of these cities. A specific element of the design brief for these buildings was to create spaces that could be used for public speaking, although many were designed first and foremost for music performances and almost all were also designed to house other social events. The Sofiensaal in Vienna was a case in point (see Figure 4.2).

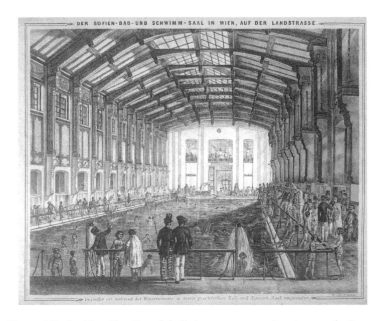

Figure 4.2 Sophiensäle: Grand hall in use as a swimming pool; *Source*: Austrian National Library/Picture Archive, Vienna

It functioned as a swimming pool in summer, which was then covered over for the winter season, to produce a ballroom and auditorium seating two thousand (Dobnig 2002: 7–11) – in which Loos gave a spirited defence of his 'House on the Michaelerplatz' in 1910. Some of these halls were built at the behest of the municipal authorities, while others were constructed by private associations. Amongst those wealthy enough to build their own premises complete with multi-purpose hall were the Associations of Architects and Engineers. In Vienna, the Association of Architects and Engineers entered into a joint project with the Lower Austrian Trade Association, which resulted in two connecting halls being created in a new complex on the Eschenbachgasse, completed in 1872 (Stoeckl 1899: 45). Three years later, the Association of Architects in Berlin began work on its new headquarters in the Wilhelmstrasse, the Architektenhaus ('House of Architects') (Bürckner 1913: 183). When completed, the building encompassed a number of meeting rooms and lecture halls, the largest being the 'Schinkel Hall', with a capacity of four hundred (Adams 1913: 234).

All these halls were available for hire, and so often housed public speaking events not directly organised by the associations themselves. Loos, for example, gave a lecture on 'Architecture' in the Architektenhaus on 8 December 1910, organised by the Verein für Kunst, and on 'My Struggles' in the Lower Austrian Trade Association's hall on 4 April 1911, as part of a series of talks organised by the Association for Adult Education (Rukschcio and Schachel 1982: 152–7). Competition for the associations came from the many commercially run halls constructed in this period, such as the massive complex of halls in Berlin's Zoological Garden (Architekten-Verein zu Berlin and Vereinigung Berliner Architekten 1896: 523; Klös and Klös 1990: 171) or the new concert hall complex in Vienna, designed by the architectural partnership of Ferdinand Fellner and Hermann Helmer (*Deutsche Bauzeitung* 1911: 148), which was the venue for a number of performances by Loos and Kraus (Rukschcio and Schachel 1982: 238–9; Timms 2005: 411).

While these halls were located in the city centre, there were also many meeting halls to be found in the suburbs. Most inns and taverns had larger rooms that could be rented out for meetings and lectures, and many breweries also opened large beer halls that were often used for political meetings, such as the 'Tivoli Hall' in Berlin-Kreuzberg (Architekten-Verein zu Berlin and Vereinigung Berliner Architekten 1896: 525). In certain circles, however, there was some concern about meetings and lectures taking place in premises licensed to sell alcohol, and an article appeared in the *Jahrbuch für das deutsche Vortragswesen* of 1912/13 discussing the desirability of banning smoking and alcohol during meetings. The author concluded, however, that only when dedicated community halls were built, would it be possible to use such a ban to distinguish clearly between education and entertainment (Fuchs 1912/13: 119–20). Although by the beginning of the twentieth century there were a number of community halls in Vienna, it was not always easy to gain access to them, especially for certain political purposes (Taschwer 1995: 13). Faced with such difficulties, the SDAP decided to construct its own premises, and in 1900, the Viennese Association of Architects and Engineers announced an architectural competition to design a suitable building to be located in the working-class district of Favoriten. First prize in the competition went to Otto Wagner's pupils Hubert and Franz Gessner, whose plans for an Arbeiterheim, or Workers' Home, included a hall designed to accommodate social gatherings and public lectures, as well as political meetings (*Der Architekt* 1901a,

Wiener Bilder: Ein Concert im Neuen Arbeiterheim. Nach dem Leben gezeichnet von C. Zimmer.

Figure 4.3 Arbeiterheim. A concert in the big hall, 1902; *Source*: Austrian National Library/Picture Archive, Vienna

1901b; Lux 1903) (see Figure 4.3). In the 1920s, both Kraus and Loos spoke in the Arbeiterheim; Kraus, at a public meeting organised by the SDAP (Timms 2005: 320), and Loos, at the invitation of the Heimkehrer, one of the local associations affiliated with the Settlement Movement (Novy and Förster 1991: 59).

Perhaps unsurprisingly, given the different uses for which the halls were designed, tension between the demands of commerce and the demands of culture shaped discourse about these spaces. In most cases, this debate centred on the use of space, but in the case of Bruno Schmitz's opulent Weinhaus Rheingold, built between 1905 and 1907, discussion of this issue informed the design. The original plan for the Weinhaus Rheingold had been to create a grand entertainment complex in the Bellevue Strasse, encompassing both concert halls and a variety of meeting rooms. Planning permission for this ambitious undertaking was refused, but was granted for the erection of a large-scale 'wine restaurant' (H[ofmann] 1907: 86). In a monograph dedicated to the Weinhaus Rheingold, Schliepmann argued that even though commerce would seem to have triumphed over art when planning permission was only granted for a wine restaurant, Bruno Schmitz was able to remain true to many of his original plans and create a building that was

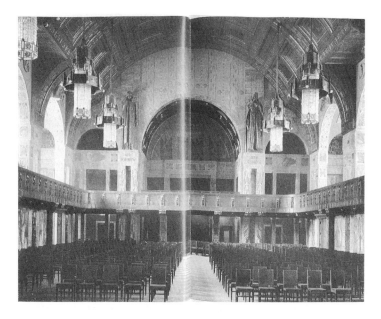

Figure 4.4   Weinhaus Rheingold, Kaisersaal. Architect: Bruno Schmitz; *Source*: Schliepmann [1907]

'a "holy place" of great, serious and truly German art' (1907: 7). In its final form, the building extended over 5000 square metres, and boast a number of rooms of differing sizes, which were eventually used for public lectures as well as to house the gastronomic enterprise for which planning permission had been granted. Of the halls, the most impressive was the largest, the 'Kaisersaal' ('Emperor's Hall'), which Schliepmann singled out as the building's 'piece de resistance', describing it as 'a fairy-tale, a dream of magnificence and beauty'(7) (see Figure 4.4).

In his review of the building, Theodor Heuss focused on the monumentality of the Kaisersaal (cited in Güttler 1980: 62). Meanwhile, although in a rather less flattering tone, in 'Cult of Distraction', first published in 1926, Kracauer wrote of 'the barbaric pomposity of Wilhelminian secular churches – like the Rhinegold, for example, which seeks to give the impression that it harbors the Wagnerian Nibelungen treasure' (1995: 323). These descriptions are not surprising, since Schmitz was an architect celebrated above all for his ability to lend a sense of permanence to innovative forms and heralded as the founder of a new monumental direction in German art (James-Chakraborty 2000: 26; Schliepmann (1907: 3). Unlike Schmitz's main monumental work, the Battle of the Nations Monument in Leipzig, the Kaisersaal in the Weinhaus Rheingold was designed to fulfil a function beyond its representative role as an aid to public memory. According to the simple scheme to differentiate between art and architecture proposed by Loos in his lecture on 'Architecture', because the 'Kaisersaal' was designed to serve a particular function, it could not properly be defined as a monument, and therefore as a work of art ([1931] 1982: 101). Similarly, Lefebvre seeks to differentiate between what he terms the 'poetry of the monument' and 'buildings, the homogenous matrix of capitalist space' (1991: 227). Unlike Loos, however, he argues that both aspects of architecture can coexist in any one building, creating tension between art and commerce and, since 'the most beautiful monuments are imposing in their durability', between the permanent, and the constant turnover typical of consumer capitalism (221).

Like many of the other grand halls built around the beginning of the twentieth century, the aura of permanence with which the monumental Kaisersaal was imbued derived from it being a type of building indebted to the spatial practice of earlier periods, and in particular, to Renaissance architecture. Writing in the late nineteenth century, the influential cultural historian Jakob Burckhardt described the Renaissance great hall (or 'public palace') as an important form of public space, identifying, in particular, the open colonnade as 'an expressive indication that the building in question is public property' ([1867] 1985: 149–50). His reflections on the use of space in the Italian Renaissance coincided with the emergence in architectural history of a new concern with the perception of space, as opposed to structure or style, which was to be found in the work of theorists such as August Schmarsow (1903, 1905) and Heinrich Wölfflin ([1888] 1964), the latter of whom had studied with Burckhardt in Basel. Wölfflin provided an account of the perception of space in the Renaissance that focused on stability and permanence, arguing that Renaissance architecture 'sought permanence and repose in everything' (58) and that the impact of Renaissance architecture is slow, quiet and enduring, meaning that 'we want to linger for ever in its presence' (38). In the great halls of the Renaissance period, this sense of stability was to be found in the harmony of proportions, the oblong floor-plan and the flat ceiling that functioned to 'calmly close off space', turning the interior into a 'structurally closed entity' (64–5). At this point, it should be noted that what is of interest for this study is not what Wölfflin has to say about the Renaissance and the Baroque per se, but the implications that his ideas would have had at the beginning of the twentieth century for the development of the architecture of communication. In terms of representations of space, architects of late nineteenth and early twentieth century great halls designed in neo-Renaissance style were making use of the received idea of a connection between Renaissance architecture and durability to enhance the monumental status of their buildings.

Unlike contemporaneous buildings such as the grand halls of the Lower Austrian Trade Association and the Association of Architects and Engineers in Vienna, the Kaisersaal was not executed in strict neo-Renaissance style. With its soaring vaulted ceiling emphasising the vertical dimensions of the space, it could be argued that its architecture owed rather more to contemporary understandings of the spatial properties of the Gothic or the Baroque, than of the Renaissance. Again according to Wölfflin, Baroque architecture, like Gothic architecture, articulated an urge for upward movement and so 'never offers us perfection and fulfilment, or the static calm of "being", only the unrest of change and the tension of transience' ([1888] 1964: 62). Despite the sense of monumentality and permanence that the Kaisersaal induced in commentators such as Schliepmann, it was also partly designed with reference to historicist styles associated with movement and transience, illustrating Lefebvre's claim that 'monumental "durability" is unable [...] to achieve a complete illusion' (1991: 221). The idea of transience is not limited to the perception of space dependent on a knowledge of historicist architecture, however; it was also present in the ornamentation of the Kaisersaal, which was adorned with a series of high reliefs designed by the sculptor, Franz Metzner, and depicting dynamic muscular human bodies (Schliepmann 1907) (see Figure 4.5). This depiction of the human form would seem to celebrate movement and, by extension, transience, and yet these were figures whose heads were set horizontally, so that on first glance it appeared as though one was gazing upon a series of beheaded figures. The dynamism of the athletic human body frozen in time, captured in stone and apparently headless, provides a telling allegory of the dialectic of permanence and transience that characterised Schmitz's architectural work.

The dialectic of permanence and transience that is a central formal property of the Kaisersaal can also be traced in the use of space for

Figure 4.5   Weinhaus Rheingold, high relief sculpture. Artist: Franz Metzner;
Source: Schliepmann [1907]

public speaking there and in other similar halls. During the course of lectures, talks and speeches, the spatial relationship between speaker and audience in such halls was proscribed by a number of architectural elements that served not only to separate the speaker from the audience, but also to privilege the speaker, thereby facilitating dissemination. As locations for public speaking, monumental grand halls were designed on the principle of the 'Synoptikon', drawing the gaze of the audience to the stage, podium or lectern at which the speaker would be located. As Lefebvre points out, these architectural features are objects invested with power and authority according to the spatial practice of Western societies (1991: 225). By standing on the stage, or at the lectern, the speaker gained authority to disseminate knowledge and ideas to an audience. In their design, halls such as these would seem to cement a sense of permanence in the relationship between speaker and audience, which served to privilege dissemination as the dominant form of public speaking in such locations.

Other architectural features of such halls, however, placed in question any straightforward correlation between a static speaker/audience relation, on the one hand, and public speaking as dissemination, on the other. In the complex of halls constructed in the Zoological Garden in Berlin, the promenade, which was designed to facilitate the circulation of some ten thousand to twelve thousand people, introduced space for movement to the communicative event (Architekten-Verein zu Berlin und Vereinigung Berliner Architekten 1896: 523) (see Figure 4.6). Although the majority of halls were not designed to include a promenade on this scale, many did incorporate direct access to an enclosed terrace or garden, or to other 'break-out spaces' such as those detailed in Otto Wagner's plans for a 'Social Palace for Vienna', which included a raked theatre, two large halls, a restaurant, a café and a garden (1908). This remained unbuilt, but spaces such as the Weinhaus Rheingold fulfilled the remit envisaged by Wagner, bringing together education and entertainment in one event, while upholding spatial and temporal barriers between the two. In gardens, terraces and promenades, the spatial relationship between speaker and audience, and indeed, between individual members of the audience, is fluid rather than static, enabling 'conversational proximity' as well as 'visual proximity' (Simmel 1997: 117). Lefebvre argues that 'monumental space permits a continual back-and-forth between the private speech of ordinary conversations and the public speech of discourses, lectures, sermons, rallying-cries, and all theatrical forms of utterance' (Lefebvre 1991: 224). In terms of the communicative event of the lecture located in the monumental space of the great hall, we might want to qualify Lefebvre's claim, by striking the adjective 'continual', for the periods for sitting still and listening, and for moving around and entering into conversation are largely prescribed in the rules of the lecture as 'language-game'. In addition, we would want to recall Warner's point that the dominance of the figure of conversation

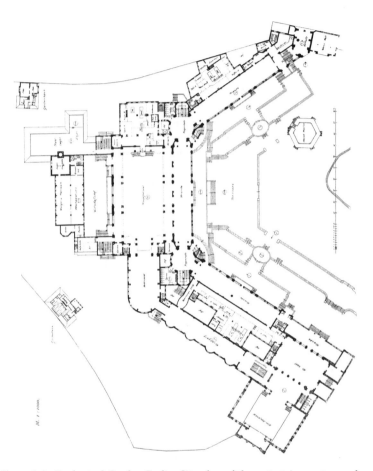

Figure 4.6   Zoological Garden Berlin. Site plan of the entertainment complex showing the promenade; *Source*: Heck and Heinroth 1912

detracts from our understanding of the way in which discourse circulates; even in 'break-out spaces', dissemination can be encountered, while conversations, however, snatched, can take place during public speeches. In both situations, as in any address to a public, 'onlookers' will be addressed, as well as be 'parties to argument' (2002: 90). While not a simple process of mapping dissemination onto permanence and dialogue onto transience, it is the case that the dialectic of permanence and transience that characterises the 'monumental space' of the hall underpins a view of modern public speaking as a communicative event comprising both dissemination and dialogue.

The theatre, the cabaret and the radio studio: Mobilising the auditorium

The late nineteenth and early twentieth centuries saw a boom in theatre construction in both Berlin and Vienna (Yates 1996: 159–63; Koneffke 1999: 9). Many prominent architects turned to designing theatres, but amongst the most prolific were Oskar Kaufmann, and the partnership of Helmer and Fellner. While providing space for public speaking was not the primary function of most mainstream theatres, they were often also used for lectures and readings, particularly during the day. In 1927, for example, Loos gave an afternoon lecture on men's fashion in Kaufmann's newly renovated Renaissance Theatre (Lang 1927). As spaces used for public speaking, theatres, like grand halls, contained elements facilitating both stasis and movement. In traditional theatre design, the design of auditoria is governed by the principle of sightlines and predicated on an afternoon static relationship between auditorium and stage, and between individual members of the audience, while the foyer, like the promenade, is predicated on the idea of the circulation of individuals through space. Manfred Semper stated that the primary purpose of the foyer was to allow the audience space for the 'exchange of ideas' (1904: 151). He then proceeded to reflect on how to design a foyer suitable for this purpose, arguing that mobility was paramount:

> in the better theatres, the public prefers to spend the intermissions conversing while strolling about. It is, however, tiring to have to turn round after having taken only a few steps, or to have to walk in circles, as is the case with a square foyer [...]. Therefore, it is sensible to give the hall a shape that allows people to promenade: this means a rectangular form. It should be wide enough to allow at least two rows to promenade abreast.
>
> Semper (1904: 153–4)

He also discussed the new architectural practice of making the foyer accessible from the first gallery as well as the dress circle, mentioning that Heinrich Seeling, the architect of the Theater des Westens in Charlottenburg (1895–6), placed windows in the wall separating the access route to the second circle from the foyer. Semper argued that this development was not without importance, but could cause distress as there would be some en route to the second circle who would not be able to refrain from casting 'longing glances into the Paradise closed off to them' (156). Just as only those of a certain social standing were able to gain access to the inner sanctuary of central coffee houses such as the Romanisches Café, so only certain theatre-goers enjoyed the luxury of a planned place for perambulatory conversation in the intervals.

While grand halls were nearly always conceived as multi-purpose spaces, in traditional theatres, the auditorium was of a rigid layout, fixing the relationship between audience and speaker, and between members of the audience over time as well as in time. Around the beginning of the twentieth century, however, theatre reformers set out to challenge this aspect of theatre design, providing a critique of the traditional 'picture-frame' theatre. Architects such as Peter Behrens and Heinrich Tessenow and, later, Oskar Strnad, Walter Gropius, Hans Poelzig and Friedrich Kiesler joined forces with directors and stage designers to seek ways of breaking down the Cartesian 'fourth wall' between stage and auditorium, and setting the auditorium in motion. Their challenge to traditional theatre design was informed first, by progressive and avant-garde tendencies in art and architecture, together with a new political definition of society (Koneffke 1999: 11); and second, by new ideas about the nature of communication.

Despite (or perhaps because of) the number of theatres being built in Berlin and Vienna around 1900, the impetus for theatre reform came not from these cities, but from smaller provincial artistic centres. Bayreuth's Festival Theatre designed for Richard Wagner by Otto Brückwald, and built between 1872 and 1876, generated the first model for a new relationship between audience and actor in the German-speaking world, but although the seating arrangement in the Festival Theatre, modified from designs found in Classical Antiquity, served to improve visual contact, it did little to overcome the gulf between actor and audience (Anderson 2000: 270). The next step on the road to combining theatre reform with theatre architecture was taken in the Artists' Colony in Darmstadt, established in 1899. Behrens devoted much of his time there to thinking about the role and shape of the ideal theatre. Although his design was never realised, in 1900, he published a brochure entitled *Feste des Lebens und der Kunst: eine Betrachtung des Theaters als höchsten Kultursymbols* (Festivals of Life and Art: A Consideration of the Theatre as the Highest Cultural Symbol) that included a detailed description of his ideal theatre. The building was to have been circular, symbolising the 'oneness of actors and viewers' (Anderson 2000: 57). As in the Festival Theatre in Bayreuth, the seating was to approximate that used in ancient Greece, meaning that the audience would have a clear connection to the broad, shallow stage. Additionally, Behrens's design included a processional area that was to be used both for actors, and for the arrival and departure of the audience, linking forestage and auditorium. Here, the gulf between actor and audience was reduced, but the relationship between individual members of the audience during the performance remained static. Although he had considered the importance of providing 'free and beautiful spaces for communion among the participants during intermissions' (59), they did not appear in the final plans for his theatre project; perhaps, as Anderson suggests, 'the plan was so idealized that a subsidiary function could not be allowed to disturb the absolute centralization' (59).

Behrens's theatre in Darmstadt remained unbuilt, but it did influence later designs for revolutionary theatres, such as Tessenow's performance space built in the Garden City Hellerau in 1911–2. Like Behrens's theatre, Tessenow's design was informed by ideas of the importance of rhythm, dance and mime (Anderson 2000: 59; Koneffke 1999: 44). His inspiration came from collaboration with Adolphe Appia, a prominent stage designer; Alexander Salzmann, a lighting specialist and Emile Jacques-Dalcroze, the initiator of Rhythmic Gymnastics (Koneffke 1999: 43–4). At the centre of his building was a large multi-purpose performance space. While it was laid out in the shape of a cross, the interior appeared as a simple rectangular hall, which could be extended on both sides. Like Behrens in Darmstadt, Tessenow strove to create a space that would overcome the traditional barrier of the proscenium arch to unite stage and auditorium. His solution was to construct a bare performance space that was linked to the auditorium through the creative use of lighting, so that both performers and audience 'shared the experience of inhabiting a glowing box' (James-Chakraborty 2000: 73).

Revolutionary ideas in theatre architecture were produced, tried and tested outside Berlin and Vienna, but there, too, they soon began to exert an influence. Projects such as Kaufmann's Hebbel-Theater in Berlin (1907/08), and Hans Poelzig's Großes Schauspielhaus (or 'Theatre of Five Thousand') were designed to facilitate a new relationship between actors and audience (*Deutsche Bauzeitung* 1908; James-Chakraborty 2000: 78). Poelzig's Schauspielhaus represented a milestone in theatre architecture, as it signalled that experimental theatre design could be realised in the modern metropolis, and paved the way for architects such as Strnad, Kiesler and Gropius to further revolutionise the theatre-going experience by using new technology to integrate the audience into the 'maelstrom of things' (Koneffke 1999: 174), as they did in projects such as Strnad's 'Raumbühne' ('Spatial Stage'), the concept for which was published in 1920; Walther Gropius' 'Totaltheater' ('Total Theatre'), designed in 1926/27 for Erwin Piscator and Friedrich Kiesler's 'Railway-Theatre', constructed in 1924.

In a lecture delivered to the Austrian Association of Engineers and Architects in Vienna in 1913, Strnad drew on the work of Schmarsow and others to focus on the physical and psychological impact of space and movement, arguing that in domestic architecture, providing opportunities for movement was an essential part of creating comfortable living space, and crucial for intensifying the architectural experience of the observer (Strnad 1917; Long 2001). He devoted time and effort to translating these concerns to the sphere of theatre, developing the idea of a *Raumbühne* in the shape of a circular stage (Strnad 1920). His designs remained, however, unrealised. Similarly, Gropius' *Totaltheater*, which included a moving stage that could be used as a sunken stage, arena or proscenium stage, remained unbuilt (Probst and Schädlich 1987: 31–4). In contrast, Kiesler, artistic director of the 1924 Vienna International Exhibition of New Theatre Technology, produced a *Raumbühne* that was entirely workable. This raised, circular stage without traditional walls was constructed in the Konzerthaus in Vienna as part of the 1924 exhibition and was used to stage a number of different events, including theatre and dance productions, as well as a set of lectures given by speakers such as the architect and filmmaker, Fernand Léger; the film critic, Béla Balázs; and Theo van Doesburg, founder of the art movement, De Stijl.

It proved to be an ideal platform for public speaking, offering a number of different positions for the lecturer (Lesák 1988: 111–63) (see Figure 4.7). Like Strnad, Kiesler's idea was to bring movement to the audience's experience of the theatre. In the catalogue for the 1924 exhibition, he published a description of an ideal *Raumbühne*, under the

Figure 4.7 Raumbühne in the Konzerthaus in Vienna, 1924: Platform for public speaking. Architect: Friedrich Kiesler; *Source*: Lesák 1988: 118

title 'Railway-Theater', suggesting that this kind of theatre might employ the new technology of the roller coaster to set both the stage and the auditorium in motion. 'Railway', proclaimed Kiesler, 'is the culmination of the theatres, halls, stadiums, cinemas, circuses, dance

Figure 4.8 'Everything is spinning, everything is moving': *Die Raumbühne*. Caricature by L. Tuzynsky (originally in *Der Goetz von Berlichingen*, 24 October 1924); *Source*: Lesák 1988: 155

events, and the unity of actor and audience' (n.d.: 11, cited in Lesák 1988: 60). Just as on a roller coaster, the audience were to be able to experience the theatrical effect of space and speed for themselves (Kiesler [1924] 1975; Koneffke 1999: 146–51) (see Figure 4.8). The design of the 'Railway-Theater', like other incarnations of the *Raumbühne*, was influenced by theories of architecture such as those put forward by Schmarsow, who argued that the 'essence of our experience of architecture [resides] in bodily movement through space rather than stationary observation' (Schmarsow, cited in Long 2001). Changing theoretical conceptions of space in the 1920s meant that in theatre architecture, 'spatiality was being thematised in all dimensions: events colonised the vertical; multidimensionality, simultaneity, circular and spiralling movements were to make it possible to experience the voluminous nature of the location' (Koneffke 1999: 174).

While in mainstream and avant-garde theatres, ever more elaborate construction techniques were employed to bring an experience of movement to the auditorium, in other, non-mainstream theatres, the experience of inhabiting the auditorium was characterised by bodily movement through space because there was no clear delineation between it and the foyer. This was the case in so-called 'Promenade Theatres' such as 'Unter den Linden' in Berlin, described by Semper as part theatre, part restaurant – a space in which the performance was only one of the distractions on offer, and the foyer and other spaces, such as the conservatory, were occupied during the performance, rather than only in the intermissions (1904: 163). Another example of the 'promenade theatre' was the Concordia Theatre, built in 1891 to a design by Gustav Ebe, who was experimenting with some of the ideas that he later presented in *The Architectural Lessons of Space* (1900). It was featured in the *Deutsche Bauzeitung*'s review of significant new buildings in Berlin in 1891 because of its unique design that allowed the entire space to be opened up to create a single room that stretched through the entire depth of the building, from the stage to the front wall of the foyer (F. 1891: 453).

The Cabaret Fledermaus in Vienna, designed by Josef Hofmann in 1907, was not so much a cross between restaurant and theatre, as between coffee house and theatre. It consisted of two rooms – the bar and the theatre, which was a

> complete little theatre for three hundred spectators, as intimate as the theatre in a millionaire's mansion. [...] There [were] boxes in the rear stalls and in the gallery, as well as space for standing and moving around, and in the stalls there [were] tables and portable armchairs.
>
> Hevesi ([1909] 1986: 243)

This hybrid space, as Hevesi noted, facilitated social interaction different to that circumscribed by the spatial practice related to either theatre or coffee house: '[i]n a place like this, one can act as if in a club and surrounded by those of like mind, in other words, of like voice. There is lively interaction with the stage, which, through the participation of talented dilettantes, has new appeal' (244). Here, he provides evidence to support Kern's assertion that cabaret was characterised by the removal of classical theatre's Cartesian fourth wall (1983: 200). Yet nineteenth century theatre reform had already sought to bridge the gap between audience and performer. The architectural innovation of cabaret theatres such as Fledermaus was not so much the loss of the fourth wall, as the introduction of movement to the auditorium, which was not mooted as a possibility in mainstream theatre architecture until the 1920s. According to Kern, encouraging movement in the auditorium of the cabaret, 'highlight[ed] what Lewis Erenberg has called "the anarchistic possibilities of the entire room"' (200).

Performances taking place in the Cabaret Fledermaus, however, called into question the desirability of introducing movement to the auditorium. In a short sketch, 'The Ten Commandments: A Cabaret Revue', Egon Friedell and Alfred Polgar focused on interactions between the members of a cabaret audience, and between the audience and the action on stage (Friedell and Polgar 1986). Foregrounding consumption as the rationale for social interaction, the sketch cast doubt on the possibility of meaningful audience interaction. It presented a picture of modern social life that closely mirrored Simmel's analysis of the alienated metropolitan dweller in 'Metropolis and Mental Life' (1997: 178–9), suggesting that Friedell and Polgar were as cynical as Richard Sennett about the possibility of productive audience participation in theatre in the early twentieth century (1976: 218). Their cynicism, however, may be an oversimplification; some reports of cabaret-like public performances, such as those given by Loos, suggest that audiences did respond to what was being said on stage (*Wiener Allgemeine Zeitung* 1927). The response may have been couched in the form of disruptive heckling, but it still represented audience participation.

A necessary precondition for audiences responding to public performances was the ability to hear the speaker. Architects of theatre reform in the early twentieth century seemed to privilege the visual over the aural, perhaps because the architectural reception of the science of acoustics was still only partial at this time; a number of articles published in the *Deutsche Bauzeitung* bemoaned architects' lack of knowledge in the field of acoustics, and their tendency to leave acoustics to chance, despite the considerable technological progress being made in the field (Unger 1909; Petzold 1929). Yet in ancient Greece, the study of acoustics was integral to theatre architecture, and until the early Renaissance, there was a belief that 'the phenomena of sound and music were inherently linked to architecture through the underlying harmony of the universe' (Thompson 2002: 18). As the scientific world view came to dominate during the sixteenth and early seventeenth centuries, this belief in the divine ratios of the cosmos was exchanged for one in which science, architecture and music went their separate ways. By the late eighteenth century, scientists had built up a substantial body of experimental literature on acoustics, but little of this was of practical use to architects. The commercialisation of theatre, however, in the late eighteenth and early nineteenth centuries, provided an impetus for architects to devote themselves to the problem of acoustics (20). Now that theatre was being established as a public institution, it was incumbent upon architects to design spaces that would enable all members of the audience to hear well (Meyer 1998: 112), which they did by basing their designs on the work of theorists such as Pierre Patte, Franceso Algarotti and George Saunders, who used geometry in their attempt to establish the form that would best facilitate the movement of sound rays through space (Thompson 2002: 20–4).

Throughout the nineteenth century, the geometrical method was followed in investigating the acoustical properties of particular spaces, and there was a general consensus that good sound was dependent on form, even if there was no agreement on what that ideal form might be (Thompson 2002: 24). At the beginning of the twentieth century, however, Wallace Sabine, assistant professor of physics at Harvard University, developed a new theory, conceiving sound 'not as geometric rays, but as a body of energy, capable of not only reflection, but also absorption' (Thompson 1999: 258). Using this more dynamic model of sound, and focusing on the role of reverberation, Sabine changed the way acoustics were studied, shifting the emphasis from the shape of a particular space to the materials with which that it was clad (258–9). Spatial acoustics had always recognised that movement is important to the perception of sound, since sound has to travel from speaker to listener. Sabine's defining contribution was to shift the focus from encouraging movement to controlling it, by exploring ways of arresting unwanted movement. Analogously, in their cabaret sketches, Friedell and Polgar suggested that in order to facilitate meaningful dialogical communication in new theatre spaces, some kind of controls (or 'language-game' rules) would need to be placed on the fluidity encouraged by the hybrid space of the cabaret.

The logical conclusion to draw from work on the desirability of controlling movement to improve acoustics was to strive for the complete elimination of unwanted movement, which was the goal of modern sound techniques in the early twentieth century. Modern sound, particularly for radio, was efficient, because through a combination of the use of new soundproofing materials and forms of technological mediation, it was stripped of all unnecessary reverberations: '[c]lear, direct, and nonreverberant, this modern sound was easy to understand, but it had little to say about the places in which it was produced and consumed' (Thompson 2002: 3). The use of the plural 'places' is instructive; for the first time in the history of public speaking, radio technology made it possible to separate production from consumption, speaker from audience.

This innovation led to the construction of spaces devoted to the production of sound, such as Poelzig's Haus des Rundfunks (House of Radio) (1929–31) (see Figure 4.9). At the heart of the complex, which was situated on the edges of the existing city, in what Max Osborn called the 'District of the Future', lay three recording studios, designed according to the demands of acoustics (Noack 1987: 130–1). The building was subjected to significant criticism related to the placing of these studios. Paul Westheim remarked that Poelzig 'uses offices to protect the recording studios from the outside world, just as the sensitive parts of the brain are protected by the skull' (1994: 18). The critical tone of this remark was reiterated the following year in Kracauer's review of the building, in which he pointed to the architectural similarities between Poelzig's building and the Karstadt department store on Hermannplatz, which he maintained, was more like a fortress than a shop (1994: 12). He then suggested that formally, the Haus des Rundfunks characterised the commodity character of the 'intellectual achievements' being created therein (13). Like Westheim, Kracauer was aiming his critique at the separation of street and recording studio, which symbolically separated speaker from audience. His contribution was to focus on the role of commodification in bringing about the dissociation of speaker and audience, drawing implicitly on Simmel's account, in 'Metropolis and Mental Life', of the way in which the capitalist money economy serves to alienate buyer from seller (1997: 176).

In contrast to Kracauer, Benjamin suggested that the separation of speaker from audience might be seen as radio's strength

Figure 4.9 Berlin, Masurenallee 8–14. 'Haus des Rundfunks' (Berliner Rundfunk);
Source: German Federal Archive, Bild-F005427-0045

(Gilloch 2001: 169–70). Other contemporary evidence, however, suggests that both audiences and speakers valued face-to-face communication over flexibility of reception. From 1924 onwards, a series of Radio Exhibitions were held in Berlin, taking place in the Haus der deutschen Funkindustrie (House of the German Broadcasting Industry) designed by Heinrich Straumer as a shop window for the industry (B. L. 1925; Noack 1987: 124). In the catalogue of the 14th Exhibition held from 30 July to 8 August 1937, Albert Wischek wrote:

> [t]he amazing thing about these exhibition halls is that here the magical force connecting each individual to the radio broadcast constantly manifests itself. Here, I see the most profound reason for the success of these radio exhibitions. Radio producers and listeners come face to face as equals.
>
> Wischek (1937: 11)

Braunmühl reiterated this view later in the same volume, arguing that radio is disadvantaged vis-à-vis direct face-to-face communication

(1937: 19). In an address speech given at the opening ceremony of the 7th Radio Exhibition held in Berlin in 1930, Albert Einstein characterised radio as 'this wonderful tool for making announcements', suggesting that radio was associated solely with monological communication at a distance. The architecture of radio, however, also included space for more conventional forms of public speaking – both the Haus der deutschen Funkindustrie and Poelzig's Haus des Rundfunks contained conventional lecture theatres and meeting rooms – demonstrating that when used for public speaking, spaces housing radio technology, like cabarets and new theatres, provided space for dialogue. The rise of mediated communication in Berlin and Vienna was accompanied by the creation of new spaces for sociability, demonstrating that an ongoing commitment to immediate communication lay at the heart of the modern media-dominated city.

The adult education establishment: Empowerment and control

In contrast to the sites discussed so far, buildings designed to house the emerging field of adult education contained purpose-built single-use spaces for public speaking. Perhaps counter-intuitively, however, this did not seem to be the most important factor in the design of these buildings. Instead, technology (especially visual technology) and geography dominated, but this is entirely concomitant with the way in which spatial boundaries in the modern city were created through the interplay of technology, geography and politics. In 1889, the Urania Society opened its first purpose-built educational establishment in Berlin. The building in the exhibition park in Moabit, a working-class suburb, was conceived as 'a palace for modern scientific adult education' (Ebel and Lührs 1988: 20) and included an observatory and laboratory space, as well as a 'Scientific Theatre' (Wissenschaftliches Theater). Crowned with three domes, housing the telescope and other astronomical instruments, the building was designed in neo-Renaissance style. In 1896, a second building was opened in the Taubenstrasse, located in the centre of Berlin, just off the main thoroughfare of the Friedrichstrasse. It housed laboratory space, a new Scientific Theatre with seating for seven hundred, and also, located directly above this space, a smaller lecture theatre with a capacity of two hundred (Ebel and Lührs 1988: 36).

As a speech site, the Scientific Theatre was similar in design to other traditional theatres used for public speaking; here, too, movement was confined to the stage, while the galleried auditorium was designed to house a static audience. The innovation here, however, was that the movement on the stage did not comprise moving bodies, but moving things. Combining painted flats and new technology, such as diaramas and electric lighting, to give the illusion of three-dimensional space and motion, the Scientific Theatre was designed to demonstrate to the audience the wonders of the natural world, packaged in popular presentations such as 'From the Earth to the Moon' and 'The Story of the Prehistoric World' (Ebel and Lührs 1988: 33). In its use of visuals and objects to popularise scientific discourse, the Scientific Theatre functioned in a similar manner to other nineteenth-century institutions such as museums and zoos, which functioned by 'caging Nature's caprices in thick walls of faultless display' (Collins 1988: 728). Emphasising its credentials as a location of popular entertainment, the Scientific Theatre's immediate precursor was the Panorama, a favoured distraction in both Berlin and Vienna in the late nineteenth century. While the Panorama, however, consisted of 'individual viewing stations located in a public space' (Crary 2001: 136), the audiences in the Scientific Theatre were seated as a collective, and a lecturer standing to the side of the forestage delivered a monological narrative to accompany the spectacle.

In popularising science, the Scientific Theatre played its role in the 'reenchantment of nature' (Daum 1998). This was, apparently, in direct contrast to the role of the lecture theatre located above the Scientific Theatre in the new Urania building in the Taubenstraße. This space was utilised for public lectures by prominent scientists, such as Hertz, Auerbach, Einstein and Planck, and explorers, such as Nansen and Amundsen, whose audiences were party to nature's disenchantment (Henning 1964: 38; Gesellschaft Urania 1913: 36–7). The vertical hierarchy at work in the building served to distinguish the two lecture theatres, each of which had its own distinct audience: a wide and varied general public waiting to be entertained in the Scientific Theatre; a smaller group privy to more specialised knowledge in the lecture theatre above. The symbolic and practical distinction between the two lecture theatres demonstrates the way in which public space for the dissemination of scientific knowledge can be divided up according to 'conditions of knowing' (Livingstone 1995: 21). The initial idea in constructing a second Urania location had been to separate 'edutainment' from education completely, with the lectures for specialists taking place in the original building in Moabit, while the more spectacular Scientific Theatre performances would move to the new building in the Taubenstraße. This, however, would have been tantamount to locating 'edutainment' in the city centre, while banishing bourgeois science to the periphery; at the beginning of the twentieth century, this was not a sustainable move. Moreover, in terms of representations of space, the distinction between the two lecture theatres was perhaps not as great as might be suggested by considering the use of space alone. The lecture theatre on the upper floor was a wide, shallow space equipped with a large projection screen at the front of the room. In other words, like the Scientific Theatre, it was a space for the dissemination of knowledge that had been designed to privilege the visual over the aural (see Figure 4.10).

As was the case with theatres and public halls, in both Urania buildings, the foyer was a space in which dialogue could take place, but here, the exchange of ideas was not limited to fleeting encounters in the foyer. The idea driving the popular performances in the Scientific Theatre was to awaken people's curiosity, which, once stimulated, could be satisfied by practical experiments carried out in laboratory space (Ebel and Lührs 1988: 21). This move serves to underpin the dominance of the visual over the aural – already suggested in the form of the presentations in the Scientific Theatre – since work in laboratory space 'privileges the sedentary gaze of the observer' through the use of a range of technological devices serving the purposes of 'opticism': lenses, prisms, microscopes, cameras and diaramas (Livingstone 1995: 20–4). It also, however, serves to complicate Livingstone's description of the linear transition from experiment to dissemination, according to which

> transmission from the sphere of private trial to the arena of public discourse [...] from private to public, from the solitary to the communal, from 'trying' to 'showing', from delving to demonstrating, was at once a move from the context of scientific discovery to the context of justification, and an exercise in refinement for public consumption.
>
> Livingstone (1995: 22)

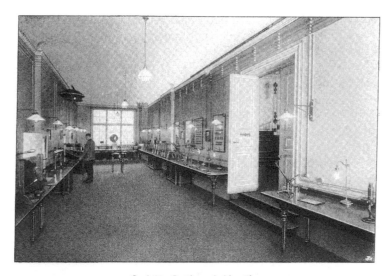

Saal für Optik und Akustik.

Der Theatersaal für populär-wissenschaftliche Vorträge in der Taubenstraße.

Figure 4.10 Urania, Berlin: Scientific Theatre and laboratory for optics and acoustics; *Source*: Gesellschaft Urania 1913

By adding another dimension in which experiments could be replicated and tested by the public, the Urania building was a space that facilitated not only the dissemination of scientific knowledge, but also dialogue with that knowledge. It was a space in which the dialectical relationship between professionalisation and popularisation, identified by Daum as typical of scientific culture around 1900, could flower (1998: 12). Here, then, the 'continual back-and-forth between the private speech of ordinary conversations and the public speech of discourses, lectures, sermons, rallying-cries, and all theatrical forms of utterance' that Lefebvre identified as characteristic of monumental space, has its correlate in the scientific sphere (1991: 224).

In Berlin, the Urania's attempt to create separate buildings for the dissemination of professional and non-professional scientific knowledge faltered. Had the popular Scientific Theatre been located in the first Urania building, in the exhibition site in Moabit, however, while the 'serious' lecture theatre had been moved to a new building in the centre of the city, the distinction between the two spaces may have been more strictly observed. In Vienna, adult education establishments were constructed on the periphery of the city, while important established institutions for the production and dissemination of knowledge, such as the university, museums and prestigious schools, were located in the city centre. Indeed, the early history of the adult education movement in Vienna is located in peripheral halls and meeting rooms, leading Taschwer to describe it as a struggle for space. The city government, particularly under the Christian Socialist mayor, Karl Lueger, who held office from 1897 to 1910, was not well disposed towards the idea of adult education, and during the 1890s, it became increasingly difficult for the Viennese Association for Adult Education to make use of municipal space. The association was forced to search for alternative spaces in which it could focus on providing its own form of education, which led first, to the appropriation and renovation of a variety of spaces and second, to the creation of a number of new spaces for adult education in Vienna's working-class districts, including the Volksheim in Ottakring and the Volksbildungshaus in Margarethen (Taschwer 1995: 12–16).

The Volksheim in Ottakring celebrated its official opening on 5 November 1905 (Filla 1992: 87) (see Figure 4.11). Like the Urania Berlin, the division of space in the building served to facilitate both dissemination and dialogue; while in formal lecture theatres,

Figure 4.11 Frontal view of the newly built Volksheim in Ottakring, 1905;
Source: Austrian National Library/Picture Archive, Vienna

dissemination was the dominant form of communication, spaces such as laboratories, refreshment rooms and the library were designed to allow dialogical communication to flourish. The building was designed by Franz Ritter von Neumann jr. in the then dominant Jugendstil aesthetic, providing a visual representation of the dialogical dimension of the building. The fluidity of natural forms was a central Jugendstil motif, symbolising the idea that education facilitates social mobility through overcoming apparently fixed boundaries between classes and status groups. Paradoxically, however, the flowing lines of the Jugendstil building can be held to represent the interests of those who funded its construction. The association 'Volkshochschule Wien Volksheim' was established by Baron Rothschild and enjoyed the financial support of upper middle-class social reformers such as Emil and Bertha Zuckerkandl (Meysels 1984: 83). Their primary aim in funding adult education was to prevent social revolution through education and, in particular, through the dissemination of evolutionary thought, for Social Darwinism played an important role in shaping the world view of the European upper classes in the period 1890–1914 (Mayer 1981: 290). In the German-speaking world, it was above all the controversial figure, Ernst Haeckel, who was responsible for the popularisation of Darwin's theories (Daum 1998), and in whose work (Haeckel 1899–1904) the connection between popular evolutionary thought and the Jugendstil aesthetic becomes readily apparent. Designing the Volksheim in Jugendstil may have had more to do with social control than would first seem to be the case. Although the balance of power in the city was altered by the creation of modern suburban spaces for the production and consumption of knowledge, this also allowed new forms of social control to be imposed there. Spaces such as the Volksheim embodied this tension between empowerment and control.

In a publication celebrating the Volksheim's tenth anniversary, testimonies written by current and former students emphasised the perception of the building as a 'home' ('Heim'), the very presence of which was empowering. Reminiscing about her time at the Volksheim, Louise Gahler (1911: 14) remarked: 'Soon I had something to do every evening. I looked forward to this time and from then on nothing stopped me from going to my now beloved home'. The Volksheim was not the only new speech site erected in the Viennese suburbs in the first decade of the twentieth century to bear the designation 'home'; Hubert and Franz Gessner's headquarters for the SDAP in Favoriten was known as the Arbeiterheim ('Workers' Home'). The importance of labelling this building a 'home' was not lost on the architectural critic and apologist of the conservative *Heimatkunst* movement, Joseph August Lux. Writing in the *Deutsche Bauzeitung*, he observed that '[c]lass consciousness and party loyalty notwithstanding, the household gods of domesticity and hospitality cannot be ignored in a home [Heim], not even in a workers' home [Arbeiterheim]' (Lux 1903: 209). Playing with the idea of 'home', both the Volksheim and the Arbeiterheim were predicated on a new relationship between public and private space. In the latter, this found its expression in the architects' practical and symbolic use of sliding walls, allowing the same space to function either as a collection of small rooms or as one large space, depending on the occasion. As Lux (1903: 210) pointed out, the use of moveable walls was both practical and symbolic. This new relationship between private and public may have been typical of certain late nineteenth-century bourgeois speech sites, such as the coffee house (Segel 1993: 34), but it marked a new departure in the design of spaces for education and politics.

Acknowledging this point, Taschwer argued that the Volksheim distinguished itself from other educational establishments in existence in the early twentieth century by offering people a 'home' ('Heimat') rather than merely a 'transit space' ('Durchgangsort') (1995: 20). This implies that the Volksheim was a place in which the emphasis was on dwelling rather than mobility. Yet in its use of space and architectural style, the building was based on an idea of fluid space that facilitated and represented movement. This is, of course, paradoxical, but it is a paradox that was fundamental to the dominant Jugendstil aesthetic of the building. In the notes for his *Arcades Project*, Benjamin included a section on 'Painting, Jugendstil, and the New' (1999: 543–61). Amongst the material gathered here are short excerpts taken from an article on Jugendstil by Dolf Sternberger, which make the point that there is a line of connection between this particular aesthetic style, the idea of the private home, and social control. Having described how the furnishings in the modern Jugendstil home have become increasingly immovable, Sternberger concludes that '[i]n this way, all permanent contents of the home are removed from the sphere of exchange, but this means that the inhabitant of the home loses his freedom to move and instead is rooted to the ground and property that he owns' (cited in Benjamin 1999: 550; translation amended). The Jugendstil design of the Volksheim, then, signified not only mobility, but also stasis.

By 1925, the Viennese socialist newspaper, the *Arbeiterzeitung*, had identified the Volksheim as one of a chain of new socialist fortresses situated in Vienna (Felt 2000: 205). This stylisation of the building signified the empowerment of the working classes in Red Vienna, but it also provided an indictment of the stasis of the rationalist scientific world view that had encroached upon the suburbs, leading to the colonisation of the 'indigenous' oral culture of the outer suburbs by the rational bureaucratic written culture emanating from the city centre (Maderthaner and Musner 1999: 38–50). As a location of oral culture based in the outer suburbs, funded by private capital in order to disseminate a rational scientific world view, and designed according to the rhetoric of both the stability of the traditional home and the mobility of the modern structure of feeling apparently signified by its Jugendstil aesthetic, the Volksheim serves to complicate the picture proposed by Maderthaner and Musner. This institution was representative of the system encroaching upon lifeworld, but like the Arbeiterheim, it simultaneously provided a space in which the distinction between private and public space could be blurred, in which the dialogical conversations of the private sphere were brought into the public sphere, relativising the dominance of dissemination in the rational-technical sphere.

The salon: Fragmented public space

While educational establishments such as the Volksheim were public spaces based on the idea of providing a home away from home, the final set of spaces to be covered in this chapter moves the investigation into the home itself, examining the way in which public space can also be embedded within private space. Tracing the history of the salon back to eighteenth century Paris, feminist theorists and historians such as Hannah Arendt ([1959] 1987) and Joan Landes (1988) argued for its importance as a form of public space that played a significant role in heralding the bourgeois revolution. Arendt's work on the salons presided over by Rahel Levin Varnhagen in Berlin in the late eighteenth and early nineteenth centuries paved the way for more recent studies of the salon tradition (Sprung 1991; Siebel 1999; Gerstinger 2002). Historians such as Siebel and Gerstinger maintain that the salon tradition was in decline by the beginning of the twentieth century and this view seems to be supported in contemporary publications such as Valerian Tornius's (1921) descriptive account of a number of leading nineteenth-century Berlin salons, or Alexander von Gleichen-Rußwurm's (1908) article, *Der Salon*, which begins by stating that the traditions of the salon have been largely lost to the modern world. Despite this gloomy start, however, von Gleichen-Rußwurm's aim was to breathe new life into the salon, and there is ample evidence for a continuing, although evolving, salon tradition, at least until the end of the imperial period, that encouraged dialogue between the arts, science and politics (Sprung 1991: 410).

Bertha Zuckerkandl's salons in Vienna exemplify the versatility of the salon as a location of communication between the spheres of the arts, science, politics and commerce, both before and after the First World War. The importance of her salons, which formed a politically neutral meeting place for leading Christian Socialists and Social Democrats in the turbulent 1920s, is summed up in words attributed to her (and which Meysels (1984) takes as his title): 'Austria resides in my salon'. Her first salon was located in her home in the Nußwaldgasse, in the noble suburb of Döbling. The late nineteenth century saw the bourgeoisie in both Vienna and Berlin colonising certain suburban areas, in which they were able to commission architects to erect fine villas. An important element in the design of the majority of these private dwelling houses was the creation of public space. Muthesius was one of the foremost architects of the bourgeois villa at this time. His work was informed by his experiences in England, where he became fascinated with English country houses such as Plas Dinam, designed by Eden Nesfield in the 1890s. Posener notes that in this house

> the hall has retained its medieval shape, though it has become a hall in the modern sense, i.e. the main communication space in the house. It would be correct to say it has *also* become the main communication space in the house, for the hall, unlike the German 'Diele', retained its functions as a living room.
>
> Posener (1972: 22)

This suggests that the hall was a central space dependent on a tension between space designed to be moved through and space in which to dwell.

This tension informed the shape of public space in many of the architect-designed dwelling houses constructed in the early twentieth century. In works such as the Scholl House and the Strauß House, Josef Frank produced public spaces conceived primarily as spaces to be moved through facilitating communication in the form of dialogue (Welzig 1998: 129). In contrast, Loos's private dwelling houses favoured the stasis of the gaze, demonstrating a theatricality that cast the house as 'the stage of everyday life' (Heynen 1999: 83). As in the picture-frame theatre, the occupants are divided into actors and audience, with specific spaces for each. In his Moller House, for example, the ladies' lounge provides a static vantage point from which the action in most of the main public rooms can be observed (44). Like a theatre box, the ladies' lounge combined the greater intimacy of a small, enclosed space with the representative function of a raised platform that at least offered the possibility of communication as dissemination. This design feature lends credence to Siebel's (1999: 81) observation that at the beginning of the twentieth century, the salon was not only a place of communication, but also a representative space that allowed a particular public to demonstrate its social and economic status. Like the World Expositions and other trade fairs, salons provided space for both communication and display.

Zuckerkandl's second salon, operating after 1918, was located in central Vienna. She invited politicians, artists and other public figures to join her at home in the Oppolzergasse (Meysels 1984: 183). The salon, which she called her 'library', was located between the dining room and the bedroom of her four-room apartment, designed and furnished by Josef Hofmann. The way in which furniture and space work together in the salon to facilitate a particular form of communication, and, concomitantly, the influence of communicative structures on the design and location of furniture forms the central theme of Siebel's (1999) study of the Berlin salon. A similar account of the bourgeois interior was offered by von Gleichen-Rußwurm (1908: 233), who devoted the first pages of his article to the importance of the reception room itself, and the 'geographic situation' of chairs and armchairs, which, if wrongly choreographed, could destroy conversation. He maintained that in a room stuffed full with souvenirs, photographs and porcelain figurines, it was unlikely that the conversation would be able to escape from chatter about servants and other domestic problems, while conversely, a typical Bohemian room, heated with a smoking stove and boasting a broken teapot, often encouraged the flow of enthusiastic conversation.

In Zuckerkandl's salon, the single most important piece of furniture was her sizeable divan, which could accommodate up to ten people. According to Zuckerkandl, it was upon this divan – a product of the Wiener Werkstätte, naturally – that 'Austria came alive' (cited in Meysels 1984: 217). Like the lectern in the lecture hall, the divan in the salon is an example of what Lefebvre is describing when he writes of objects that are invested with power and authority according to the spatial practice of Western societies (1991: 225). The practised hostess drew on the power of the divan to allow her to initiate and master the conversation (Siebel 1999: 24). The rules of engagement in the eighteenth-century salon were based on a strict demarcation between private conversation and general conversation. Only the latter, involving all those present, was acceptable in the salon (Siebel 1999: 24). While the fragmentation of public space in the villas built around

1900, dividing the available space into ladies' lounge, gentlemen's lounge, dining room, music room and so on, may seem to signal modifications to these rules of engagement, salons did continue to provide a forum for public speaking, in the form of both general conversation addressed to a public and also, befitting the theatricality of spaces such as those designed by Loos, readings and lectures. The authors associated with Young Vienna read from their works in Zuckerkandl's salon, and in the interwar years, Hofmannsthal was still performing there, giving, for example, a reading of his *Welttheater* (World Theatre) in 1922 (Meysels 1984: 213). Three years earlier, as we saw in chapter two, Mendelsohn had given a series of eight illustrated talks to a private audience at Molly Phillipson's salon in Berlin (Heinze-Greenberg and Stephan 2000: 14–44). Indeed, the fragmented form of public space characteristic of the modern salon can be said to have encouraged the construction of an urban public through discourse, by providing a spatial setting in which dissemination and dialogue coexisted.

Deciphering the space of public speaking

Taking the Berlin Trade Exhibition as his point of departure, but writing about exhibition architecture in general, Simmel (1997: 256) notes that the modernity of this form of architecture lies in 'the entirely new proportion between permanence and transience' that is typical of both its structure and its aesthetic character. Deciphering the space for public speaking that was appropriated or constructed in the early twentieth century reveals that speech sites, in all their multiple manifestations, were predicated on a relation between permanence and transience, and on the relation between their spatial correlates, stasis and movement. The presence of this relation, which was at times structural, at other times codified in aesthetic appearance, suggests that like the exhibition site, speech sites were at the vanguard of the modern city's architecture.

Yet these sites were also indebted to tradition. The very fact that they were recognisable as speech sites was due to the aspect of spatial practice that provides the taken-for-granted shared sense of space, without which people would be unable to make sense of the world they inhabit. In terms of the speech sites under consideration here, this sense of spatial practice was encoded in the memory of historic

spaces such as the forum or the arcade, as well as architectural elements, such as the lectern. Spatial practice, however, is not so much
about tradition as determination in advance, as about

> tradition [...] as the site that occasions both an understanding of
> dominance – the categories and concepts which are handed down
> and which thus determine thinking within and as tradition – and
> the possibility of a thinking, which, while it maintains (houses) the
> dominant, is neither reducible to nor explicable in terms of it.
>
> Benjamin (1997: 290)

In this sense, spatial practice emerges as a vital force that changes
over time, even as it provides the very condition of possibility of such
change. In the speech sites presented here, the element of change is
contained in the sense of movement being introduced, whether through
architectural innovations, such as the sliding walls of the Arbeiterheim
or the roller coaster effect of Kiesler's *Raumbühne*; aesthetic features,
such as the Jugendstil design of the Volksheim; or the way that space
was used, such as protestors moving through parks in direct opposition
to their designers' desire to create spaces that would provide respite
from the endless processes of circulation that characterise modern
urban life.

This chapter set out to examine the connections between metropolis, speech site and public speaking. The speech sites presented here
as an integral part of the emerging metropolis are aesthetic objects
that, in line with Seel's (2005: 92) remarks on 'atmospheric appearing', affect the character of their setting, casting the metropolis as an
entity shaped by the immediate nature of public speaking, as well as
by mediated communication (the latter, of course, being the familiar
argument about the relationship between metropolis and communication). At the same time, the character of the metropolis can be
discerned in the figure of circulation that characterises individual
speech sites, as well as the network form of the eclectic collection of
spaces assembled here. In other words, there is a reciprocal relationship between the modern city and the network of speech sites that it
houses. What, however, of public speaking as an activity? In Chapter 3,
we saw that there was a mimetic relationship between the form of
modern public speaking and the form of the metropolis. In this chapter, the emphasis has been on the relation between the speech site

and public speaking. Just as the metropolis was the setting for speech sites, so the latter form the setting for public speaking as an aesthetic object. Public speaking affected the character of speech sites; indeed, in many cases, it was the activity itself that transformed a particular space into a speech site, since only some of the spaces under investigation here were designed specifically with public speaking in mind, and only a very few were constructed exclusively for that purpose. Modern public speaking was characterised by the performance of intimacy, achieved through a form of speaking that was based on aesthetic language and comprised both dissemination and dialogue. The speech sites examined in this chapter bear witness to these formal attributes in the way that they provide spaces for both dissemination and dialogue. At the same time, the form of modern public speaking is intuitable from the character of the speech sites themselves, in the way that they demonstrate a complex set of relations between permanence and transience, stasis and movement, control and empowerment. There is, then, a set of complex relations between location, speech and the emerging metropolis that allows us to see that public speaking lies at the very heart of the modern metropolis, constructing that entity even as it is constructed by it.

Epilogue: Public Speaking and the City of the Future

> Future of public space depends upon the ability
> to mix discourse and architecture in a new area of
> endeavour called *discourse architecture*.
>
> Sack (2005: 243)

The power of the spoken word

Potsdamer Platz, Ground Zero, Kartal-Pendik, Fiera Milano, City in the Desert. These iconic names denote a series of masterplans for the (re)development of global cities produced by 'starchitects' such as Renzo Piano, Daniel Libeskind, Zaha Hadid and Rem Koolhaas. In his opening address to the 1908 Architecture Congress in Vienna, Otto Wagner expressed disquiet at the power that developers were increasingly able to wield over architects (Hevesi 1986: 293–4). A century later, it seems that global city developments rise or fall on their ability to brand themselves through association with a big name architect. Offering provocative and ambitious visions for new urban formations, these architects assume a role akin to that of the Loosian 'Über-architect'. Like this figure, and the early twentieth century architects it inspired, they occupy this position thanks not only to their flair in fashioning the built environment, but also to the result of their ability to contribute to the discursive construction of the city by appearing in public on the global stage; if Loos was at home on the European express train, these contemporary architects make their home on intercontinental flights.

A number of these 'starchitects' first made their mark through writing and speaking about architecture and the city, rather than through their contributions to the built environment. Libeskind, for example, entered the public domain as a 'conceptual architect', whose paper designs and maquettes were held to be visionary, but ultimately not realisable – 'virtual', in the sense outlined by Grosz (2001). In 1989, he won a competition to build the Jewish Museum in Berlin. It was completed a decade later, to a typically complex design, weaving together multiple layers of meaning and illusion, and it marked the beginning of his career as a practising architect (Libeskind 1999). That it was built at all is testament to his skill in communicating difficult ideas in visual, textual and oral form. Since the building of the Jewish Museum, he has realised many other renowned projects, but at the same time, he continues to give lectures on architecture and the city, as detailed in the extensive list of engagements maintained on his website (Libeskind 2008). According to the agency managing his public speaking activities,

> [o]n stage, Daniel Libeskind is a dazzling presenter – a whirlwind of energy, ideas, theory, maxims, and philosophy. Libeskind speaks without condescension, drawing you into a fascinating conversation about the buildings you want to live and work in, and the kinds of cities we aspire to.
>
> Lavin Agency (2008)

This implies that, like Simmel and Loos, Libeskind's performances are predicated on the performance of intimacy, and an understanding of the force of presentations involving both dissemination and dialogue.

In his 2002 Proms Lecture on 'Music and Architecture', held at the V&A in London and broadcast on BBC Radio 3, Libeskind adopted the figure of conversation as a rhetorical strategy, demonstrating his ability to translate the formalist aesthetic characteristic of his architectural designs to the form of the lecture. His presentation consisted of a set of improvised answers to questions on the relationship between music and architecture that had been prepared in advance by his staff and handed to him in sealed envelopes. In a manner reminiscent of Simmel's style, Libeskind performed spontaneity in a lecture presented as dialogue; unlike Simmel, however, Libeskind interacted with his audience, rather than merely engaging in dialogue with himself (Architecture on 3 2008). In answer to a question from the audience, he made an argument for the 'virtuality' of music and architecture, maintaining that in both, texts transcend performance to retain the promise of other possible interpretations. In terms of architecture, he was alluding to the necessary disjunctions between the plan and its realisation, and the building and its use, invoking the tensions between representational space, representations of space and spatial practice that, according to Lefebvre (1991), triangulate the production of social space.

While Libeskind assumed the mantle of the 'Über-architect' to put forward his aesthetic vision of the city in spoken form, Rem Koolhaas sought to shrug off what he saw as the restrictions imposed on the professional architect when advancing his ideas on the city in a lecture on 'Metropolitan Apotheosis', part of the 1999 'Sounding the City' series, broadcast on BBC Radio 3 from the Festival Hall in London (Architecture on 3 2008). Casting himself, instead, as a researcher of the 'urban condition' able to observe the phenomenon of the city without the pressure of transforming it that is incumbent upon the professional architect, he proceeded to offer a critical account of the twentieth century's 'destruction of the city'. According to his diagnosis, the city as we have known it has ceased to exist; it has been 'replaced by a new model, no longer – or not yet – city', which bears some resemblance to the vision of the city offered by Scheerbart (1909a) almost a century earlier. Yet almost immediately after pronouncing the demise of the city, Koolhaas claimed that old cities – Paris, New York, Rome – continue to exist. Their problem is that they suffer from the strength of the 'afterimage', making it impossible for them to function as cities in the sense of 'laboratories of uncertainty'. He then turned his attention to the virtual world, arguing that this destroys the city even as it seals its inevitability. His lecture, then, was constructed on a series of paradoxical claims and counterclaims, underlining the fact that in talks such as this, he, like Simmel, Loos and others, was engaged in 'poetic world-making'. At the same time, however, he rejects what he calls the 'myth of the visionary', which implies that a single solution can be found for the puzzle that is the urban condition. While this fiction might still appear reasonable in the context of 'old cities', the irrelevance of the planners' perspective (and so the bird's-eye view of the visionary) is, Koolhaas maintained, palpable in 'no longer – or not yet – cities', such as Lagos or Shenzhen.

Koolhaas and Libeskind choose to intervene in debates on architecture and the city by appearing in public. Their implicit belief in the power of the spoken word also appears to inform their architectural practice, as both have designed contemporary speech sites, such as Libeskind's Creative Media Centre in Hong Kong (which, with its crystalline structure, is reminiscent of Taut's unbuilt designs from the early 1920s) and Koolhaas's 2003 design for the Beijing Central Business Centre. The latter's central premise echoes an argument advanced in this study:

> The increasing ubiquity and mobility of information technology paradoxically stresses the importance of face-to-face human interaction so that, at the dawn of the 21st century, business is communication.
>
> Office for Metropolitan Architecture (2008)

Here, Koolhaas is reiterating a proposition that has been taken up in sociological discourse by John Urry (2003) writing on the ubiquity of 'meetingness' in the modern world, and that forms the basis of Graeme Furness's (2004) work on the 'power of the spoken word' in the present. In designing spaces that facilitate sociability and association, Libeskind, Koolhaas and others are giving form to a mode of thinking about the city that sees its continued importance in fostering and housing what Apel (1980) calls 'communication communities'. Much of this thinking has developed in response to a perceived erosion of public space, which it seeks to counter by listening to tradition and reconstructing prime sites of bourgeois sociability, such as the coffee house and the salon.

Assembling in electronic space

In contrast, other thinkers appear keen to move beyond this rather limited view of the speech–space–city triad, embracing the new possibilities offered by computer technology and the new media. The Arabianranta development in Helsinki is an example of an 'intelligent city', where all residents have access to networked computer technology through the installation of a fibre optic cable that has been provided as standard along with other public utilities such as water and electricity (Shaw 2003). This development has been styled as a 'Living Laboratory', where ways of using the new media to improve communication and participation in local government and decision-making have been tested, with the direct aim of improving the city and the urban experience (Lahti, Kangasoja and Huovila 2006). While projects such as these focus on the possibilities for using new kinds of communication in a specific set of circumstances, the ways that this development is (and will be) inhabited open up a myriad other opportunities, some of which do not remain at the level of the possible as 'a performed version of the real', but take things into the realm of the virtual as 'the space of the emergence of the new'. As Grosz notes, drawing on Deleuze, the difference between the possible and the virtual lies in their relationship to the actual:

> The transition from the possible to the real is a predictable one, not involving anything new or unexpected. The relationship between the virtual and the actual is one of surprise, for the virtual promises something different to the actual that it produces, and always contains in it the potential for something other than the actual.
>
> Grosz (2001: 12)

A networked development such as Arabianranta creates the condition of possibility for its residents to contribute to the construction of virtual publics, or 'global digital assemblages' (Sassen 2006: 326). The crucial issues for the present study are the nature of the connection between these new publics and the conception of the city, and the role that public speaking plays in the construction of virtual publics.

Sassen (2006: 316) puts forward one point of connection between new publics and the city, arguing that 'current conditions in global cities are creating [...] rhetorical openings for new types of political actors that may have been submerged, invisible or without a voice'. Modifying the conclusions about the form of modern public speaking drawn in Chapter 3, she argues that these openings allow the 'production of "presence" of those without power' (315), and notes that the city itself is partly constituted by such processes. In a move that is ostensibly paradoxical, she suggests that the importance of the 'global digital assemblage' lies in its ability to give greater weight to the local, which it does by revealing that the latter is actually connected to a web of related localities. Ways of producing 'presence' include participating in such 'assemblages' and engaging in the different modes of appearing in public offered by digital networks such as the Internet.

Making Things Public, an exhibition curated by Bruno Latour and Peter Weibel at the Center for Art and Media in Karlsruhe in 2005, offered critical reflection on the way that digital networks facilitate new ways of appearing in public as part of a larger assessment of 'assembling [...] under the provisional and fragile Phantom Public' (Latour 2005: 41). Much of Latour's introductory essay is concerned with the question of assembly. He puts forward a strong argument for the construction of spaces for assembling 'disorderly voices, contradictory interests and virulent claims', the construction of spaces that go beyond the 'existing globe or dome of some earlier tradition of building parliaments' (39, 41). In other words, he suggests that the digital age requires a rethinking of public space and the creation of blueprints for new kinds of speech sites that attempt to transcend the constraints of current spatial practice, posing the rhetorical question: 'What would a [...] space be that would not be "neo"? What would a truly contemporary style of assembly look like?' (31). The exhibition did not set out to provide a single answer to this question; instead, it collected a set of possible and virtual responses to it. Like the Berlin Trade Exhibition of 1896 and the Vienna Imperial Jubilee Exhibition of 1898, the *Making Things Public* exhibition was simultaneously a representation of actual and possible forms of communication, and a site in which new directions in communication could emerge. As Weibel (2005: 1026) argues – echoing Simmel's (1997: 255–8) essay on the Berlin Trade Exhibition – the exhibition itself functioned as 'a new type of political gathering' in which visitors engaged in constructing the public sphere.

One section of the *Making Things Public* exhibition was influenced by ideas of the rediscovery of rhetoric's importance and an associated search for 'a new eloquence' (Latour and Weibel 2005: 854–5). That search led Steve Dietz (2005) to the web. Under the banner 'Fair Assembly', he presented a project designed to extend the reach of the exhibition as assembly by constructing a 'participatory platform' that would allow anyone working at the 'intersection of information gathering and opinion making' (911) to have their web presence included as part of the *Making Things Public* exhibition. In electronic space – a collection of 'picto-textual social artefacts embodied in electronic stagings of texts, images, and graphics through software and hardware' (Latham and Sassen 2008: 10) – architecture has a key role to play in the design of virtual environments, including the production of speech sites. The aim of Dietz's undertaking was to make visible the 'means by which the project makes its ideas public', and so to provoke debate on the way that the architecture of the electronic world, in the form of protocols, impinges upon the kind of assemblies enabled by Internet technologies. In other words, his installation questioned how digital culture affects the way we think about the act of assembling.

Much of the early writing on the Internet answered that question by celebrating the manner in which this technology enabled the creation of a new form of community, characterised by the meeting of minds, without the constraints of the body (Rheingold 1993). While Rheingold and others focused on the idea of the 'virtual community', Mitchell (1995) and Donath (1996) cast their reflections on new forms of sociability associated with Internet technology in terms of the city, suggesting that new forms of urban life were emerging online.

A central premise of writing on Internet-enabled communication was the bracketing out of the body in the digital world (Rheingold 1993; Mitchell 1995). Donath (1996) too presented this as the key distinction between the real city and the virtual city, but her thesis, which focused on ways of inhabiting the virtual city, looked at how new forms of 'sociable media' enabled central elements of face-to-face communication, such as presence and recognition, to operate in electronic space. Her work with the Sociable Media Group at MIT Media Lab takes these questions as the point of departure for a sustained investigation of the potential contained in the new media's unique communicative capacity to support both dissemination, and dialogue, and of the spaces in which this potential can be glimpsed.

Podcasts or simultaneous webcasts offer one simple way of using Internet-enabled communication to facilitate the circulation of the public lecture. This is to use the Internet as an additional form of broadcast media, similar to radio or television, but with the added advantage of enabling wide access to archived material. Using this kind of technology, the talks given by Koolhaas in 1999 and Libeskind in 2002 remain accessible to us, lending the ephemerality of the public performance an air of durability. In these cases, however, the idea of 'assembly' plays very little part; the audience for these talks in electronic form remains a collection of diverse individuals separated by time and space, and with no obvious means of gathering around the event. In contrast, manifestations of the 'metaverse', such as Second Life, offer possibilities for constructing spaces for public speaking that facilitate assemblies taking place in real time involving actors from across the globe.

Around 1900, spaces constructed for adult education signalled a new departure in the provision of urban speech sites. A century later, research shows that Second Life is increasingly being used by educators for meetings, conferences and teaching, taking advantage of technology such as 'built-in text chat messaging features and external third party applications like streaming media and VOIP technology' to construct events based on dissemination and dialogue (Jennings and Collins 2007: 181). Leading education establishments are in the vanguard of developing speech sites in electronic space. To take one example, Harvard's Berkman Center for Internet and Society has a Second Life presence (Berkman Island) on which it has constructed an environment that 'looks and feels like Harvard all dressed up for graduation day' (Nesson and Nesson 2008a: 279). The site includes the simulation of a formal classroom, but, apparently, classes seldom take place there; instructors have found that the open-air amphitheatre just outside offers a more usable speech site (Nesson and Nesson 2008b). Lectures and talks can take place entirely within Second Life, but the form also offers the possibility of more complex gatherings based on the interpenetration of the real and the virtual worlds.

On 12 November 2008, Charles and Rebecca Nesson gave a talk on 'Second Life: Open Education and Virtual Worlds', organised by the Berkman Center and held in Harvard Law School's Langdell Hall (Nesson and Nesson 2008b). The event was simultaneously webcast and streamed into Second Life, where it could be viewed on the large screen that forms the focal point of the amphitheatre on Berkman Island. The speakers, then, were addressing an audience of avatars assembled in Second Life, as well as the audience sitting before them. To complicate matters, those sitting in the audience in Langdell Hall were encouraged to bring their own laptops, so they could be taken on a tour through Second Life as the lecture unfolded. The audience of avatars included those of the ones sitting in the audience in real life, and while Charles Nesson was speaking, Rebecca Nesson's avatar was engaging other avatars in conversation in the virtual amphitheatre.

In this way, it was possible for someone watching the lecture elsewhere in the world to engage in conversation in real time with the avatars of people sitting in the audience at Harvard – 'conversational proximity' was facilitated by simulated 'visual proximity'. At one point

Figure E.1 Rebecca Nesson lecturing at Langdell Hall, Harvard, 2008, with Second Life projected on a screen in the background; *Source*: © Yvette Wohn

during the lecture, there was a strange moment for those members of the audience at Harvard who were unfamiliar with Web 2.0 and applications such as Second Life: when the screen in the lecture hall switched to a view of the amphitheatre on Berkman Island, the real audience became aware of the virtual audience watching the event as it unfolded, and saw that they were indeed being joined by a number of people from elsewhere (including the present author, sitting in her home in Scotland).

The unfolding of this event in real time points to the way that electronic space is transformed into a place – in this case, a speech site – through the 'occasioning of space' (Blum 2003: 187). In this, it is just like physical space. One difference between the lecture that takes place only in physical space, and the lecture that is experienced simultaneously in electronic space, however, is the speed in which the latter begins to circulate beyond its immediate place of delivery. The process of the circulation of discourse that constructs a public (Warner 2002: 90) begins as the lecture is occurring, enabled by the 'hypermobility' of the lecture (Sassen 2006: 344). Another difference is that streaming the lecture into electronic space eradicates the temporal distinction between dissemination and dialogue, while the spatial distinction is between physical and electronic space, rather than between two physical spaces (such as the auditorium and the foyer). Strikingly, however, speech sites in electronic space are usually indebted to existing spatial practice, such as the amphitheatre on Berkman Island.

Beyond simulations of the built environment

Many of the speech sites constructed in Second Life are simulations of already existing spaces and places, and so remain in thrall to early twentieth century ideas of sociability, association and assembly. Even projects dedicated to exploring the potential of Second Life for new architectural initiatives do not appear to move significantly beyond this, perhaps because, as Cicognani suggests, 'displacement and ambiguity' remain the norm in online environments and can only be countered by designing spaces that strive for 'metaphorical coherence' (2003: 97). The innovative Studio Wikitecture is an open group dedicated to 'the application of an open source paradigm to the design and production of both real and virtual architecture and urban planning', with the declared aim of

> Improving Architecture and City Planning by Harnessing the Ideas behind...Mass Collaboration, Social Networking, Wikis, Folksonomies, Open Source, Prosumers, Networked Intelligence, Crowd Sourcing, Crowd Wisdom, Smart Mobs, Peer Production, Lightweight Collaboration, Emergent Intelligence, Social Production, Self-Organized Communities, Collective Genius, Loose Networks of Peers, Collaborative Infrastructures, Open platforms, Wiki Workplace, Open Innovation, Horizontal Networks, Collective Intelligence, Global Innovation Networks, Swarm Intelligence, Decentralized Collaboration, Participatory Culture, Web 2.0...and the like.
>
> Studio Wikitecture (2008)

The group's commitment to open source is important. If the 'freedom to associate' and the 'freedom of speech' were the focus of debates about public space in the late nineteenth and early twentieth centuries, at the beginning of the twenty-first century, a related concern is the question of access to electronic space, which is, increasingly, undergoing 'corporate-consumerist territorialisation' (Wise 2003: 128). As Sassen points out, however, this is not a one-way process, since 'global digital assemblages' of different kinds also serve to 'shape questions of territory, authority, and rights' (2006: 326–7). Demonstrating the connection between the open source movement and the construction of public electronic space, Studio Wikitecture's first collaborative projects in Second Life revolved around constructing assembly spaces, beginning with a rudimentary gathering place, and proceeding to the design of a virtual classroom for the University of Alabama. The top three schematic designs for the latter all retain skeuomorphic structures – such as columns, walls and raked seating – which means that they are immediately recognisable as speech sites, but do not primarily focus on how electronic space differs from physical space (Studio Wikitecture 2008).

In contrast, many of the projects developed by the Sociable Media Group at MIT set out to play with the essential differences between electronic space and the built environment, designing virtual gathering places that would function in ways not possible in the real world. In one development, a meeting space has been designed to resemble a football pitch rather than a conference room. In this space, the location of the avatar in the space is crucial, as people position their avatars at certain places on the field to express how strongly they agree or disagree with the topic being discussed. In this example, the way that space is inhabited is harnessed for its ability to create meaning (Naone 2007). This too, however, has its precursor in the real world, where people attending a lecture can express basic reactions to the speaker by, for example, standing up and applauding, or leaving the room.

Other initiatives leave behind the notion of digital architecture as ways of enclosing digital space – in the same way that architecture can be described as enclosing space – and focus instead on the realm of protocols and algorithms. This is the approach taken by Warren Sack (2005) in his analysis of 'very large-scale conversations', one of a number of ways of assembling in cyberspace as explored in the volume on 'digital formations' by Sassen and Latham (2005). Sack offers a view of the 'architecture of discursive space' constructed from the interpersonal networks, topics, and ideational relationships that characterise news groups, Usenet, forums and other similar forms of

Internet-enabled communication (244). Architecture, of course, can be divided into the tectonic and the aesthetic, and Sack discusses both elements. At the level of structure, he explores how certain kinds of conversation are supported by 'network architectures', looking at the way in which new forms of communication technology engender new forms of talk, just as Chapter 3 did for public speaking around 1900. In terms of aesthetics, he sets out to visualise the very large-scale conversations taking place in electronic space. The resulting images, or 'Conversation Maps', serve as a reminder of the durability of such conversations, which, unlike the face-to-face conversation, are archived; their recall is not limited to the operation of memory. The 'Conversation Map', however, is more than a representation; it also functions as an interface, steering and summarising discussions (265).

There are, of course, a number of very large-scale conversations taking place about the urban experience. In blogs such as Metablog, Perfect City, and Studio Wikitecture; Internet sites such as the World Architecture Community; and forums such as Cyburbia, the city of the future is being discursively constructed. Plotting these discussions on a 'Conversation Map', particularly a version expanded to provide a 'technology of the self' for very large-scale conversations (Foucault 1997: 224–35; Sack 2005: 277), would provide a way of visualising the contemporary discursive construction of the city, tapping into the myriad conversations and ideas proposed about that entity, both actual and virtual, in electronic space. The city of the future, then, need not be conceived merely as a simulation of a built environment; instead, it can be visualised as a complex network of speech sites, as an entity formed through digital speech. This city, as it is constantly re-imagined and reconstructed through very large-scale conversations in electronic space, and as it shapes and steers that form of public speaking, is a virtual entity that contains the potential to surprise the actual city.

Notes

1 Look Who's Talking

1. Jephcott translates 'Bürger' as 'bourgeois', losing the sense of 'citizen' that is implicit in the German, and important for the development of my argument.
2. This is close to Habermas's (1989) conception of the ideal bourgeois public sphere as a discursive entity based on reason and the ideal of the gentleman.
3. For a comprehensive list of Kraus's public performances, see Wagenknecht (1985).
4. From 1925, Kraus labelled his readings of dramatic works, 'Theater der Dichtung', but the first examples of such performances are to be found around 1912 (Knepler 1984: 13).
5. From 1925, these were published in the *Fackel*, and a volume of *Zeitstrophen* was published in 1931, dedicated to Adolf Loos on his sixtieth birthday (Knepler 1984: 225–6).
6. Both the film and a collection of recordings of Kraus's lectures are available as supplements to the catalogue of an exhibition on Kraus by the Deutsches Literaturarchiv in Marbach (Pfäfflin and Dambacher 1999).
7. As a result of the Social Democrats' defeat and the changing political climate in Germany, Kraus came out in favour of the authoritarian government led by Dollfuss, which resisted National Socialism from a conservative and patriotic Austrian standpoint (Timms 2005: 473–91).

2 Architects and the Urban Public

1. 'Ornament and Crime' started life as a lecture first delivered in Berlin in 1909, was published in French in 1913, but did not appear in print in German until 1929. For further details of the publication history of Loos's essays and lectures, see Chapter 1 of Stewart (2000).
2. The other lectures in the series were: Hugo Häring, 'Architectural Problems of our Times' (1 February); Adolf Rading, 'American Architecture' (8 February); Walter Curt Behrendt, 'The New Architectural Sensibility' (15 February); Hans Poelzig, 'The Architecture of Culture' (22 February); Heinrich Tessenow, 'Streets and Squares' (1 March); Peter Behrens, 'Urban Architecture' (8 March).
3. The debate can be traced in leading German and Austrian architectural publications of the time, such as *Deutsche Bauzeitung* and *Der Architekt*.
4. The architectural association in Berlin constructed its headquarters in the Wilhelmstrasse, completing the project in 1876, while the Austrian association of engineers and architects built on the Eschenbachgasse, completing the building in 1872.

5. A report of 'Ornament und Verbrechen' was carried in *Fremdenblatt*, on 22 January 1910 and later reprinted in *Konfrontationen* (Opel 1988: 37–9). An essay with this title was published in the Frankfurter Zeitung in 1929 and reprinted in *Trotzdem* (Loos [1931] 1982: 78–88). Herwarth Walden's journal, *Der Sturm*, carried a report of 'Über Architektur' (1/41: 330) and an excerpt from the lecture (1/42: 334). A text bearing the title 'Architektur' was published in *Trotzdem* (Loos [1931] 1982: 90–104). A report of 'Mein Haus am Michaelerplatz' appeared in the *Neue Freie Presse* on 12 December 1911 and was later reprinted in *Konfrontationen* (Opel 1988: 71–2). A full text version of this lecture, together with many of the slides used was published retrospectively (Rukschcio 1985).
6. A summary of the proceedings of the Seventh International Congress of Architects can be found in the *Journal of the Royal Institute of British Architects*, 13 (1905/06): XLII–XLIII.
7. This text, first published in *Trotzdem* in 1931, is a report of the lecture given by Loos in the Haus des Deutschtums on 12 November 1926 based on notes taken by Gustav Schleicher. See also Loos (n.d.).

3 Appearing in Public

1. A report of this lecture can be found in the *Berliner Tagblatt* of 17 March 1916. True to Simmel's style, this lecture probably grew out of a series of lectures that he held in Easter Europe and Russia in 1912 (reported in the *St Petersburger Monatsblatt* Nr. 463, the *Ostsee Zeitung* of 28 September 1912 and the *Potsdamer Tageszeitung* of 5 October 1912).
2. As far as can be ascertained, the first performances of these lectures were as follows: 'Ornament and Crime' – Vienna, 21 January 1910, organised by the Akademischer Verband für Literatur und Musik (Rukschcio and Schachel 1982: 147); 'Über Architecture' – Berlin, 8 December 1910, organised by the Verein für Kunst (*Der Sturm* 1/41: 330); 'On Walking, Standing…' – Vienna, 18 March 1911, organised by the Städtischer Verband für Literatur und Kunst (*Neues Wiener Journal* 19 March 1911). There is some speculation that the first performance of 'Ornament and Crime' may have taken place earlier than 1910 (Topp 2004: 207), but I have not been able to substantiate this.

4 Locating the Voices

1. Although much of Burckhardt's conception of the Renaissance has been attacked by later historians (see, for example, Cohn 1995), his work was extremely influential in Germany in the late nineteenth century, and so is likely to have influenced Schwechten.
2. Excerpts from this lecture were published in *Der Sturm* on 15 December 1910, under the title 'Über Architektur', while a different version of the text appeared in Trotzdem (Loos [1931] 1982) under the title 'Architecture'.

Works Cited

AAC-F (1899–1936) Austrian Academy Corpus: AAC-Fackel. Online Version *Die Fackel*, ed. K. Kraus. AAC Digital Edition 1. http://www.aac.ac.uk (date accessed 10 October 2008).

Adams (1913) 'Bericht des Regierungs- und Baurats Adams an den Bibliothekausschuß des Architekten-Vereins', *Deutsche Bauzeitung* 8/46: 232–6.

Adorno, T. W. (1991) 'The essay as form', in *Notes to Literature*, vol. 1, ed. R. Tiedemann, trans. S. W. Nicholson. New York: Columbia University Press, 3–23.

Adreßbuch der deutschen Rednerschaft (1886–1912). Berlin: Gesellschaft für Verbreitung von Volksbildung.

Altenberg, P. (n.d.) 'Vortragsabend'. Handwritten manuscript. Handschriftensammlung, Wiener Stadt- und Landesbibliothek.

Amanshauser, H. (1985) *Untersuchungen zu den Schriften von Adolf Loos*. Vienna: UGWO.

Anderson, S. (2000) *Peter Behrens and a New Architecture for the Twentieth Century*. Cambridge, MA: MIT Press.

Apel, K.-O. (1980) *Towards a Transformation of Philosophy*. London: Routledge and Kegan Paul.

Arbeiterzeitung (1928) 'Vorlesung Alfred Polgar', 16 December.

Architecture on 3 (2008) BBC Radio 3: Programme Archive. http://www.bbc.co.uk/radio3/architecture/progarchive.shtml (date accessed 10 November 2008).

Architekten-Verein zu Berlin and Vereinigung Berliner Architekten (1896) *Berlin und seine Bauten*, 3 vols. Berlin: Wilhelm Ernst & Sohn.

Architekten-Verein zu Berlin (1924) *Hundert Jahre Architekten-Verein zu Berlin, 1824–1924*. Berlin: Wilhelm Ernst & Sohn.

Arendt, H. (1958) *The Human Condition*. Chicago: University of Chicago Press.

—— ([1959] 1987) *Rahel Varnhagen*. Munich: Piper.

Arnold Schoenberg Center (2003) Exhibition: Schoenberg, Mahler, Zemlinsky, Schreker, May–September 2003. http://www.schoenberg.at/4_exhibits/asc/zemlinsky/asc_2003_e.htm (date accessed 1 October 2008).

Auerbach, A. (1912) 'Allerlei Sprechkünste', *Die Schaubühne* 8/4: 101–4.

Ausstellungs-Commission (1898) *Jubiläums-Ausstellung Wien 1898. Officieller Führer*. Vienna: Verlag der Ausstellungs-Commission.

Avery, G. C., ed. (2002) *Feinde in Scharen. Ein wahres Vergnügen dazusein. Karl Kraus – Herwarth Walden: Briefwechsel 1909–1912*. Göttingen: Wallstein.

B. L. (1925) 'Das Haus der deutschen Funkindustrie in Berlin-Charlottenburg', *Deutsche Bauzeitung* 59/14: 105–10.

Bab, J. (1906) 'Die Körperkunst', *Die Schaubühne* 2/52: 631–3.

Bahr, H. (1897) *Renaissance. Neue Studien zur Kritik der Moderne*. Berlin: Fischer.

—— (1911) 'Tagebuch', *Der Strom. Organ der Wiener Volksbühne* 3: 80–1.

—— (1971) *Hermann Bahr: Briefwechsel mit seinem Vater*, ed. A. Schmidt. Vienna: H. Bauer.

Beaulieu, H. von (1912) 'Vortragsbildung. Ein Gespräch', *Kunstwart* 25/9: 156–9.

Behne, A. (1915) *Die Kunstschätze in den östlichen Kriegsgebieten*. Berlin: Zentralbildungsausschuß der Sozialdemokratischen Partei Deutschlands.

Behrens, P. (1900) *Feste des Lebens und der Kunst*. Leipzig: Diederichs.

Benjamin, A. (1997) 'Eisenman and the Housing of Tradition', in *Rethinking Architecture*, ed. N. Leach. London: Routledge, 286–301.

—— (2000) *Architectural Philosophy: Repetition, Function, Alterity*. London: Continuum.

Benjamin, W. (1966) *Briefe*, ed. G. Scholem and T. Adorno, 2 vols. Frankfurt am Main: Suhrkamp.

—— (1972) *Kritiken und Rezensionen*, vol. 3, *Gesammelte Schriften*, ed. R. Tiedemann and H. Schweppenhäuser. Frankfurt am Main: Suhrkamp.

—— (1974) *Abhandlungen*, vol. 1, *Gesammelte Schriften*, ed. R. Tiedemann and H. Schweppenhäuser. Frankfurt am Main: Suhrkamp.

—— (1991) *Walter Benjamin. Aufsätze, Essays, Vorträge*, vol. 2.3, *Gesammelte Schriften*, ed. R. Tiedemann and H. Schweppenhäuser. Frankfurt am Main: Suhrkamp.

—— (1996–2003) *Walter Benjamin Selected Writings*, 4 vols. Cambridge, MA: Belknap Press.

—— (1999) *The Arcades Project*, trans. H. Eiland and K. McLaughlin. Cambridge, MA: Belknap Press.

Beraneck (1912) 'Der österreichische Ingenieur- und Architektenverein 1848–1911', *Jahrbuch des österreichischen Ingenieur- und Architektenvereins*, 29–43.

Berliner Architekturwelt (1901/02) 'Das neue Romanische Haus', 4: 193–208.

Berliner Gewerbe-Ausstellung (1896) *Illustrierter Amtlicher Führer durch die Berliner Gewerbe-Ausstellung 1896*, 2nd edn. Berlin: Verlag der Expedition des Amtlichen Führers.

Berman, M. (1983) *All That is Solid Melts Into Air*. London: Verso.

Bilke, M. (1981) *Zeitgenossen der Fackel*. Vienna and Munich: Löcker.

Blaß, E. (1928) 'Das alte Café des Westens', *Die literarische Welt* 35: 269.

Blau, E. (1999) *The Architecture of Red Vienna, 1919–1934*. Cambridge, MA: MIT Press.

Bletter, R. H. (1975) 'Paul Scheerbart's architectural fantasies', *Journal of the Society of Architectural Historians* 34/2: 83–97.

—— (1981) 'The interpretation of the glass dream – expressionist architecture and the history of the crystal metaphor', *Journal of the Society of Architectural Historians* 40/1: 20–43.

Blondel, E. (1991) *Nietzsche: The Body and Culture*. London: Athlone Press.

Blum, A. (2003) *The Imaginative Structure of the City*. Montreal: McGill-Queen's Press.

Blümner, R. (1907) 'Drama und Schaubühne', *Die Schaubühne* 3/2: 433.

———— (1926/27) 'Absolute Schauspielkunst', *Der Sturm* 17/3: 47.

Böhringer, H. and K. Gründer, eds (1976) *Ästhetik und Soziologie um die Jahrhundertwende: Georg Simmel*. Frankfurt am Main: Vittorio Klostermann.

Bourdieu, P. (1984) *Distinction: A Social Critique of the Judgement of Taste*. Cambridge, MA: Harvard University Press.

Bowlby, R. (1985) *Just Looking: Consumer Culture in Dreiser, Gissing and Zola*. London: Routledge.

Brauneck, M. (1974) *Literatur und Öffentlichkeit im ausgehenden 19. Jahrhundert*. Stuttgart: Metzler.

Braunmühl, H. J. von (1937) 'Rundfunk und Akustik', in *Amtlicher Führer zur 14. Großen Deutschen Rundfunkausstellung*, ed. I. Kaul. Berlin: Eher, 19.

Brühl, G. (1991) *Die Cassirers: Streiter für den Impressionismus*. Leipzig: Edition Leipzig.

Buber, M. ([1923] 2004) *I and Thou*. London: Continuum.

Burckhardt, J. ([1867] 1985) *The Architecture of the Italian Renaissance*, trans. J. Palmes. London: Secker & Warburg.

Bürckner (1913) 'Das Vereinshaus des A.V.B.', *Deutsche Bauzeitung* 8/34: 183–7.

Cacciari, M. (1993) *Architecture and Nihilism. On the Philosophy of Modern Architecture*, trans. S. Sartarelli. New Haven: Yale University Press.

Canetti, E. (1982) *Die Fackel im Ohr*. Frankfurt am Main: Fischer.

Cassirer, E. (1957) *The Philosophy of Symbolic Forms*, vol. 3, *The Phenomenology of Knowledge*, trans. R. Manheim. New Haven: Yale University Press.

Cicognani, A. (2003) 'Architectural Design for Online Environments', in *Virtual Publics: Policy and Community in an Electronic Age*, ed. B. Kolko. New York: Columbia University Press, 83–111.

Cohen, L. ed. (2005) *'Gerade weil Sie eine Frau sind...': Erkundungen über Bertha von Suttner, die unbekannte Friedensnobelpreisträgerin*. Vienna: Braumüller.

Cohn, S. (1995) 'Burckhardt revisited from social history', in *Language and Images of Renaissance Italy*, ed. A. Brown. London: Oxford University Press, 217–34.

Collins, H. M. (1988) 'Public experiments and displays of virtuosity: The core-set revisited', *Social Studies of Science* 18: 725–48.

Crary, J. (2001) *Suspensions of Perception: Attention, Spectacle and Modern Culture*. Cambridge, MA: MIT Press.

Csokor, F. T. (1927) 'Ernst Toller in Wien', *Die literarische Welt* 3/6: 47.

Czech, H. and W. Mistelbauer (1989) *Das Loos Haus*. 3rd edn. Vienna: Löcker.

Dallago, C. (1912) 'Karl Kraus: Der Mensch', *Der Sturm* 3/115–6: 77–9; 3/117–8: 90–1.

Damaschke, A. (1912) *Volkstümliche Redekunst*. 13.-14. Tsd. Jena: Gustav Fischer.

Dann, O. ed. (1984) *Vereinswesen und bürgerliche Gesellschaft in Deutschland*. Munich: Oldenbourg.

Daum, A. (1998) *Wissenschaftspopularisierung im 19. Jahrhundert. Bürgerliche Kultur, naturwissenschaftliche Bildung und die deutsche Öffentlichkeit 1848–1914*. Munich: Oldenbourg.

De Certeau, M. (1988) *The Practice of Everyday Life*. Berkeley: University of California Press.

Der Architekt (1901a) 'Wettbewerb für ein "Arbeiterheim" im X. Bezirk in Wien', 53: 261–3.

———— (1901b) 'Vermischtes: Preisausschreiben', 53: 237–8.

Der Sprecher (1911) 'Das Wesen der Großstadt', 1/3: 33.

Dessoir, M. (1902) 'Rede und Gespräche', *Die Zeit*, 29 March.

———— (1940) *Die Rede als Kunst*. Munich: Ernst Reinhardt.

Deutsche Bauzeitung (1891) 'Arbeiter-Wohnungen in Berlin' 25/27: 162–3; 28: 170–1; 30: 181–3; 33: 200–1; 40: 241–3.

———— (1896) 'Bau- und künstlerische Vorträge der Berliner Gewerbe-Ausstellung', 30/282–83: 282.

———— (1908) 'Hebbel-Theater', 42/23: 253–4.

———— (1910a) 'Allgemeine Städtebau-Ausstellung Berlin 1910', 44/1–2: 145–6.

———— (1910b) 'Vermischtes. Vorträge aus Anlaß der Allgemeinen Städtebau-Ausstellung in Berlin 1910', 44/32: 240.

———— (1911) 'Vermischtes. Der Neubau eines Konzerthauses mit staatlicher Akademie für Musik in Wien', 45/18: 148.

———— (1919a) 'Erster Deutscher Architektentag am 27. Juni 1919 im Haus des "Vereins Berliner Künstler" in Berlin', 53/46: 253–5.

———— (1919b) 'Vermischtes. Berliner Siedelungs-Politik', 53/55: 312.

———— (1922) 'Die Freie Deutsche Akademie des Städtebaus', 56/46: 286–7.

———— (1923) 'Aus dem Vereinsleben. Freie Deutsche Akademie des Städtebaus', 57/22: 111–2.

———— (1926) 'Die Baukunst unserer Zeit', 60/9: 88.

———— (1927a) 'Vermischtes. Schinkelfest des Architekten- und Ingenieurvereins Berlin', 61/27: 240.

———— (1927b) 'Die deutsche Bauausstellung 1930. Eine 10 jährige Dauerausstellung der deutschen Bauwirtschaft', 61/62: 520.

———— (1929) 'Vermischtes. Die endgültige Ausgestaltung der Bauausstellung Berlin', 62/50: 440.

Dietz, S. (2005) 'Fair Assembly', in *Making Things Public. Atmospheres of Democracy*, ed. B. Latour and P. Weibel. Cambridge, MA: MIT Press, 910–15.

Dobnig, M. J. (2002) *Architecture and Aura. Entwicklung eines Entwurfprozesses am Beispiel der Sofiensäle*. Unpublished Diplomarbeit. Technische Universität Wien.

Dolbin, B. F. (1926) 'Adolf Loos', *Die literarische Welt* 2/52: 11.

Donath, J. (1996) *Inhabiting the Virtual City: The Design of Social Environments for Electronic Communities*. Sociable Media Group, MIT. http://smg.media. mit.edu/People/judith/Thesis/ (date accessed 10 November 2008).

Düding, D. (1988) 'Einleitung: Politische Öffentlichkeit, politisches Fest, politische Kultur', in *Öffentliche Festkultur*, ed. D. Düding, P. Friedemann and P. Munich. Hamburg: Rowohlt, 10–23.

Durieux, T. (1971) *Meine ersten neunzig Jahre. Erinnerungen: Die Jahre 1952–1971*, nacherzählt v. J. W. Preuß. Berlin: Herbig.

Ebe, G. (1900) *Architektonische Raumlehre*. Dresden: Gerhard Kühtmann.

Ebel, G. and O. Lührs (1988) 'URANIA – eine Idee, eine Bewegung, eine Institution wird 100 Jahre alt!', in *100 Jahre Urania Berlin. Festschrift*, ed. Urania Berlin. Berlin: Westkreuz Druckerei, 15–70.

Ehls, M.-L. (1997) *Protest und Propaganda: Demonstrationen in Berlin zur Zeit der Weimarer Republik*. Berlin/New York: de Gruyter.

E[iselen], F. (1919) 'Architekten-Verein zu Berlin', *Deutsche Bauzeitung* 53/47: 265–6; 53/59: 341–2; 53/75: 448.

Eley, G. (1992) 'Nations, publics, and political cultures: Placing Habermas in the nineteenth century', in *Habermas and the Public Sphere*, ed. C. Calhoun. Cambridge, MA: MIT Press, 289–339.

Engel, E. (1911) 'Rednerstil', *Der Sprecher* 1/3: 25–7.

Ermers, M. ([1927] 1985) 'Eine "kunstgewerbliche" Massenversammlung', in *Kontroversen*, ed. A. Opel. Vienna: Pracher, 89–92.

F. (1891) 'Berliner Neubauten. 56. Das Theater-Gebäude der Concordia', *Deutsche Bauzeitung* 25/75: 453–4.

Felt, U. (2000) 'Die Stadt als verdichteter Raum der Begegnung zwischen Wissenschaft und Öffentlichkeit', in *Wissenschaft und Öffentlichkeit in Berlin 1870–1930*, ed. C. Goschler. Stuttgart: Franz Steiner, 185–220.

Filla, W. (1992) 'Ludo Moritz Hartmann: Wissenschaftler in der Volksbildung', in *Aufklärer und Organisator. Der Wissenschaftler, Volksbildner und Politiker Ludo Moritz Hartmann*, ed. W. Filla, M. Judy, U. Knittler-Lux. Vienna: Picus, 67–100.

Fischer, H. (1922) 'Nestroy-Feier', *Die Weltbühne* 18/1: 488–9.

—— (1962) *Karl Kraus, mit vorzüglicher Hochachtung: Briefe des Verlags der Fackel*. Munich: Kösel.

Foucault, M. (1997) 'Technologies of the Self', in *Ethics: Subjectivity and Truth; Essential Works of Foucault 1954–1984*, vol. 1, ed. P. Rabinow. New York: The New Press.

Frank, A. (1991) 'For a Sociology of the Body: An Analytical Review', in *The Body: Social Processes and Cultural Theory*, ed. M. Featherstone, M. Hepworth and B. Turner. London: Sage, 36–94.

Frank, J. (1931) *Architektur als Symbol. Elemente neuen deutschen Bauens*. Vienna: Schroll.

Freydank, R. (1988) *Theater in Berlin. Von den Anfangen bis 1945*. Berlin: Argon.

Fricke, D. (1990) 'Die Maifeiertage in den Beziehungen zwischen August Bebel und der österreichischen Sozialdemokratie im ersten Jahrfünft nach Hainfeld', in *Die Bewegung: Hundert Jahre Sozialdemokratie in Österreich*, ed. E. Fröschel, M. Mesner and H. Zoitl. Vienna: Passagenverlag.

Friedell, E. (1985) 'Adolf Loos: Zu seinem fünfzigsten Geburtstag', in *Kontroversen*, ed. A. Opel. Vienna: Prachner, 77–82.

Friedell, E. and A. Polgar (1986) 'Die zehn Gerechten: Eine Kabarettrevue', in *Goethe und die Journalisten*, ed. Heribert Illig. Vienna: Löcker, 67–72.

Frisby, D. (1985) *Fragments of Modernity*. Cambridge: Polity.

—— (2001) *Cityscapes of Modernity*. Cambridge: Polity.

—— (2002) 'The Metropolis as Text: Wagner and Vienna', in *The Hieroglyphics of Space. Reading and Experiencing the Modern Metropolis*, ed. N. Leach. London: Routledge, 15–30.

Fuchs, M. P. (1912/13) 'Trink- und rauchfreie Versammlungen', *Jahrbuch für das deutsche Vortragswesen* 1: 119–20.

Furness, G. (2004) *Orality: The Power of the Spoken Word*. London: Palgrave Macmillan.

Gadamer, H. G. (1993) *Ästhetik und Poetik I: Kunst als Aussage*, vol. 8, *Gesammelte Werke*. Tübingen: Mohr.

Gahler, L. (1911) 'Wie kam ich ins Volksheim', in *Der Schritt ins Licht. Dem Volksheim zum zehnten Jahrestag*, ed. J. L. Stern. Vienna: Hugo Heller.

Gassen, K. and M. Landmann, eds (1958) *Buch des Dankes an Georg Simmel*. Berlin: Duncker & Humblot.

Geißler, E. (1911) 'Rhetorik', *Der Sprecher* 1/1: 5–6.

—— (1914) *Rhetorik*, 2 vols. Leipzig/Berlin: B.G. Teubner.

Gerstinger, H. (2002) *Altwiener literarische Salons. Wiener Salonkultur von Rokoko bis zur Neoromantik (1777–1907)*. Hallein: Akademische Verlagsanstalt Salzburg.

Gesellschaft Urania ed. (1913) *Denkschrift zum 25 Jährigen Bestehen der Gesellschaft Urania in Berlin (1888–1913)*. Berlin: W. Büxenstein.

Gilloch, G. (2001) *Walter Benjamin. Critical Constellations*. Cambridge: Polity.

Gleichen-Rußwurm, A. von (1908) 'Der Salon', *Die neue Rundschau* 19/1: 232–46.

Goffman, E. (1963) *Behaviour in Public Places*. New York: Free Press.

—— (1969) *The Presentation of Self in Everyday Life*. London: Allen Lane.

—— (1981) *Forms of Talk*. Oxford: Blackwell.

Goldschmidt, H. E. (1984) 'Die Vorlesungen für Arbeiter', in *Karl Kraus liest Offenbach*, ed. G. Knepler. Vienna: Löcker.

Greenhalgh, P. (1988) *Ephemeral Vistas: A History of the Expositions Universelles, Great Exhibitions and World's Fairs, 1851–1939*. Manchester: Manchester University Press.

Gronberg, T. (2001) 'Coffeehouse Encounters: Adolf Loos's Café Museum', *FrauenKunstWissenschaft* 32 (December): 22–33.

Gropius, W. (1919) 'Rede zur ersten Ausstellung von Schülerarbeiten des Bauhauses im Juni 1919'. Typescript. Thüringisches Hauptstaatsarchiv Weimar. Staatliches Bauhaus Weimar Nr. 132, Bl. 5r.

—— (1987) 'Rede zur ersten Ausstellung von Schülerarbeiten des Bauhauses im Juni 1919', in *Walter Gropius Ausgewählte Schriften*, vol. 3, ed. H. Probst and C. Schädlich. Berlin: Ernst & Sohn, 73–5.

Grosz, E. (2001) *Architecture from the Outside. Essays on Virtual and Real Space*. Cambridge, MA: MIT Press.

Gruber, H. (1991) *Red Vienna: Experiment in Working-Class Culture 1919–1934*. New York: Oxford University Press.

Gumbrecht, H. U. (2004) *Production of Presence: What Meaning Cannot Convey*. Palo Alto: Stanford University Press.

Güttler, P. (1980) 'Gaststätten', in *Berlin und seine Bauten*, part VIII, *Bauten für Handel und Gewerbe*, vol. B, *Gastgewerbe*, ed. Architekten und Ingenieur-Verein zu Berlin. Berlin/Munich: Wilhelm Ernst & Sohn, 53–124.

Haas, W. (1957) 'Um 1910 in Prag: Aus Jugendtagen mit Werfel, Kafka, Brod und Hofmannsthal', *Forum* 42 (Juni): 223–6.

Habermas, J. (1989) *The Structural Transformation of the Public Sphere*, trans. T. Burger. Cambridge: Polity.

—— (1997) 'Modern and Postmodern Architecture', in *Rethinking Architecture*, ed. N. Leach. London: Routledge, 227–35.

Haeckel, E. (1899–1904) *Kunstformen der Natur*. Leipzig/Vienna: Bibliographisches Institut.

Hanak, W. and M. Widrich, eds (1998) *Wien II. Leopoldstadt: Diesseits der Donau, jenseits des Kanals*. Vienna: Brandstätter.

Harvey, D. (2003) *Paris, Capital of Modernity*. London: Routledge.

Hausen, K. (1991) 'Frauenprotest und Männerdemonstration. Zum geschlechts-spezifischen Aktionsverhalten im großstädtischen Arbeitermilieu der Weimarer Republik', in *Massenmedium Straße. Zur Kulturgeschichte der Demonstration*, ed. B. J. Warneken. Frankfurt am Main: Campus, 202–30.

Heck, L. and O. Heinroth (1912) 'Die neuen Restaurations- und Saalbauten im Zoologischen Garten', *Deutsche Bauzeitung* 46: 1–6; 29–35.

Hegemann, W. ed. (1911) *Der Städtebau. Nach den Ergebnissen der allgemeinen Städtebauausstellung in Berlin*. Berlin: Ernst Wasmuth.

Heidegger, M. ([1927] 1962) *Being and Time*, trans. J. Macquarrie and E. Robinson. Oxford: Blackwell.

Heinze-Greenberg, I. and R. Stephan (2000) *Erich Mendelsohn. Gedankenwelten: Unbekannte Texte zu Architektur, Kulturgeschichte und Politik*. Ostfildern-Ruit: Hatje Cantz.

Henning, O. (1964) *Urania Berlin*. Berlin: Stapp.

Herkner, H. (1910) 'Der gegenwärtige Stand der Arbeiterfrage', *Wochenschrift des Architekten-Vereins zu Berlin* 5/9: 50–2; 5/10: 57–8.

Herneck, F. (1976) *Einstein und sein Weltbild, Aufsätze und Vorträge*. Berlin: Der Morgen.

Hevesi, L. ([1899] 1985) 'Moderne Kaffeehäuser' *Kontroversen*, ed. A. Opel. Vienna: Prachner, 10–2.

⸺ ([1909] 1986) *Altkunst-Neukunst. Wien 1894–1908*, reprint ed. O. Breicha. Klagenfurt: Ritter.

⸺ ([1899] 1988) 'Kunst auf der Straße', in *Konfrontationen*, ed. A. Opel. Vienna: Prachner, 12.

Heynen, H. (1999) *Architecture and Modernity*. Cambridge, MA: MIT Press.

Hildebrandt, G. (1927) 'Hofmannsthal's Vortrag in München', *Die literarische Welt* 3/5: 39.

Hofmann, A. (1901) 'Zur Stellung der Architektur im öffentlichen Kunstleben Deutschlands', *Deutsche Bauzeitung* 35/36: 225–6.

⸺ (1907) 'Der Neubau des Weinhauses "Rheingold" der Aktien-Gesellschaft Aschinger in der Bellevue- und der Potsdamer Straße zu Berlin', *Deutsche Bauzeitung* 41/13: 85–6; 16: 109–10; 18: 121–2; 37: 257–9; 38: 261–2; 39: 269–70.

⸺ (1908) 'Die Großstadt als baukünstlerischer Organismus', *Baukunst* 42/23: 146–8.

⸺ (1919) 'Die Stellung des Baukünstlers im Leben und in der menschlichen Gesellschaft', *Deutsche Bauzeitung* 53/77: 457–8; 79: 465–8; 80: 475–8.

Hofmannsthal, H. von (1927) 'Das Schrifttum als geistiger Raum der Nation', *Die neue Rundschau* 7: 11–26.

⸺ (1991) *Erfundene Gespräche und Briefe*, vol. 23, *Sämtliche Werke. Kritische Ausgabe*. Frankfurt am Main: S. Fischer, 7–20.

Hubrich, H.-J. (1981) *Hermann Muthesius. Die Schriften zu Architektur, Kunstgewerbe, Industrie in der "Neuen Bewegung"*. Berlin: Gebr. Mann.

Huelsenbeck, R. (1982) 'Erste Dadarede in Deutschland gehalten am 22. Januar 1918', in *Richard Huelsenbeck*, ed. R. Sheppard. Hamburg: Hans Christians Verlag, 54–7.

Ikelaar, L. ed. (1996) *Paul Scheerbarts Briefe von 1913–1914 an Gottfried Heinersdorff, Bruno Taut und Herwarth Walden*. Paderborn: Igel.

Jahrbuch des österreichischen Ingenieur- und Architektenvereins (1912) 'Vereinsnachrichten' 64: 111.

Jahrbuch für das deutsche Vortragswesen (1912–1937). Berlin: Gesellschaft für Verbreitung von Volksbildung.

James, K. (1997) *Erich Mendelsohn and the Architecture of German Modernism*. Cambridge: Cambridge University Press.

James-Chakraborty, K. (2000) *German Architecture for a Mass Audience*. London: Routledge.

Janik, A. and S. Toulmin (1973) *Wittgenstein's Vienna*. New York: Simon and Schuster.

Jara, C. (1995) 'Adolf Loos's "Raumplan" Theory', *Journal of Architectural Education* 48/3: 185–201.

Jaspers, K. (1933) *Man in the Modern Age*, trans. E. Paul and C. Paul. London: Routledge.

Jelavich, P. (1996) *Berlin Cabaret*. Cambridge, MA: Harvard University Press.

Jennings, N. and C. Collins (2007) 'Virtual or Virtually U: Educational Institutions in Second Life', *International Journal of Social Sciences* 2/3: 180–6.

Joël, K. (1913) 'Geselligkeit und Geisteskultur'. *Die neue Rundschau* 24/1: 779–803.

Johnston, W. M. (1972) *The Austrian Mind: An Intellectual and Social History, 1848–1938*. Berkeley: University of California Press.

Judson, P. (1996) *Exclusive Revolutionaries: Liberal Politics, Social Experience, and National Identity in the Austrian Empire, 1848–1914*. Ann Arbor: University of Michigan Press.

K. (1909) 'Redekunst', *Kunstwart* 22/12: 340–2.

Kafka, F. (1953) *Letters to Milena*, trans. T. Stern and J. Stern, ed. W. Haas. London: Secker and Warburg.

Kassal-Mikula, R. and C. Benedik (2000) *Das ungebaute Wien: Projekte für die Metropole 1800 bis 2000*. Vienna: Historisches Museum.

Kern, S. (1983) *The Culture of Space and Time 1880–1918*. Cambridge, MA: Harvard University Press.

Kessler, H. G. (1982) *Tagebücher 1918 bis 1937*, ed. W. Pfeiffer-Belli. Frankfurt am Main: Insel Verlag.

Kiesler, F. ([1924] 1975) 'Das Railway-Theater', in *Internationale Ausstellung neuer Theatertechnik, Katalog, Programm, Almanach*, ed. F. Kiesler. Reprint Vienna: Löcker.

—— (n.d.) 'Railway', *Pásmo* 5/6: 11.

Kittler, F. (1990) *Discourse Networks, 1800/1900*, trans. M. Metteer and C. Cullens. Stanford: Stanford University Press.

—— (1999) *Gramophone, Film, Typewriter*, trans. G. Winthrop-Young and M. Wutz. Stanford: Stanford University Press.

Klausmann, C. (1998) 'Grund- und Bürgerrechte Ausblick', in *1848: Aufbruch zur Freiheit*, ed. L. Gall. Berlin: Nicolai, 233–53.

Klös, H.-G. and U. Klös, eds (1990) *Der Berliner Zoo im Spiegel seiner Bauten 1841–1989*. Berlin: Heenemann.

Kluge, A. (2001) *Der unterschätzte Mensch*, vol. 2., *Geschichte und Eigensinn*. Frankfurt am Main: Zweitausendeins.

Knepler, G., ed. (1984) *Karl Kraus liest Offenbach*. Vienna: Löcker.

Koneffke, S. (1999) *Theater-Raum: Visionen und Projekte von Theaterleuten und Architekten zum anderen Aufführungsort 1900–1980*. Berlin: Riemer.

K[ornig], O. (1929) 'Alfred Polgars Arbeitervorlesung', *Arbeiterzeitung* 25th October.

Kracauer, S. (1964) *Strassen in Berlin und Anderswo*. Frankfurt: Suhrkamp.

—— (1994) 'Sendestation: Das Haus', in *Hans Poelzig: Haus des Rundfunks*, ed. Sender Freies Berlin. Berlin: ARS Nicolai, 11–13.

—— (1995) *The Mass Ornament: Weimar Essays*, ed. and trans. T. Levin, Cambridge, MA: Harvard University Press.

Kraus, K. (1974) *Briefe an Sidonie Nadherny von Borutin, 1913–1916*, ed. H. Fischer. Munich: Publisher.

Kury, A. (2000) *'Heiligenscheine eines elektrischen Jahrhundertendes sehen anders aus...' Okkultismus und die Kunst der Wiener Moderne*. Vienna: Passagen Verlag.

L. K. (1922), 'Vortrag Adolf Loos', *Neue Freie Presse (Abendblatt)*, 5 December.

Ladd, B. (1990) *Urban Planning and Civic Order in Germany, 1860–1914*. Cambridge, MA: Harvard University Press.

Lahti, P., J. Kangasoja and P. Huovila, eds (2006) *Electronic and Mobile Participation in City Planning and Management*. Helsinki: Picaset Oy.

Landes, J. (1988) *Women and the Public Sphere in the Age of the French Revolution*. Ithaca: Cornell University Press.

Lang, H. (1927) 'Über Hosenträger, Gamaschen und den europäischen Geist. Adolf Loos im Renaissance-Theater', *Vossische Zeitung*, 1 March.

Langen, G. (n.d.) *Mitteilungen des Wandermuseums für Städtebau, Siedelungswesen und Wohnwesen*. Berlin: H.S. Hermann.

—— ed. (1916) *Städtebau, Siedelungswesen, Wohnwesen. Ein Führer durch das Wandermuseum*. Berlin: Carl Heymanns Verlag.

Latham, R. and S. Sassen, eds (2005) *Digital Formations: IT and New Architectures in the Global Realm*. Princeton: Princeton University Press.

Latour, B. (2005) 'From Realpolitik to Dingpolitik or how to make things public', in *Making Things Public. Atmospheres of Democracy*, ed. B. Latour and P. Weibel. Cambridge, MA: MIT Press, 14–41.

Lavin Agency (2008) Speakers' Bureau: The Lavin Agency. http://www.lavinagency.com (date accessed 10 November 2008).

Lazarus, M. ([1879] 1986) *Über Gespräche*, reprint ed. K. C. Köhnke. Berlin: Hensel.

Lefebvre, H. (1991) *The Production of Space*, trans. D. Nicholson-Smith. Oxford: Blackwell.

Lesák, B. (1988) *Die Kulisse explodiert: Friedrich Kiesler's Theaterexperimente und Architekturprojekte 1923–1925*. Vienna: Löcker.

Lesser, L. (1927) *Volksparke heute und morgen*. Berlin: Rembrandt-Verlag.

Lessing, J. (1900) *Das halbe Jahrhundert der Weltausstellungen: Vortrag gehalten in der Volkswirtschaftlichen Gesellschaft zu Berlin*. Berlin: Simion.

Lewin, L. (1960) 'Zur Geschichte der Lessing-Hochschule. Berlin 1914–1933', *Berliner Arbeitsblätter für die deutsche Volkshochschule* 11: 1–48.

Libeskind, D. (1999) *Jewish Museum, Berlin: Between the Lines*. Munich/New York: Prestel.

—— (2008) Studio Daniel Libeskind. http://www.daniel-libeskind.com/ (date accessed 1 December 2008).

Livingstone, D. N. (1995) 'The spaces of knowledge: contributions towards a historical geography of science', *Environment and Planning D: Society and Space* 13: 5–34.

Loew, B. (1985) *Friedrich Naumann 1860–1919*. Königswinter: Friedrich-Naumann-Stiftung.

Long, C. (2001) 'Gedanken beim Entwurf eines Grundrisses: Spatial Planning in Oskar Strnad's Hock and Wassermann Houses, 1912–1915', *Uméni* 49/6: 520–30.

Loos, A. (n.d.) Graphische Sammlung der Albertina, Vienna. Adolf Loos Archiv, Mappe 'Vorträge Loos'.

—— ([1921] 1981) *Ins Leere gesprochen*. Vienna: Prachner.

—— ([1931] 1982) *Trotzdem*. Vienna: Prachner.

—— (1983) *Die potemkinsche Stadt*, ed. Adolf Opel. Vienna: Prachner.

Ludwig, E. (1912) 'Genialität des Körpers', *Neue Rundschau* 23/2: 1589–92.

Lukács, G. ([1911] 1974) *Soul and Form*, trans. A. Bostock. London: Merlin Press.

—— ([1923] 1972) *History and Class Consciousness*, trans. R. Livingstone. Cambridge, MA: MIT Press.

Lunzer, H. (1989) 'Karl Kraus und der "Akademische Verband für Literatur und Musik in Wien"', in *Karl Kraus: Ästhetik und Kritik*, ed. S. H. Kaszynski and S. P. Scheichl. Munich: Edition Text und Kritik, 141–78.

Lux, J. A. (1903) 'Das Wiener Arbeiterheim', *Deutsche Bauzeitung* 37/33: 209–10.

Maciuika, J. (2000) 'Adolf Loos and the Aphoristic Style: Rhetorical Practice in Early Twentieth-Century Design Criticism', *Design Issues* 16/2: 75–86.

Maderthaner, W. and L. Musner (1999) *Die Anarchie der Vorstadt: Das andere Wien um 1900*. Vienna: Campus.

Mannheim, K. (1956) *Essays on the Sociology of Culture*. New York: Oxford University Press.

March, O. (1910) 'Zur Eröffnung der Allgemeinen Städtebau-Austellung in Berlin 1910', *Wochenschrift des Architekten-Vereins zu Berlin* 5: 145–6.

M[arilaun], P. ([1926] 1988) 'Die Eisenbahn hat die Menschen auseinandergebracht', in *Konfrontationen: Schriften von und über Adolf Loos*, ed. A. Opel. Vienna: Prachner, 104–6.

Marx, K. (1977) 'The Communist Manifesto' in *Karl Marx Selected Writings*, ed. D. McLellan. Oxford: Oxford University Press, 221–47.

Mattenklott, G. (1983) 'Der mythische Leib: Physiognomisches Denken bei Nietzsche, Simmel und Kassner', in *Mythos und Moderne. Begriff und Bild einer Rekonstruktion*, ed. K. H. Bohrer. Frankfurt am Main: Suhrkamp, 138–56.

Mauthner, F. (1901–1903) *Beiträge zu einer Kritik der Sprache*, 3 vols. Stuttgart: J.G. Cotta.

Mayer, A. (1981) *The Persistence of the Old Regime: Europe to the Great War.* London: Croom Helm.

McLuhan, M. (1962) *The Gutenberg Galaxy: The Making of Typographic Man.* Toronto: University of Toronto Press.

Mehring, W. (1925) 'Aufruhr im Saale der Philharmonie', *Die literarische Welt* 1/5: 50.

Mendelsohn, E. (1919a), 'Das Problem einer neuen Baukunst', Kunstbibliothek, Staatliche Museen zu Berlin – Preußischer Kulturbesitz, Erich Mendelsohn Archiv, Mss 3.

―――― (1919b) 'Vorträge im Salon Molly Philippson'. Kunstbibliothek, Staatliche Museen zu Berlin – Preußischer Kulturbesitz, Erich Mendelsohn Archiv, V 27a and b, Mss (sep.) 92.

―――― (1930) 'Das Problem einer neuen Baukunst', in *Das Gesamtschaffen des Architekten: Skizzen, Entwürfe, Bauten,* ed. H. Klotz. Berlin: Mosse, 8.

Meyer, J. (1998) *Theaterbautheorien zwischen Kunst und Wissenschaft.* Zurich: gta/Berlin: Gebr. Mann.

Meysels, L. O. (1984) *"In meinem Salon ist Österreich": Berta Zuckerkandl und ihre Zeit.* Vienna/Munich: Herold.

Miles, M., I. Borden and T. Hall (2000) *The City Cultures Reader.* London: Routledge.

Mitchell, W. J. (1995) *City of Bits: Space, Place and the Infobahn.* Cambridge, MA: MIT Press.

Moynahan, G. (1996) 'The Problems of Physiognomy and the Development of Cultural Theory in Georg Simmel and Ernst Cassirer', *Simmel Newsletter* 6/1: 44–56.

Müller, A. ([1812] 1967) *Zwölf Reden über die Beredsamkeit und deren Verfall in Deutschland.* Frankfurt am Main: Insel-Verlag.

Muthesius, H. (1900) 'Architektonische Zeitbetrachtungen: Ein Umblick um die Jahrhundertwende', *Centralblatt der Bauverwaltung* 20: 125–7; 145–7.

―――― (1902) *Stilarchitektur und Baukunst. Wandlungen der Architektur im 19. Jahrhundert und ihr heutiger Standpunkt.* Mühlheim-Ruhr: Schimmelpfang.

―――― (1907a) 'Architektur und Publikum', *Neue Rundschau* XVIII/2: 204–14.

―――― (1907b) 'Die Erziehung zur Architektur', in *Kunstgewerbe und Architektur.* Leipzig: Eugen Diederichs, 40–60.

―――― (1908a) *Wirtschaftsformen im Kunstgewerbe,* Berlin: Simion.

―――― (1908b) *Die Einheit der Architektur. Betrachtungen über Baukunst, Ingenieurbau und Kunstgewerbe.* Berlin: Karl Curtius.

Naone, E. (2007) 'Unreal Meetings', *Technology Review* 11 July 2007. http://www.technologyreview.com/Infotech/19035/?a=f (date accessed 10 November 2008).

Nedelmann, B. (1983) 'Georg Simmel – Emotion und Wechselwirkung in intimen Gruppen', *Kölner Zeitschrift für Soziologie und Sozialpsychologie,* Sonderheft 25: 174–209.

Negt, O. and A. Kluge (1993) *Public Sphere and Experience: Toward an Analysis of the Bourgeois and Proletarian Public Sphere,* trans. P. Labanyi, J. O. Daniel, A. Oksiloff. Minneapolis: University of Minnesota Press.

Nemeth, E. and F. Stadler, eds (1996) *Encyclopedia and Utopia. The Life and Work of Otto Neurath (1882–1945)*. Vienna Circle Institute Yearbook 4. Dordrecht/Boston/London: Kluwer.

Nenno, N. (1997) 'Femininity, the Primitive and Modern Urban Space: Josephine Baker in Berlin', in *Women in the Metropolis: Gender and Modernity in Weimar Culture*, ed. K. v. Ankum. Berkeley: University of California Press.

Nesson, R. and C. Nesson (2008a) 'The Case for Education in Virtual Worlds', *Space and Culture* 11/3: 273–84.

———— (2008b) 'Second Life: Open Education and Virtual Worlds'. Lecture given at Berkman Centre for Internet and Society at Harvard University on 12 November 2008. http://dev.berkmancenter.org/interactive/events/2008/11/secondlife (date accessed 1 December 2008).

Nietzsche, F. ([1883–85] (1969) *Thus Spake Zarathustra*, trans. R. J. Hollingdale. Harmondsworth: Penguin.

Noack, D. (1987) 'Bauten für den Rundfunk', in *Berlin und seine Bauten*, part 10, vol. B., *Anlagen und Bauten für den Verkehr*, vol. 4, *Post und Fernmeldewesen*. Berlin: Ernst & Sohn, 121–54.

Novy, K. and W. Förster (1991) *Einfach bauen: genossenschaftliche Selbsthilfe nach der Jahrhundertwende. Zur Rekonstruktion der Wiener Siedlerbewegung*. Vienna: Picus.

Österreichische Ingenieur- und Architektenverein (1909) *Bericht über den 8. internationalen Architekten-Kongress Wien 1908*. Vienna: Anton Scholl.

Office for Metropolitan Architecture (2008) Beijing Central Business District. Detailed planning scheme. http://www.oma.eu/index.php?option=com_content&view=article&id=3&Itemid=1 (date accessed 10 November 2008).

Ong, W. J. (1958) *Ramus, Method and the Decay of Dialogue*. Cambridge, MA: Harvard University Press.

———— (1967) *The Presence of the Word: Some Prolegomena for Cultural and Religious History*. New Haven: Yale University Press.

———— (1982) *Orality and Literacy: The Technologizing of the Word*. London: Routledge.

Opel, A., ed. (1988) *Konfrontationen. Schriften von und ueber Adolf Loos*. Vienna: Prachner.

Ostwald, H. (1905) *Berliner Kaffeehäuser*, vol. 7, *Großstadtdokumente*, ed. H. Ostwald. Berlin/Leipzig: H. Seemann.

Pauly, E. (1913/14) *20 Jahre Café des Westens*. Berlin: Richard Labisch & Co.

Petermann, T. ed. (1903) *Die Großstadt. Vorträge und Aufsätze zur Städeausstellung*, vol. 9, *Jahrbuch der Gehe-Stiftung zu Dresden*. Dresden: D. Zahn und Jaensch.

Peters, J. D. (1999) *Speaking into the Air: A History of the Idea of Communication*. Chicago/London: University of Chicago Press.

Petersen, R. (1911) 'Die Verkehrsaufgaben des Verbandes Großberlin', *Wochenschrift des Architekten-Vereins zu Berlin* 6/40–46: 223–49.

Petzold, E. (1929) 'Grundsätze der Raumakustik', *Deutsche Bauzeitung* 62/36: 327–8.

Pfäfflin, F. and E. Dambacher, eds (1999) *Karl Kraus. Eine Ausstellung des Deutschen Literaturarchivs im Schiller-Nationalmuseum Marbach*. Stuttgart: Scheufele.

Pfoser, A. (1980) *Literatur und Austromarxismus*. Vienna: Löcker.

Pirsch, V. (1985) *Der Sturm. Eine Monographie*. Herzberg: Bautz.

Posener, J. (1972) *From Schinkel to the Bauhaus. Five Lectures on the Growth of Modern German Architecture*. London: Lund Humphries.

—— (1981) *Schinkel zu Ehren. Festreden 1848–1980*. Berlin: Frölich und Kaufmann.

Probst, H. and C. Schädlich (1987) *Walter Gropius. Der Architekt und Pädagoge. Werkverzeichnis Teil 2*. Berlin: VEB.

Projekt Ariadne (2008) Austrian National Library, Projekt Ariadne. Frauenvereine. http://193.170.112.215/ariadne/vfb/vfbvereine.htm#1 (date accessed 1 October 2008).

Raabe, P. (1961) 'Die Aktion. Geschichte einer Zeitschrift', in *Die Aktion*, ed. F. Pfemferrt. Reprint ed. P. Raabe. Darmstadt: Wissenschaftliche Buchgesellschaft, 7–21.

Rasky, B. (2005) Arbeiterfesttage. Zur Fest- und Feiernkultur der österreichischen historischen Sozialdemokratie bis 1933. www.kakanien.ac.at/beitr/fallstudie/BRasky2. (date accessed 1 May 2005).

Read, A. (2000) 'Speech Sites', in *Architecturally Speaking*. London: Routledge, 119–39.

Rheingold, H. (1993) *The Virtual Community*. Reading, MA: Addison-Wesley.

Riemann, R. (1921) *Rednerschule: Die Kunst der politischen und wissenschaftlichen Rede vor der Öffentlichkeit*. Leipzig: Dietrich'sche Verlag.

Roberts, J. M. (2001) 'Spatial Governance and Working Class Public Spheres: The Case of a Chartist Demonstration at Hyde Park', *Journal of Historical Sociology* 14/3: 308–36.

Roda Roda (1913) 'Vortragsreise', *Die Schaubühne* 9/37: 855–9.

Rowe, D. (2003) *Representing Berlin: Sexuality and the City in Imperial and Weimar Germany*. Aldershot: Ashgate.

Rukschcio, B. (1985) 'Adolf Loos: Mein Haus am Michaelerplatz', in *Aufbruch zur Jahrhundertwende: Der Künstlerkreis um Adolf Loos*, ed. C. Kreuzmayer. Sonderheft 2 *Parnaß*. Linz: C. & E. Grosser.

Rukschcio, B. and R. Schachel (1982) *Adolf Loos: Leben und Werk*. Salzburg: Residenz Verlag.

Sack, W. (2005) 'Discourse Architecture and Very Large-scale Conversation', in *Digital Formations: IT and New Architectures in the Global Realm*, ed. R. Latham and S. Sassen. Princeton: Princeton University Press, 242–82.

Salten, F. (1911) *Wurstelprater*. Vienna/Leipzig: Graphische Kunstanstalt Brüder Rosenbaum.

Sample, C. (1996) 'Living Words: Physiognomy and Aesthetic Language', in *The Incorporated Self*, ed. M. O'Donovan-Anderson. Lanham, MD: Rowman and Littlefield.

Sassen, S. (2006) *Territory, Authority, Rights: From Medieval to Global Assemblages*. Princeton: Princeton University Press.

Sassen, S. and R. Latham, eds. (2005) *Digital Formations: IT and New Architectures in the Global Realm*. Princeton: Princeton University Press.

Schebera, J. (1988) *Damals im Romanischen Café*. Braunschweig: Westermann.
Scheerbart, P. (1909a) 'Dynamitkrieg und Dezentralization', *Gegenwart* LXXVI (27 November): 905–6.
―――― (1909b) 'Transportable Städte', *Gegenwart* LXXVI (9 October): 762.
―――― (1910) 'Die Stadt auf Reisen', *Das Blaubuch* V (29 September) 109–18.
―――― (1912) 'Das Ozeansanatorium für Heukranke. *Der Sturm* 123–24 (August): 128–9.
―――― ([1914] 1972) *Glass Architecture*, ed. D. Sharp, trans. J. Palmer and S. Palmer. New York: Praeger.
Scheffler, K. (1926) 'Die Zukunft der Großstädte und die Großstädte der Zukunft', *Neue deutsche Rundschau* 37: 522–36.
Scheichl, S. P. (2002) 'Die Architektur der Essays eines Architekten über Architektur: Der Essayist Adolf Loos', in *Studia austriaca* 10: 161–77.
Scheu, R. (1898) 'Redende Künste', *Die Wage* 1/16: 265–6.
―――― (1909) 'Adolf Loos', *Die Fackel* 283–84: 25–37.
Schiffermüller, I., ed (2001) *Geste und Gebärde: Beiträge zu Text und Kultur der klassischen Moderne*. Bozen: Edition Sturzflüge.
Schliepmann, H. [1907] *Professor Bruno Schmitz' Haus 'Rheingold' Berlin*. Darmstadt: Alexander Koch.
Schmarsow, A. (1903) *Unser Verhältnis zu den bildenden Künsten: Sechs Vorträge über Kunst und Erziehung*. Leipzig: Teubner.
―――― (1905) *Grundbegriffe der Kunstwissenschaft*, Leipzig: Teubner.
Schölermann, W. ([1889] 1985) 'Café Museum', in *Kontroversen*, ed. A. Opel. Vienna: Prachner.
Schorske, C. (1981) *Fin-de-Siecle Vienna: Politics and Culture*. New York: Vintage Books.
Schwarzer, M. (1995) *German Architectural Theory and the Search for Modern Identity*. Cambridge: CUP.
Schwenk, H. (1998) *Berliner Stadtentwicklung von A bis Z*. Berlin: Edition Luisenstadt.
Seel, M. (2005) *Aesthetics of Appearing*, trans. J. Farrell. Stanford, CA: Stanford University Press.
Segel, H. B. (1987) *Turn-of-the-Century Cabaret*. New York: Columbia University Press.
―――― (1993) *The Vienna Coffeehouse Wits 1890–1938*. West Lafayette: Purdue Research Foundation.
Semper, M. (1904) 'Theater', 6. Halbband, Heft 5, *Handbuch der Architektur*, ed. Eduard Schmitt. Stuttgart: Bergsträsser.
Sennett, R. (1976) *The Fall of Public Man*. Cambridge: Cambridge University Press.
―――― (1991) *The Conscience of the Eye. The Design and Social Life of Cities*. London/Boston: Faber & Faber.
Shaw, W. (2003) 'In Helsinki Village…', *Wired* 9.03. http://www.wired.com/wired/archive/9.03/helsinki_pr.html. (date accessed 10 November 2008).
Sheppard, R. (1980–83) *Die Schriften des neuen Club 1908–1914*. 2 vols. Hildesheim: Gerstenberg.
Siebel, E. (1999) *Der großbürgerliche Salon, 1850–1918: Geselligkeit und Wohnkultur*. Frankfurt am Main: Reimer.

Simmel, G. (1955) *Conflict and the Web of Group Affiliations*, trans. Kurt Wolff. Glencoe, IL: The Free Press.

—— (1990) *The Philosophy of Money*, trans. D. Frisby and T. Bottomore. London: Routledge.

—— (1995) 'Die ästhetische Bedeutung des Gesichts', in *Aufsätze und Abhandlungen 1901–1908 I*, vol. 7, *Georg Simmel Gesamtausgabe*, ed. R. Kramme. Frankfurt am Main: Suhrkamp, 36–42.

—— (1997) *Simmel on Culture*, ed. D. Frisby and M. Featherstone. London: Sage.

Simmel, H. (1976) 'Auszüge aus den Lebenserinnerungen', in *Ästhetik und Soziologie um die Jahrhundertwende: Georg Simmel*, ed. H. Böhringer and K. Gründer. Frankfurt am Main: Vittorio Klostermann, 247–68.

Sitte, C. ([1889] 1985) *City Planning According to Artistic Principles*, trans. G. Collins and C. Collins. New York: Random House.

Soja, E. (1989) *Postmodern Geographies: The Reinsertion of Space in Critical Social Theory*. London: Verso.

Sprung, H. (1991) 'Bourgeois Berlin Salons: Meeting Places for Culture and the Sciences', in *World Views and Scientific Discipline Formation*, ed. W. R. Woodward and R. S. Cohen. Dordrecht/Boston/London: Kluwer, 401–14.

Stein, P. and W. von Metzsch (1896) *Ausstellungsgedenkbuch. 'Von Schreibtisch und Werkstatt': Handel, Gewerbe und Industrie im Geiste des schaffenden Berlin*. Berlin: Siegesmund.

Stern, J. P. (1966) 'Karl Kraus's Vision of Language', *The Modern Language Review* 16/1: 71–84.

Stewart, J. (2000) *Fashioning Vienna: Adolf Loos's Cultural Criticism*. London: Routledge.

Stoeckl, C. (1899) *Der Oesterreichische Ingenieur- und Architektenverein. MDCCCIIL bis MDCCCIIC. Festschrift*. Vienna: Anton Schroll.

Strnad, O. (1917) 'Einiges Theoretische zur Raumgestaltung', *Deutsche Kunst und Dekoration* 41: 39–40, 49–50, 62, 65–7, 69.

—— (1920) 'Projekt für ein Schauspielhaus', *Der Architekt* 23: 49–64.

Stübben, J. (1924) 'Aus der Geschichte des Architekten-Vereins zu Berlin', in *Hundert Jahre Architekten-Verein zu Berlin, 1824–1924*. Berlin: Ernst.

Studio Wikitecture (2008) Studio Wikitecture: Opening Architecture. http://studiowikitecture.wordpress.com/ (date accessed 1 December 2008).

Taschwer, K. (1995) 'Orte des Wissens. Zur Topographie der Vermittlungsstätten von Wissenschaft in Wien, 1900–1938', *Spurensuche. Mitteilungen des Vereins zur Geschichte der Volkshochschulen* 3: 8–26.

Taut, B. (1919) *Die Stadtkrone*. Jena: Diederichs.

—— (1920a) *Der Weltbaumeister: Architektur-Schauspiel für symphonische Musik*. Hagen: Folkwang-Verlag.

—— (1920b) *Die Auflösung der Städte*. Hagen: Folkwang-Verlag.

Tenbruck, F. (1990) *Die Kulturellen Grundlagen der Gesellschaft*. Opladen: Westdt. Verlag.

Thompson, E. (1999) 'Listening To/For Modernity: Architectural Acoustics and the Development of Modern Spaces in America', in *The Architecture of Science*, ed. P. Galison and E. Thompson. Cambridge, MA/London: MIT Press, 253–80.

—— (2002) *The Soundscapes of Modernity*. Cambridge, MA: MIT Press.

Timms, E. (1986) *Karl Kraus, Apocalyptic Satirist: Culture and Catastrophe in Habsburg Vienna*. New Haven/London: Yale University Press.

—— (2005) *Karl Kraus, Apocalyptic Satirist: The Post-War Crisis and the Rise of the Swastika*. New Haven/London: Yale University Press.

Tönnies, F. (1887) *Gemeinschaft und Gesellschaft*. Leipzig: Fues's Verlag.

Topp, L. (2004) *Architecture and Truth in Fin-de-Siecle Vienna*. Cambridge: Cambridge University Press.

Tornius, V. (1921) *Der ästhetische Tee: die Berliner Gesellschaft von 1800 bis 1900*. Berlin: Ullstein.

Triadafilopoulos, T. (1999) 'Politics, Speech and the Art of Persuasion: Towards an Aristotelian Concept of the Public Sphere', *Journal of Politics* 61/3: 741–57.

Troch, H. (1991) *Rebellensonntag: der 1. Mai zwischen Politik, Arbeiterkultur und Volksfest in Österreich 1890–1918*. Vienna/Zürich: Europaverlag.

Ueding, G. and B. Steinbrink (1994) *Grundriss der Rhetorik: Geschichte, Technik. Methode*. Stuttgart/Weimar: J.B. Metzler.

Unger, T. (1909) 'Aus der Praxis der Raum-Akustik', *Deutsche Bauzeitung* 43/15: 98–9; 16: 107–8.

Urania Berlin e.V. ed. (1988) *100 Jahre Urania Berlin. Festschrift*. Berlin: Westkreuz Druckerei.

Urbach, D. (1971) *Die Volkshochschule Großberlin, 1920–1933*. Stuttgart: Klett.

Urry, J. (2003) 'Social Networks, Travel and Talk', *British Journal of Sociology* 54/2: 155–75.

Veigl, H. (1986) *Lachen im Keller: Von den Budapestern zum Wiener Werkl. Kabarett und Kleinkunst in Wien*. Vienna: Löcker.

Viertel, B. (1999) 'Erinnerung an Karl Kraus'. Unpublished manuscript. Excerpt in *Karl Kraus: Eine Ausstellung des Deutschen Literaturarchivs im Schiller-Nationalmuseum Marbach*, ed. F. Pfäfflin and E. Dambacher. Marbach: Deutsche Schillergesellschaft, 479–81.

Wagenknecht, C. (1985) 'Die Vorlesungen von Karl Kraus. Ein chronologisches Verzeichnis', *Kraus-Heft* 35/36: 1–30.

Wagner, O. (1908) 'Palast der Wiener Gesellschaft', *Der Architekt* 14: 114–5.

—— ([1902] 1988) *Modern Architecture: A Guide for his Students to this Field of Art*, trans. H. F. Mallgrave. Santa Monica, CA: The Getty Center.

Walden, H. (n.d.) *Sturm*-Archiv, Handschriftensammlung. Staatsbibliothek zu Berlin Preußischer Kulturbesitz. Correspondence.

Ward, J. (2001) *Weimar Surfaces: Urban Visual Culture in 1920s Germany*. Berkeley, CA: University of California Press.

Warneken, B. J. (1986) *Als die Deutschen demonstrieren lernten. Das Kulturmuster 'friedliche Straßendemonstration' im preußischen Wahlrechtskampf 1908–1910*. Tübingen: Ludwig-Uhland-Institut für empirische Kulturwissenschaft der Universität Tübingen.

Warner, M. (2002) *Publics and Counterpublics*. New York: Zone Books.

Weber, M. (1978) 'Concepts and Categories of the City', in *Economy and Society*, ed. G. Roth and C. Wittich. Berkeley: University of California Press, 1212–36.

―――― (2004) *The Vocation Lectures: 'Science as a Vocation'; 'Politics as a Vocation'*, ed. D. Owen and T. B. Strong, trans. Rodney Livingstone. Indianapolis: Hackett.

Weibel, P. (2005) 'Art and Democracy: People making art making people', in *Making Things Public. Atmospheres of Democracy*, ed. B. Latour and P. Weibel. Cambridge, MA: MIT Press, 1008–37.

Weigel, S. (1992) *Leib- und Bildraum. Lektüren nach Benjamin*. Cologne/ Weimar/Vienna: Böhlau.

Welzig, M. (1998) *Josef Frank (1885–1967): das architektonische Werk*. Vienna/ Cologne/Weimar: Böhlau.

Westheim, P. (1994) 'Das neue Berliner Funkhaus', in *Hans Poelzig: Haus des Rundfunks*, ed. Sender Freies Berlin. Berlin: ARS Nicolai, 17–19.

Whyte, I. B. (1981) *Bruno Taut. Baumeister einer neuen Welt. Architektur und Aktivismus 1914–1920*, trans. M. Walther. Stuttgart: Gerd Hatje.

―――― (1985) *The Crystal Chain Letters: Architectural Fantasies by Bruno Taut and his Circle*. Cambridge, MA: MIT Press.

―――― (2003) 'Introduction', in *Modernism and the Spirit of the City*, ed. I. B. Whyte. London: Routledge.

Wiener Allgemeine Zeitung (1927) 'Der Überfall auf das Wiener Kunstgewerbe', 22 April.

Wiener Rundschau (1898) 'Maximilian Harden', 2 (15 February): 278.

Winston, B. (1998) *Media Technology and Society. A History: From the Telegraph to the Internet*. London: Routledge.

Wischek, A. (1937) 'Die große deutsche Rundfunkausstellung in Berlin – ein Bedürfnis', in *Amtlicher Führer zur 14. Großen Deutschen Rundfunkausstellung*, ed. I. Kaul. Berlin: Eher, 11–13.

Wise, J. M. (2003) 'Community, Affect, and the Virtual: The Politics of Cyberspace', in *Virtual Publics: Policy and Community in an Electronic Age*, ed. B. Kolko. New York: Columbia University Press, 112–33.

Wittgenstein, L. (1922) *Tractatus Logico-Philosophicus*, trans. C. K. Ogden. London: Kegan Paul, Trench, Trübner.

―――― (1976) *Philosophical Investigations*, trans. C. E. M. Anscombe. 3rd edn. London: Blackwell.

Wölfflin, H. ([1888] 1964) *Renaissance and Baroque*, trans. K. Simon. Collins: Fontana.

Wymetal, Wilhelm von ([1911] 1988) 'Wiener Weihnachtsbrief', in *Konfrontationen*, ed. A. Opel. Vienna: Prachner, 74–7.

Yates, W. E. (1992) *Schnitzler, Hofmannsthal and the Austrian Theatre*. New Haven: Yale University Press.

―――― (1996) *Theatre in Vienna. A Critical History, 1776–1995*. Cambridge: Cambridge University Press.

Zeitschrift des österreichischen Ingenieur- und Architektenvereins (1906) 'Damen in technischen Vereinen', 58: 238.

Zietz, P. and H. Rüdenburg (1999) *Franz Heinrich Schwechten: Ein Architekt zwischen Historismus und Moderne*. Stuttgart: Edition Axel Menges.

Zukin, S. (1995) *The Cultures of Cities*. Oxford: Blackwell.

Index

acoustics, 150–2, 157
Adler, Viktor, 18–19
Adorno, T.W., 95
  'The Essay as Form', 92, 116
Adreßbuch der deutschen Rednerschaft,
  24, 83
  see also Jahrbuch für das deutsche
    Vortragswesen
adult education, 16, 20, 21, 24–5,
  81, 83, 84, 91, 92, 99, 135,
  154–62, 175
adult education associations
  Society for the Promotion of
    Adult Education (Gesellschaft
    für die Verbreitung von
    Volksbildung), 16, 83–4, 92
adult education establishments in
  Berlin
  Arbeiterbildungsschule, Berlin, 24
  Freie Deutsche Akademie des
    Städtebaus, 84
  Humboldt-Akademie, 20, 84
  Lessing Hochschule, Berlin, 25
  Staatsbürgerschule, Berlin, 23
  Urania Berlin, 20, 24, 25, 84, 154–8
adult education establishments in
  Vienna
  Urania Vienna, 24
  Volkshochschule Volksheim,
    Vienna, 20, 24, 44, 84,
    158–62, 166
aesthetic
  aesthetic education, 77
  aesthetic experience, 14
  aesthetic idea, 104–5
  aesthetic language, 45, 103–6,
    110, 119, 167
  of disruption, 69–70
  see also architecture, aesthetic
    dimension of; city, aesthetic
    dimension of; Jugendstil

aesthetics, 1, 45, 179
  and politics, 27, 45
  of discursive space, 178
  see also appearing
affordable housing, 62–3, 66, 81–2, 84
  see also Siedlungsbewegung;
    housing question
agora, 10, 29
Akademischer Verband für Literatur
  und Musik, 21, 30, 37, 68–70
Die Aktion, 22, 26
Albert Gutmann Konzertdirektion,
  33
Algarotti, Francesco, 151
Altenberg, Peter, 30, 35, 41
  'Lecture Evening', 114
  'Tulips', 114
Amphitheatre, 175–7
  see also Classical Antiquity
Amundsen, Roald, 155
Apel, Karl-Otto, 14, 171
appearing
  artistic, 96, 98, 100, 105
  atmospheric, 96, 119, 121, 166
  mere, 96
  see also Seel, Martin
Appia, Adolphe, 145
Arabianranta development, Helsinki,
  171–2
Arbeiterheim, 44, 66, 135–6, 160–1,
  166
Arbeiterzeitung, 25, 161
Arbeitsrat für Kunst, 57, 65, 72–4
architect as 'urban hero', 56, 95
architectural associations, 38, 57,
  59, 60, 62, 64, 65, 68, 69
  Architectural Association of Berlin
    (Architekten-Verein zu Berlin),
    57, 58, 60–1, 63, 65, 78, 180
  Architectural Committee for
    Greater Berlin, 61

architectural associations (*Continued*)
  Austrian Association of Architects
    and Engineers, 38, 57, 58,
    60, 146
  Committee for Architectural
    Development of Vienna,
    61, 68
  Union of Architects in Berlin,
    61–2, 65, 68
architectural congresses
  Eighth International Congress of
    Architects, Vienna, 1908, 60,
    67, 168
  First Congress of German
    Architects, Berlin, 1919, 67
  Seventh International Congress
    of Architects, London,
    1907, 78
architecture
  aesthetic dimension of, 53–6, 62,
    67–76, 77, 79, 165
  education and popularisation, 53,
    63, 66, 76, 77–84
  and encounter with the Other,
    77–86
Der Architekt, 68, 136
Arendt, Hannah, 10, 29, 56, 96–7,
  162
Aristotle, 10
Arts and Crafts Movement, 55, 64,
  70, 109
  see also Werkbund; Wiener
    Werkstätte
assemblage, 15, 133, 172, 178
assembly, 13, 18, 126, 128, 171,
  173–5, 177–8
association, 15, 91, 92, 133
Association for Art
  see Verein für Kunst
Association for Social Politics, 63
associations
  cultural, 21, 22, 70, 77
  political, 25, 84, 92, 136, 158
  professional, 64
  voluntary, 18, 20, 23, 36, 132
  women's, 38–9
  workers', 18, 44

  see also adult education
    associations; architectural
    associations *and under*
    individual names
auditorium, 107, 111, 134, 143–7,
  149–50, 155, 177
Auerbach, Alfred, 17
Auerbach, Felix, 155
avatar, 175–6, 178

Bab, Julius, 104
Bachofen, Johann Jakob, 42
Bahr, Hermann, 21, 33–4, 38, 49,
  94–5, 100, 106
Bakhtin, Mikhail, 95
Balázs, Béla, 146
Baroque, 61, 139
Bauhaus, 69, 72, 74
BBC Radio, 3, 169–70
Beaulieu, H. von, 15–17, 38
Bebel, August, 18, 98
Behne, Adolf, 83, 92
Behrens, Peter, 51, 52, 56, 67–8, 73,
  144–5, 180
Bekessey, Imre, 41, 43, 44
Bell, Alexander Graham, 8
Benjamin, Andrew, 69, 165–6
Benjamin, Walter
  on Adolf Loos, 69–71, 85
  on the flaneur, 12, 102
  and the Freistudentischen
    Bund, 22
  on Jugendstil, 161
  on language, 103
  on radio, 152
  on world exhibitions, 3
Benjamin, Walter, works by
  Arcades Project, 3, 48, 102, 161
  'Eduard Fuchs, the Collector and
    the Historian', 69
  'Erfahrung und Armut', 69
  'Karl Kraus', 29–30, 33, 37,
    40–3, 85
  'Karl Kraus reads Offenbach'
  One Way Street, 40, 48, 69
  'Paris, City of the Nineteenth
    Century', 71

'Problems of Socio-Linguistics', 103
'The Work of Art in the Age
   of its Technological
   Reproducibility', 27, 55, 69
Beraneck, 61, 64, 68
Berkman Center for Internet and
   Society, Harvard, 175–7
Berlin
   Charlottenburg, 144
   Friedrichshain, 123, 125
   Grünewald, 128
   Kaiser Wilhelm Memorial Church,
      130
   Kurfürstendamm, 128
   Moabit, 154, 156, 158
   Neukölln, 127
   Rixdorf, 81
   Tiergarten, 124–5
   Treptowerpark, 123, 125–6
   Wedding, 127
   Westend, 127
   see also speech sites in Berlin
Berlin Trade Exhibition, *see*
   exhibitions; Simmel, Georg
Berliner Tageblatt, 79
Berman, Marshall, 11
Biedermeier, 131–3
Bierbaum, Oskar Julius, 22
Bismarck, 27, 45
Blaß, Ernst, 129
Blondel, E., 73, 98
Blum, Alan, 10, 13, 15, 31–9, 43, 49,
      100, 112, 117, 121–2, 126, 176
   see also scene
Blümner, Rudolf, 99–100, 103, 106
Bodenreform, 83, 86
   see also Damaschke, Adolf
body, 98, 102, 104, 107–8, 109,
      111–2, 114, 119, 139, 174
Borutin, Sidonie Nadherny von, 114
Bowlby, Rachel, 38
Brno, 31, 113
Bruckner, Ferdinand, 106
Brückwald, Otto, 144
Buber, Martin, 10
Building society 'Ideal', 81
Burckhardt, Jakob, 130, 138, 181

cabaret, 21, 26, 27, 115, 122, 143,
      149–51, 154
   Austrian Social Democratic
      Political Cabaret, 27
   Fledermaus, 22, 149–51
   Jewish-political cabaret, 27
   Nachtlicht, 22
   Schall und Rauch, 22
Cacciari, Massimo, 12, 42, 48, 55,
      70–1, 122, 132
cafés, 72, 115, 128–33
   see also speech sites
Canetti, Elias, 39
capitalism, 3, 29, 45, 46, 67, 69, 71,
      138, 152
Carlyle, Thomas, 90
Cartesian fourth wall, 115,
      144, 150
Cassirer, Ernst, 112–3
Cassirer, Paul, 26, 30, 122
Chartists, 19, 125
Cicognani, Anna, 177
circulation, 66, 85–6, 115, 119, 123,
      126–7, 166
   of commodities, 46, 59, 126
   of discourse, 2, 14, 50, 174, 176
   of ideas, 11, 14, 51, 57, 59
   of images, 7
   of individuals, 7, 11, 14, 46, 49,
      59, 126, 132, 141, 143
   of knowledge, 11, 14
   of messages, 7
   of sounds, 7
   of speakers, 59
city
   as aesthetic entity, 10, 49, 56,
      67–76, 79, 179
   electronic, 12
   exhibitions, 2–10, 51–2, 78–83,
      131–2, 165, 173
   and female sexuality, 42
   imagined, 11, 73, 82, 121, 179
   mobile, 73, 82
   modern, 14–15, 39, 48, 50, 51–2,
      56–9, 65–7, 69, 71, 76–7, 91,
      95, 113, 116, 119, 122, 127,
      130, 132, 154, 165–6

city (*Continued*)
  as a place for encountering
      the Other, 49–50, 56,
      77–86
  as a place of corruption, 43
  as site for production of new
      norms, 117
  as site of production, 3, 57
  virtual, 174, 179
  as visual construction, 12
  world city, 2–3
city planner, 10, 58, 60, 79, 81, 121,
    123, 124, 170
city planning, 61, 67, 68, 79, 81–4,
    86, 121, 123, 177
Classical Antiquity, 144
coffeehouse, *see* café
Cohn-Wiener, Ernst, 83
commerce, 49, 136, 138, 162
communication
  communities, 14, 17
  dialogical, 92, 95, 111, 151,
      159, 162
  disembodied, 7
  embodied, 8, 85, 98, 102, 112
  face-to-face, 8, 67, 153, 171,
      174, 179
  immediate, 8, 9, 12, 102, 132–3,
      154, 166
  indirect, 89, 98
  mass, 7, 10
  mediated, 131–2, 154, 156, 166
  technology, 2, 4–5, 7, 12, 90, 93,
      131, 179
  see also media
communicative event, 91, 126–7,
    141, 143
community, 36, 40, 63, 76, 86, 174,
    179
conference, 9, 60, 65, 83, 175
Conférence, 94, 111
consumption, 8, 15, 47, 150, 152,
    156, 160
conversation, 14, 60, 72, 88, 92–6,
    107, 114, 169, 179
  maps, 179

very large-scale, 178–9
conversational proximity, 133, 141,
    176
counterpublic, 14, 84–6
Crary, Jonathan, 155
cultural capital, 15, 32
cultural criticism, 17, 21, 47, 52, 69,
    92, 106, 117
cultural transfer, 11, 50, 57, 59–60
cyberspace, 178

Dada, 27, 103
Damaschke Adolf, 83, 86, 87, 90, 91,
    95, 98, 100, 120
Danton, 27
Darmstadt, Artists' Colony, 73, 144–5
De Certeau, Michel, 10, 41
De Stijl, 146
debating clubs, 25–6, 38
decadence, 23, 94
Dessoir, Max, 94–5, 100
destruction, 69, 72, 84–5, 123
destructive character, 70
  see also Benjamin, Walter; Loos,
      Adolf; Kraus, Karl
Deutsche Bauzeitung, 9, 52, 54, 62–3,
    65, 67, 79, 83–4, 135, 146,
    149, 150, 160
dialectic
  of concealing and revealing, 110
  of empowerment and control,
      154, 160, 167
  of permanence and transience,
      120, 133, 139–40, 142, 165,
      167
  socio-spatial, 11
  of stasis and motion, 9, 122, 123,
      143, 165, 167
dialogue, *see* dissemination
Dietz, Steve, 173–4
digital, 172–4, 178–9
Dilthey, Wilhelm, 93
discourse architecture, 168
dissemination, 14, 17, 24, 49, 60,
    82–3, 86, 111, 127, 140–2,
    155–6, 158–9, 162, 163

and dialogue, 91–100, 115, 117,
    122, 127, 128–33, 142–3,
    158–9, 162, 165, 167
Dix, Otto, 69
Doesburg, Theo van, 146
Donath, Judith, 174
Dresden, 1, 31, 38
    First German Municipal
        Exhibition, 2, 4, 8–9, 81, 101
Durieux, Tilla, 26
Durkheim, Emile, 110

Ebe, Gustav, 149
Eberstadt, Rudolf, 79
Einstein, Albert, 20, 154, 155
electronic space, 171, 173, 175–9
Eley, Geoff, 9, 19, 44
Emperor Franz Josef, 3, 78
Engel, Eduard, 88
Erenberg, Lewis, 150
Exhibitions
    Bauhaus 1919, 74
    Berlin Trade Exhibition, 2–9, 165,
        173
    Chicago World's Fair
    Fifth Exhibition of Allotments,
        Affordable Housing and
        Domestic Architecture,
        Vienna, 1923, 82
    First German Municipal
        Exhibition, Dresden, 2, 4, 8–9,
        81, 101
    Fourteenth Great German Radio
        Exhibition, Berlin, 153
    General Municipal Exhibition,
        Berlin, 51–2, 78–81
    International Exhibition of
        Building, Leipzig, 81
    London Great Exhibition, 2
    Making Things Public, Center for
        Art and Media in Karlsruhe,
        173–4
    Paris Expositions Universelle, 2, 9
    Philadelphia, 1875, 8
    Seventh Great German Radio
        Exhibition, Berlin, 1930, 154

    Ten-Year Architectural Exhibition,
        Berlin, 1931, 83
    Vienna Imperial Jubilee
        Exhibition, 2–7, 131–2
    Vienna International Exhibition
        of New Theatre Technology,
        1924, 146–8, 173
    Werkbund Exhibition, Cologne,
        72
    World Exhibition, Brussels, 25
experience
    collectively secured (Erfahrung),
        117
    lived (Erlebnis), 10, 41, 52, 64, 117
    of space, 131, 145, 146, 148–9
    urban, 10–12, 15, 49, 52, 59, 64,
        115, 117, 119, 172, 179
    see also aesthetic experience
Expressionism, 26, 69, 99, 103

Die Fackel, 30–1, 33–4, 37, 39, 42,
    44–7, 180
fashion, 79, 111, 143
Fechter, Paul, 101, 109
Fellner, Ferdinand, 135, 143
Festival Theatre, Bayreuth, 144–5
Festsaal, *see* Grand Hall
Fichte, 54
First World War, 24, 92, 101, 162
    aftermath, 25, 45, 54, 57, 64–5, 73
    anti-war protest, 26, 44–7
    patriotism, 26
Fischer von Erlach, 61, 116
Fischer, Heinrich, 41, 44
flâneur, 47, 102
Fontane, Theodor, 93
forum, 130, 165
Foucault, Michel, 179
Fourier, Charles, 71
foyer, 144–5, 149, 156, 177
Frank, Josef, 51, 55, 83, 84, 163
Frank, Leonhardt, 26
Frank, Philipp, 9
Frankfurter Zeitung, 29, 181
Fraser, Nancy, 11
Freistudentischen Bund, 18, 22

Friedell, Egon, 113, 150–1
Frisby, David, 2, 8, 12, 38, 42, 47, 62, 112, 113, 123, 128
Furness, Graeme, 171

Gadamer, Hans Georg, 104–5, 110
Garden City, 66, 79, 84, 145
Gassen, Kurt, 106
Geißler, Ewald, 39, 91, 103
gender, 37–9
Genzmer, Felix, 79
George, Stefan, 106, 111
Gesamtkunstwerk, 74, 98
Gessner, Franz, 135, 160
Gessner, Hubert, 135, 160
gesture, 40, 41, 97–8, 102, 110
Gibson, Charles Dana, 133
Giese, Erich, 59
Girardi, Alexander, 26
Gleichen-Rußwurm, Alexander, 162, 164
Goecke, Theodor, 62–3, 79
Goethe, Johann Wolfgang von, 16, 27, 30, 31, 35, 53–4, 101, 117
Goethe Society and the Argonauts, 27
Goffman, Erving, 93, 104, 110, 120
Gorki, Maxim, 21
Gothic, 73, 139
grand halls, 58, 133–44
Gropius, Walter, 51, 65, 71, 76, 144, 146
    Inaugural address to students of the Bauhaus, 74
    Opening manifesto of the Bauhaus, 72
Grosz, Elizabeth, 169, 172
Grosz, George, 69
Gumbrecht, Hans Ulrich, 96, 102, 114

Haas, Willy, 22, 40
Habermas, Jürgen, 10, 44, 52, 95, 128, 180
Hadid, Zaha, 168
Haeckel, Ernst, 160
Hagel, Alfred, 28

Harden, Maximillian, 17, 21, 23, 25, 34
Hardt, Ludwig, 26
Hartmann, Ludo, 24
Harvey, David, 10, 11
Haussmann, Baron, 12, 123
Hegemann, Werner, 79, 81
Heidegger, Martin, 56, 70
Heimatkunst Movement, 160
Heller, Hugo, 21
Helmer, Hermann, 135, 143
Herkner, Heinrich, 63–4
Hermann, Georg, 109
Hertz, Heinrich, 15
Hesse, Hermann, 21
Heuss, Theodor, 25, 137
Hevesi, Ludwig, 60, 67, 131–2, 149, 168
Hiller, Kurt, 22
historicist architecture, 68, 129, 139
Hobrecht, James, 59
Hoddis, Jakob van, 22
Hoffmann, Adolf, 65
Hofmann, Albert, 54, 58, 62, 67–8, 78, 84
Hofmann, Josef, 149, 164
Hofmannsthal, Hugo von, 22, 26, 27, 38, 98–9, 165
housing question, 62–7
Huelsenbeck, Richard, 27
hypermobility, 177

illusion, 109–10
imagined community, 59, 126
industrialisation, 57, 123
intelligent city, 171
interwar period, 27, 64, 66, 165

Jacobsohn, Siegfried, 22
Jacques-Dalcroze, Emile, 145
Jagow, Traugott von, 125
Jahrbuch des österreichischen Ingenieur-und Architektenvereins, 58
Jahrbuch für das deutsche Vortragswesen, 16–17, 24, 49, 91, 135

see also Adreßbuch der deutschen Rednerschaft
Janik, Allan, 89
Jansen, Hermann, 79, 81
Jaspers, Karl, 91
Jelusic, Mirko, 99
Jesenka, Milena, 7
Jöel, Karl, 93
Jugendstil, 159–61, 166

Kafka, Franz, 7, 49, 93
Kampffmeyer, Hans, 83, 84
Kant, Immanuel, 45, 54, 77, 89
Kaufmann, Oskar, 143, 145
Kautsky, Karl, 64
Kelsen, Hans, 24
Kerr, Alfred, 41
Kessler, Harry Graf, 19–20, 26, 127
Kierkegaard, Soren, 89
Kiesler, Friedrich, 144, 146–8, 166
Kinesis, 104, 107–10
Kirchner, Ernst Ludwig, 69
Kittler, Friedrich, 7, 12, 89–90
Kluge, Alexander, 9, 19, 46
Knepler, Georg, 29, 31, 47
Koolhaas, Rem, 168, 170–1, 174
Kracauer, Siegfried, 12, 42, 127–8, 137, 152
Kraus, Karl, 15, 21, 22, 25, 27–50, 61, 69, 71, 85, 94, 99, 121, 122, 135, 136
    amateur film of public performance, 31
    lecture tours, 30–1
    Offenbach performances, 30–1, 40, 42
Kraus, Karl, works by
    'Beauty in the Service of the Salesman', 114
    'Ein Kantianer und Kant' ('A Kantian and Kant'), 45
    'Für Lammasch' (For Lammasch), 45
    'Man frage nicht ...', 31
    'Reklamefahrten zur Hölle' ('Promotional Trips to Hell'), 46

'Sittlichkeit und Kriminalität' ('Morality and Criminality'), 42
'Das Techno-Romantische Abenteur' ('The Techno-Romantic Adventure'), 45–6
'Theater der Dichtung' ('Theatre of Poetry'), 30, 40–2
'Der Traum ein Wiener Leben' ('Viennese Life as a Dream'), 48–9
'Die Welt der Plakate' ('The World of Posters'), 41–2
'Zeitstrophen', 30, 180
'Zwei Hundert Vorlesungen und das Geistige Wien' ('Two Hundred Lectures and the Viennese Intelligentsia'), 35–6
Krause, Friedrich, 79
Kroner, Richard, 105
Kunstschule *Der Sturm*, 99
Kunstwart, 15, 88, 91

Lagos, 170
Langen, Gustav, 81–3
language, 29, 41, 46, 88–9, 91, 92, 94, 112, 117
    crisis, 89
    mimetic and semiotic dimensions of, 103–4
    ordinary, 92–4
    scepticism, 89
    see also aesthetic language
language-game, 13–15, 17, 21, 127, 141, 151
Lasalle, Ferdinand, 18, 45, 98
Lassar, Oskar, 9
Latour, Bruno, 173
Lavin Agency, 169
Lazarus, Moritz, 93
League of Free Students
    see Freistudentischen Bund
lectern, 20, 30, 63, 88, 94–5, 106, 108, 141, 164, 165
lecture series, 23, 25, 26, 31, 43, 49, 51–2, 56, 61, 63, 65, 70, 74–6,

77, 79, 81, 82, 87, 92, 113, 115, 135
lecture tours, 20, 22, 60
Lefebvre, Henri, 1, 11, 120–1, 138–9, 141, 158, 164, 170
Léger, Fernand, 146
Lenin, 27
Leonhard, Rudolf, 103
Lessing, Julius, 2, 9
Libeskind, Daniel, 168–71, 174
Liebknecht, Karl, 19–20
Liebknecht, Wilhelm, 18, 24
lifeworld, 14, 43, 119, 161
Lihotsky, Grete, 84
linguistic theory, 103
Die literarische Welt, 27, 40
Loewensen, Erwin, 22
London, 2, 45, 67, 78, 113, 121
Loos, Adolf, 11, 31, 41, 47, 51, 55, 66, 68–9, 89–91, 121, 138, 165, 168, 169, 170
    aesthetic of disruption, 69–71
    critique of communication, 130–3
    Haus am Michaelerplatz, 115–6, 181
    Haus Moller, 163
    lectures and performances, 53, 70, 84–5, 113–19, 131–2, 135–6, 143, 150
    on the Über-Architekt, 53–4, 68, 168
    Raumplan theory, 131
    see also Café Museum
Loos, Adolf, lectures and written work by
    'Architecture', 53, 131–2, 135, 138, 181
    'Between the Charleston and the Blackbottom', 115
    'The Day of the Settler', 85
    'The Exhibition Style', 3
    Ins Leere gesprochen, 88–9
    'The Man with the Modern Nerves', 70, 113
    'The Modern Settlement', 84–5
    'My House on the Michaelerplatz', 70, 113–4, 116, 134

'The Old and the New Style in Architecture', 53
'On Walking, Standing, Sitting, Eating and Drinking', 115
'Ornament and Education', 53
'Ornament und Crime', 51, 70, 115–6, 118
'The Technical, Artistic and Cultural Meaning of Thrift', 114
Trotzdem, 181
Lower Austrian Trade Association, 134–5, 139
Ludwig, Emil, 101, 105, 109, 111
Lueger, Karl, 18–19, 24, 158
Lukács, Georg, 10, 116
Lux, Joseph August, 136, 160
Luxemburg, Rosa, 27, 45

Mach, Ernst, 89, 98, 104
Mahler, Gustav, 70
Mann, Heinrich, 21
Mann, Thomas, 21
March, Otto, 62, 78–9
Marx, Karl, 40, 63–4
Mauthner, Fritz, 89
May Day, 18–19, 25–6, 124–5
McLuhan, Marshall, 87
meaning effects, 97–8, 102
    see also presence effects
media, 15, 45, 89, 154, 171, 173–5, 178
    see also communication
Mehring, Walter, 27
Meidner, Ludwig, 69
Meier-Graefe, Julius, 22
Mendelsohn, Erich, 51, 65, 74–6
Messel, Alfred, 62
Metzner, Franz, 139–40
Michaelis, Karin, 37
Mietskaserne, 62
    see also affordable housing; housing question
Mitchell, W. J., 174
mobile museum (Wandermuseum), 81–2
modernity, 2–3, 7, 12, 42, 46, 52, 57, 61, 68–9, 89, 100, 113,

115–7, 123, 126, 129, 131–3,
    165
monological speech, 94, 154–5
Montesquiou-Fezensac, Comte
    Robert de, 94
monumental space, 76, 78–9, 90,
    122, 137–41, 143, 158
Morris, William, 78, 121
Müller, Adam, 87
Museum for Settlement and Urban
    Planning, 82
Museum for Social and Economic
    Affairs, Vienna, 82–3
    see also Neurath, Otto
Mussolini, 27
Muthesius, Hermann, 51, 53, 59,
    81, 163
Muthesius, Hermann, lectures by
    'Architectural Observations on the
        Current Times', 54, 77
    'Architecture and the Public', 53,
        77, 81
    'Economics and the Arts and
        Crafts Movement', 64
    'The Education of the Public in
        Architecture', 53, 78
    'The Unity of Architecture', 64

Nansen, Fridtjof, 155
National Assembly, Frankfurt, 18, 23
Naumann, Friedrich, 17–18, 23–4,
    26, 49
Negt, Oskar, 9, 19
Neise, Hansi, 26
Nesfield, Eden, 163
Nesson, Charles, 175
Nesson, Rebecca, 175–6
Nestroy, Johann, 30, 31, 35, 41
network, 14, 22, 58–60, 64, 117, 166
    digital, 171–3, 177–9
    of language-games, 13, 17, 127
    of speech sites, 59, 122, 166, 179
    transport, 4, 45, 59
Neue Freie Presse, 3, 16, 47, 114, 181
Neue Rundschau, 16, 91, 93
Neuer Club, 21
Neues Wiener Tagblatt, 16

Neumann, Franz Ritter von jr., 159
Neurath, Otto, 66, 82–4
New York, 170
Nietzsche, Friedrich, 21, 42, 53–4,
    68, 73, 89, 93, 98, 102, 132
nihilism, 71, 132
Nobel Prize for Peace, 38

occult, 17, 20
Offenbach, Jacques, 30–1, 40, 42
Office for Metropolitan Architecture,
    171
    see also Koolhaas, Rem
Olbrich, Josef Maria, 61, 131
Ong, Walter, 87
open source, 177–8
operetta, 41, 47, 99
    see also Offenbach, Jacques
oral culture, 87, 90, 131, 133, 161
Osborn, Max, 152
Ostwald, Hans, 129

Pan, 22
paradox, 97–8, 100, 112, 117
Paris, 2, 9, 31, 67, 71, 113, 115, 123,
    162, 170
Parliament, 47, 64, 88, 129
parliamentary debate, 18
Patte, Pierre, 151
Pauly, Ernst, 128
perception
    of architecture and space, 73, 78,
        138–9, 151
    of intimacy, 100–13, 167, 169
    performance, 10, 14, 17, 22, 23,
        26, 31, 33–4, 36–8, 40–1,
        44–6, 73, 85, 96–119, 145,
        149, 167, 170, 174
    sensuous, 73, 98, 102, 104, 106,
        107
performativity, 39, 41, 96, 97, 100
Peters, Jan Durham, 10, 89, 93, 95
Petersen, Richard, 59, 81
Pfemfert, Fritz, 22, 129
physiognomy, 48, 98, 102–4, 109–10
Piano, Renzo, 168
Piscator, Erwin, 146

Planck, Max, 155
podcasts, 174
podium, 22, 35, 41, 99, 141
Poelzig, Hans, 51–2, 56, 83, 144,
    146, 152, 154
  Großes Schauspielhaus, 146
  Haus des Rundfunks, 152–4
Polgar, Alfred, 25, 150–1
political parties
  Austrian Christian Socialist Party,
    24, 158, 162
  Austrian Social Democratic Party
    (SDAP), 18–19, 24, 27, 44, 66,
    135, 136, 160, 162, 180
  German Democratic Union, 125
  German Social Democratic Party
    (SPD), 24, 62, 92, 125
Posener, Julius, 58, 163
pragmatics, 97–8, 102
Prague, 22, 31, 113
presence, 15, 96–9, 102, 105, 109,
    114, 119, 120, 131, 138, 160,
    172, 174
presence effects, 96, 98, 102, 114
  see also meaning effects
private space, 132, 160, 162
private sphere, 42–3, 162
promenade, 141–3, 149
prostitution, 42, 48
public
  poetic construction of, 14
  urban, 9, 14, 49, 51–2, 57, 61, 62,
    66, 77, 81, 84, 86, 119, 132,
    165
  see also counterpublic
public intellectual, 15, 29, 32, 50
Public Park Movement, 123
public space, 122, 138, 155, 162–5
public speaking
  aesthetic dimension of, 11, 21–2,
    91, 95–100, 102–5, 109–10, 119
  at exhibitions, 2, 8–9, 79–81
  formal connection to the modern
    city, 59, 91, 115–7
  manuals, 86, 91–2
  political, 14, 17–20, 23–7, 38,
    43–5, 64–5, 90, 124–7, 136

  training in, 88, 91, 99
  see also adult education
public sphere, 11, 25, 29, 30, 31,
    34, 38, 44, 56, 78, 96–7, 162,
    173, 180
  and expansion of discursive space,
    19–20, 44, 86

Raimund, Ferdinand, 30, 31, 35
rational-technical, 14, 49–50, 55–7,
    60, 62, 67, 69, 71, 79, 95,
    104, 162
Raumbühne, 146–8, 166
Read, Alan, 78, 121
recitation, 16–17, 21–2, 26, 99
Red Vienna, 66, 161
Reichspost, 40
Reinhardt, Max, 22, 99
Renaissance, 130, 138–9, 150, 154,
    181
Renner, Karl, 18, 24
representational space, 121, 124,
    127, 170
representations of space, 121, 124,
    139, 156
  see also city planning
revolution
  of 1848, 9, 18, 23
  of 1918 / 1919, 19–20, 65, 72, 127
Rheingold, Howard, 174
rhetoric, 27, 39, 48, 87, 90, 95, 99,
    103, 114, 172, 173
rhetorical education, *see* public
    speaking, training in
Rickert, Heinrich, 101, 111
Riecke, Ilse, 25
Riemann, Robert, 19
right to associate and right to free
    speech, 9, 90
Rilke, Rainer Maria, 21, 26
Robespierre, 27
Roda Roda, 22
Rome, 67, 130, 170
Rowe, Dorothy, 42, 69

Sabine, Wallace, 151
Sack, Warren, 168, 178–9

salon, 69, 76, 93, 106, 122, 162–5, 171
Salzmann, Alexander, 145
Sample, Colin, 103–4, 107, 110
Sassen, Saskia, 172–3, 177–8
Saunders, George, 151
scene, 12, 15, 17, 21, 23, 27–41, 43,
    49, 71, 89, 100, 106, 112, 116,
    129
Schäfer, Carl, 9
Die Schaubühne, 17, 22, 45
    see also Die Weltbühne
Scheerbart, Paul, 21, 71–3, 76, 82, 170
Scheffler, Karl, 47, 52, 63, 64
Schenzhen, 170
Scheu, Robert, 29, 97–100, 112, 117
Schiller, Friedrich, 54
Schinkel Memorial Lectures, 54, 58,
    67, 77
Schleiermacher, Friedrich, 54
Schliepmann, Hans, 128, 136–9
Schmarsow, August, 138, 146, 148
Schmitz, Bruno, 136–9
Schnitzler, Arthur, 21, 38
Schober, Johann, 41, 43
Schoenberg, Arnold, 70
Schölermann, Wilhelm, 131
Schreiber, Adele, 25
Schultze-Naumburg, Paul, 81
Schumacher, Fritz, 81
Schwechten, Franz, 129–30, 181
science, popularisation of, 21, 24,
    155–8
Second Life, 175–8
Seel, Martin, 96–100, 109, 119, 122,
    166
Seeling, Heinrich, 143–4
Sennett, Richard, 10, 150
Settlement Movement
    (Siedlungsbewegung), 66,
    84–5, 136
Settlers' School, 84
Shakespeare, 30, 35
Sholem, Gersholm, 40
Simmel, Georg, 1, 2, 54, 63, 70, 89,
    91, 121, 169–70, 173, 181
    on conversational and visual
        proximity, 133, 141, 176

lecturing style, 101–13
network of social circles, 64
war-time lecturing activities, 26, 101
Simmel, Georg, lectures and written
    works by
    'The Aesthetic Significance of the
        Face', 110–11
    'Berlin Trade Exhibition', 3, 8,
        165, 173
    'Bridge and Door', 130
    'Goethe and Love', 101
    'Metropolis and Mental Life', 1,
        7–8, 10, 12, 59, 91, 101, 107,
        112–3, 117, 150, 152
    'The Philosophy of Fashion', 111
    'Sociology of the Senses', 102,
        104, 106, 107, 110, 120
    'The Sociology of Sociability', 15,
        133
Singer, Kurt, 106
Sitte, Camillo, 123
sociability, 8–9, 15, 93, 133, 154
Sociable Media Group, MIT, 174, 178
Social Darwinism, 54, 159–60
Socialist Law, 62
Society of Economists, 2, 64
Socrates, 32, 93, 117
Sombart, Werner, 64, 70, 105
Sozialistischer Studentenbund, 26
spatial practice, 66, 121, 123, 124,
    138, 141, 149, 164, 165–6, 170
spatial relations, 15, 56, 107,
    110–13, 120, 133, 141
spatial stage, *see* Raumbühne
speech sites as aesthetic object, 166
speech sites elsewhere
    Berkman Island, 175–6
    Kelmscott House, London, 121
    Langdell Hall, Harvard Law
        School, 175–6
    Paulskirche, Frankfurt, 18, 23
    Sorbonne, Paris, 31, 70, 113
    Speakers' Corner, Hyde Park, 19,
        125, 127
    University of Alabama virtual
        classroom in Second Life, 178
    University of Munich

speech sites in Berlin
Architektenhaus, 134–5
Café des Westens, 72, 115
Concordia Theatre, 149
Friedrichshain, Volkspark, 125
Haus der deutschen Funkindustrie, 153–4
Haus des Rundfunks, 152, 153–4
Humboldt University, 26
'Kaisersaal' in the Weinhaus Rheingold, 137–40
Paul Cassirer Art Gallery, 26, 30, 122
Philharmonic Hall, 23, 27
Police Headquarters, Berlin, 19
Rahel Levin Varnhagen's salon, 162
Renaissance Theatre, 143
Romansiches Café, 129–30, 144
Schloßplatz, 19, 122, 127
'Scientific Theatre', Urania, 154–8
Singakademie, 93
Theater des Westens, 143–4
Tiergarten, 124–5
Tivoli-Hall, Kreuzberg, 135
Treptowerpark, 125–6
Unter den Linden Theatre, 149
Vortragssaal Aktion, 22
Weinhaus Rheingold, 136–41
Zoological Garden, 135, 141–2
speech sites in Vienna
Arbeiterheim, Favoriten, 136, 160–1, 166
Beethoven-Saal, 37
Bertha Zuckerkandl's salons, 162, 164–5
Bösendorfersaal, 33, 38
Cabaret Fledermaus, 149–50
Café Museum, 131–3
Konzerthaus, 31, 36, 122, 146–7
Lower Austrian Trade Association, Grand Hall, 134–5, 139
Prater, 26, 34, 122, 124
'Railway-Theater', 146–8
Schwarzwaldschule, 131
Schwedenkino, 31
Sophiensaal, 70, 114, 115, 134

Volksbildungshaus, Margarethen, 158
Volksheim, Ottakring, 24, 44, 158–62, 166
see also adult education establishments
Der Sprecher, 16, 49, 88
Spykman, Nikolas, 105
Stahl, Fritz, 79
Stammtisch, 69, 72, 73
Stefan, Paul, 21
Steinbrink, Bernd, 87
Sternberger, Dolf, 161
Strauss, Richard, 99
Stresemann, Gustav, 25
Strnad, Oskar, 144, 146
Stübben, Joseph, 58, 61, 63, 81
Studio Wikitecture, 177–9
Der Sturm, 99, 103
see also Kunstschule *Der Sturm*
Suffrage Stroll, 124–5
Susman, Margarete, 109, 111
Suttner, Bertha von, 38
synoptikon, 133, 140

Taut, Bruno, 51, 65, 71–6, 171
Glass House, 72
Taut, Bruno, written works by
Die Auflösung der Städt, 73
Die Stadtkrone, 73
Der Weltbaumeister, 73–5
Taut, Max, 84
Tessenow, Heinrich, 144–5
The Torch, see *Die Fackel*
theatre, 21, 25–6, 47, 73, 99, 109, 113, 122, 124, 141, 143–51, 155, 159, 163
Thode, Henry, 17, 20, 23
Thompson, Emily, 151–2
Timms, Edward, 28, 31, 36, 42–5, 47–8, 135, 136
Toller, Ernst, 25
Tönnies, Ferdinand, 63
Tornius, Valerian, 162
Toulmin, Stephen, 89
Tractatus Logico-Philosophicus, 10, 89

Tranquillini, Emil, 61
transport, 2, 4, 7, 45–6, 58–9, 61, 72–3, 82

Über-Architekt, der, 53–4, 68, 168
Ueding, Gert, 18, 87–90
Ullmann, Ludwig, 21
urban planning, *see* city planning
Urry, John, 171

Verein Freie Volksbühne, Berlin, 23, 25
Verein für Kunst, 21, 30, 46, 53, 64, 70, 71, 181
Vereine, *see* associations
Vienna
  Danube, 61
  Döbling, 163
  First District, 61–2
  Hofburg, 116
  Karlskirche, 61
  Karlsplatz, 61
  Leopoldstadt, 34
  Prater, 26, 34, 122, 124
  Ringstrasse, 47, 90, 131
  Schönbrunn, 61
  Secession building, 61, 90, 131
  Town Hall, 82–3
  Türkenschanzpark, 123
visual proximity, 133, 141, 176
visual technology, 28, 47–8, 154–6
  Panorama, 155
  ready-to-view slideshows, 84, 92
visual-aural relation, 106–11
vocalization, 104, 105–10
Volkswirtschaftlichen Gesellschaft, *see* Society of Economists
vorlesen, 100
vortragen, 99–100

Wagner, Martin, 66, 83
Wagner, Otto, 51, 54, 62, 67, 69, 123, 135
  city railway, 61
  lectures and addresses, 60, 67, 79, 116

Modern Architecture, 51
  'Social Palace for Vienna', 141
Wagner, Richard, 144
Wahlrechtsspaziergang
  see Suffrage Stroll
Walden, Herwarth, 21–2, 30, 46, 70, 71, 72, 99, 129
Wandermuseum, *see* mobile museum
Warner, Michael, 10, 14, 34, 49, 52, 57, 84–6, 96, 97, 112, 119, 141, 176
  poetic world-making, 98, 117–9, 170
Weber, Max, 18–20, 54, 57
Weibel, Peter, 173
Weininger, Otto, 42
Die Weltbühne, 22, 45
  see also Die Schaubühne
Werdandi-Bund, 23
Werkbund, 72, 81
Werner, Heinz, 103
Westheim, Paul, 152
Wiener Rundschau, 16, 23
Wiener Werkstätte, 70, 164
Wiesenthal, Grete, 22
Wille, Bruno, 25
Wittgenstein, Ludwig, 10, 13, 89
  see also language-game
Wittig, Paul, 58
Wohnungskultur, 53
Wölfflin, Heinrich, 138–9
Workers Council for Art, *see* Arbeitsrat für Kunst
Workers' Home, *see* Arbeiterheim
written culture, 161
Wyneken, Gustav, 26

Die Zeit, 3, 94
Zeitschrift des österreichischen Ingenieur- und Architektenvereins, 38
Zuckerkandl, Bertha, 159, 162, 164–5
Zuckerkandl, Emil, 159
Die Zukunft, 23